W9-BYC-282

The Need to Kill

INSIDE THE WORLD OF THE SERIAL KILLER

The Need to Kill

INSIDE THE WORLD OF THE SERIAL KILLER

DR. STEVEN A. EGGER

Library of Congress Cataloging-in-Publication Data

Egger, Steven A.
    The need to kill : inside the world of the serial killer / Steven A. Egger.
        p. cm.
    Previously published in a different form as 'The Killers among us : an examination of
serial murder and its investigation'.
    "First printing".
    Includes bibliographical references.
    ISBN 0-13-143344-X
        1. Serial murders. 2. Serial murderers. 3. Serial murder investigation. I. Egger. Steven
A. Killers among us. II. Title.

    HV6515.E345 2003
    364.152'3--dc22   2003060932

Editorial/Production Supervision: *MetroVoice Publishing Services*
V.P., Editor-in-Chief: *Tim Moore*
Marketing Manager: *John Pierce*
Manufacturing Manager: *Maura Zaldivar*
Cover Design Director: *Jerry Votta*
Cover Design: *Nina Scuderi*
Interior Design: *Gail Cocker-Bogusz*
Full-Service Project Manager: *Anne R. Garcia*

© 2003 Pearson Education, Inc.
Publishing as Prentice Hall
Upper Saddle River, NJ 07458

**Prentice-Hall offers excellent discounts on this book when ordered
in quantity for bulk purchases or special sales. For more information,
please contact: U.S. Corporate and Government Sales, 1-800-382-3419,
corpsales@pearsontechgroup.com. For sales outside of the U.S., please contact:
International Sales, 1-317-581-3793, international@pearsontechgroup.com.**

Previously published in a different form as *The Killers Among Us:
An Examination of Serial Murder and Its Investigation*. First edition
published by Prentice Hall 1998; second edition published 2002.

Printed in the United States of America

First Printing

ISBN 0-13-143344-X

Pearson Education LTD.
Pearson Education Australia PTY, Limited
Pearson Education Singapore, Pte. Ltd.
Pearson Education North Asia Ltd.
Pearson Education Canada, Ltd.
Pearson Educación de Mexico, S.A. de C.V.
Pearson Education—Japan
Pearson Education Malaysia, Pte. Ltd.

To my mother, for her love, creativity, and support.

CONTENTS

Acknowledgments

I would like to acknowledge the assistance of the following people, without whom this book would not have been possible:

- Professor José Sanmartin, director of the Queen Sofia Center for the Study of Violence; Valencia, Spain, for inviting me to speak and share my research with others at the International Workshop on Violence and Psychopathy in November 1999.

- Richard Griffiths of CNN Special Reports, Producer of *Murder by Number*, a two-hour television program on serial murder, and Cable News Network, Inc., for providing me with the original transcripts and research material used in producing *Murder by Number*, first broadcast in January 1993.

- Professor David Canter, University of Liverpool, for inviting me to England to present at the second International Conference on Investigative Psychology in April 1993; at the third conference in September 1994; at a special conference in May 1995 to share my ideas and concepts with police officials from around the world; and in September 1998 at the fifth International Conference, entitled *New Directions in Offender Profiling*.

- Leo Meyer, deputy director of the Illinois Department of Corrections (retired), for his interest in my research and for taking me on tours of both death row facilities in Illinois, where in front of one cell I had a brief conversation with the late John Wayne Gacy.

- Captain Bobbie Prince of the Texas Rangers (retired) and the late Sheriff Jim Boutwell of Williamson County, Texas for their patience and support of my interviews with serial killer Henry Lee Lucas.

- Jim Sewell, director of the Florida Law Enforcement Executive Institute, Florida Department of Law Enforcement, for valuing my research, inviting me to speak at the Institute in Tallahassee, and introducing me to Paul Decker.

- Paul Decker, deputy warden of Starke Prison in Florida, for providing me with the opportunity to interview serial killer Ottis Toole.

- Michael Reynolds, author of *Dead Ends,* the true account of serial killer Aileen Wuornos, for his continued support and willingness to discuss some tough issues with me at any time.

- To my colleagues who have researched the difficult phenomenon of serial murder: Eric Hickey, Candice Skrapec, Ron Holmes, Philip Jenkins, Richard Krause, Jack Olsen, Roy Hazelwood, Robert Ressler, D. Kim Rossmo, Jack Levin, James Fox, Stephen Giannangelo, and others who continue to observe and study this phenomenon.

- To Canadian anthropologist and writer Elliott Leyton, considered by many of us who have studied this horrific crime to be the "father" of serial murder research, for his willingness to share his analysis of the serial murder phenomenon and his encouragement of my research.

- And to all homicide investigators everywhere, but especially to Sergeant Frank Salerno (retired) of the Los Angeles County Sheriff's Office, who has investigated many serial murder cases, including the "Night Stalker" and "Hillside Strangler" cases; to Lieutenant Ray Biondi (retired), who investigated the Sacramento "Vampire Killer" and the Gerald Gallego serial murder cases; and to Robert Keppell (retired) of the Washington State Attorney General's Office, who worked on the Ted Bundy case and on the Green River Task Force, and who recently developed the Homicide Investigative Tracking System for his state.

- To the researchers, law enforcement officers, and students who attended the First International Conference on Serial and Mass Murder at the University of Windsor, Ontario in April 1993. For the first time, many of us who study and write about serial murder were together at the same time and place, agreeing or agreeing to disagree on a number of issues.

- To Thomas Guillen of Seattle University in Seattle, Washington and Tory Creti of the University of North Texas in Denton, Texas for their review of the manuscript.

- To all the students at the University of Illinois at Springfield who took my serial murder course and who were frustrated with so many questions and so few answers. By asking all those questions, we learned from each other.

- To Bob Ladendorf for his interest and the continued support he has provided to me through his personal clipping service.

- To the National Crime Faculty at Bramshill Police College in England, who were gracious hosts to my wife, Kim, and me in May 1996.

- And finally, to Kim, my best friend, colleague, and partner, for her sociological research and steadfast support for my research and writing. Without her and her research support, none of this would ever have been published.

ABOUT THE AUTHOR

Dr. Steven A. Egger is a Professor of Criminology at the University of Houston Clear Lake and Professor Emeritus of Criminal Justice at the University of Illinois at Springfield. He was project director of the Homicide Assessment and Lead Tracking System (HALT) for the State of New York, the first statewide, computerized system to track and identify serial murderers. He has been researching serial murder since 1983.

He authored *The Killers Among Us: Examination of Serial Murder and Its Investigations, Second Edition* and *Serial Murder: An Elusive Phenomenon*. Dr. Egger has lectured on serial murder in England, Canada, the Netherlands, and Spain.

Dr. Egger has worked as a police officer, homicide investigator, police consultant, and law enforcement academy director. He holds a Ph.D. in Criminal Justice from Sam Houston State University, where he completed the world's first dissertation on serial murder.

With his wife, Kim Egger, he is currently working on an encyclopedia of serial murder that will include entries on over 1,300 serial killers.

CONTRIBUTORS

Kim A. Egger studied at Purdue University and has a B.S. in Psychology from the University of Illinois at Springfield. She is currently pursuing a master's degree in law and psychology. She has co-authored, with Steven Egger, a chapter on the victims of serial murder in a monograph on victimology. For the past ten years, she has been developing a database on serial killers, which currently holds information on 1,246 serial murderers. She has lectured at Purdue University, the University of Illinois at Springfield, and Brazosport College, Texas.

Don Larsen is a detective with the Springfield, Illinois Police Department. He holds a B.S. in Criminal Justice from the University of Illinois at Springfield.

Linda Kreuger was formerly a part-time patrol officer with the Sangamon County Sheriff's Office. She is currently employed in Rehabilitation Administration for the state of Illinois. She holds a master's degree in rehabilitation from Southern Illinois University.

Michael Miller is the author of more than fifty nonfiction books on topics as varied as music theory, business management, and computer use. He is also president of the Molehill Group, a writing/consulting firm based in Carmel, Indiana.

PREFACE

As a society, we have very little tolerance for homicide. When we can see some logic or rational reason for the killing, however, our tolerance for such an act is somewhat greater. It is much harder to find the rationale for an act of murder when the killer and the victim appear to have been strangers.

The reasoning behind the murder of a stranger defies our understanding. Such murders tend to increase our level of fear because of the apparent randomness with which victims are chosen. It cannot be denied that we are a violent society, prone to killing our friends, loved ones, and even acquaintances. But to kill a stranger, unless it is during the commission of another crime, is a definite threat to our society, an act that places us all at risk. A killer who intentionally chooses a stranger as his victim threatens our very social order.

THE MYTHS OF SERIAL MURDER

The Silence of the Lambs, released in 1991, was an extremely popular movie and winner of several Academy Awards. Unfortunately, this movie has probably done more than any other single film, book, or television program to promote the mythology of serial murder—and to obscure the facts of the phenomenon.

It's regrettable that most attempts at objectivity or factual reporting on serial murder are colored with the sensationalism of fiction writers and journalists competing for the public's interest. Serial killers are typically presented as randomly killing strangers on our city streets, in our parks, or on university campuses; reliable factual reporting of these crimes is marred by the hype and horror seen in newspaper columns and in the thirty-second sound bites of prime-time television programs.

Movies, novels, and the press have all promoted a number of myths regarding serial murder. Chief among these myths are the following:

- All serial killers had terrible childhoods, were beaten by their parents, and were sexually abused.
- Serial killers are "mutants from hell" who do not resemble the average person in appearance and mannerisms.
- Serial killers prey on anyone who crosses their paths and spend no time at all selecting their victims.
- Serial killers have an uncanny ability to elude the police for long periods of time.
- The serial killer fits the profile of a sex-starved man-beast, driven to kill because of a horrible childhood and the way society has treated him. He has had an unusual relationship with his mother. He travels alone across large geographic areas of the country and has an in-depth knowledge of police criminal investigative procedures, which allows him to elude local, state, and federal law enforcement. He is an insane and cowardly maniac who preys on the weak and helpless.
- The Federal Bureau of Investigation investigates all serial murderers because most of them cross state lines.

Like all myths, these contain some degree of truth. But myths are not really helpful in dealing with the serial killer. In fact, myths make understanding these killers and catching them all the more difficult.

THROUGH A MIRROR, DARKLY

It's important when analyzing the serial murder phenomenon to focus on the facts and not on the myths perpetuated by the media. Contrary to the images fed to us in *The Silence of the Lambs* and other works of fiction and nonfiction, the serial killer is not a hero but rather the mirror image of our potential selves. He can be seen as just like us, except that his avocation happens to be killing. We may develop a twisted infatuation with the fact that this person has killed and killed and killed again. We may marvel at his ability to commit the unthinkable, even though we ourselves have harbored such thoughts. To commit murder time and time again, to satiate the killer's continuing taste for death, has resulted in society's own insatiable fascination with these acts.

And here's the scariest part: Once caught, the serial killer who appears on our television screens and on the pages of our newspapers does not appear abnormal. We may label him insane or a "wacko," but deep down inside we see him as very much like ourselves—yet somehow different. It is this difference-yet-similarity that captures our attention and fascinates us.

My goal in writing this book is to provide a better understanding of these killers among us. To that end, I'll explore the theories behind serial murder, present detailed case studies of some of the most notorious serial killers of the past twenty years, and discuss how serial murders are investigated. You'll learn who these killers are and why they kill and kill and kill; you'll also learn what law enforcement is doing to track down and catch these deadly criminals.

It is my hope that when you're finished reading this book, you'll have a clear sense not only of the killers who perpetrate these crimes but also of their victims. There is no role for myth in the understanding of serial murder; the facts of the phenomenon are sobering enough.

THE PHENOMENON

1

THEY ARE ALL AROUND US

In modern society, we create strangers of each other—and as we become strangers, we begin to see others more as objects and less as human beings. This is not only a result of our alienation but also comes from our ever-present fear of the stranger.

In anticipation of falling prey to the stranger or perhaps from the memories of prior victimization, we remain a part of society yet hold ourselves apart from most of its members. We try to convince ourselves that we have control over our own lives but as we move about increasingly among strangers, we have little control over these individuals. And to the extent that we are seen as prey by some of these strangers, we are reminded that predators are all around us.

It is a realization that can make us feel truly isolated—and very much alone.

DEFINING SERIAL MURDER

The serial murder phenomenon dates back at least to the late 1880s, when Herman Webster Mudgett, alias Henry Howard Holmes, killed twenty-seven women in his "Murder

Castle" in Chicago, Illinois. Mudgett, who was hanged in 1896, is considered by some to be America's first serial killer.

Back then and for the next hundred years, serial murder was often described as "lust murder." The term *serial murder* was first used some time in 1982 or 1983; no one knows for sure who coined the term, but it has been with us ever since.

Numerous efforts have been made to define the phenomenon of serial murder. The national media began to define serial murder in early 1984, when *Newsweek* magazine differentiated between "serial" and "mass" murder by describing the former as an act in which the killer explodes in one homicidal rampage. That same year, an article in *Life* magazine reported that "unlike traditional mass murderers, who suddenly crack under pressure and kill everybody in sight, serial murderers kill and kill and kill, often for years on end." Nevertheless, until about 1989 the news media continued to refer to serial murder as "mass murder," even though the two are decidedly different.

Mass murder is a single horrific incident in which a killer annihilates a number of victims. Mass murderers are people like Richard Speck, who killed seven nurses in Chicago, Illinois on a single evening in July 1966 or James Oliver Huberty, who walked into a McDonald's restaurant in San Ysidro, California and killed twenty patrons before turning a gun on himself.

Serial murder is very different from mass murder. For the law enforcement community, *serial murder* usually refers to sexual attacks and the resulting death of young women, men, or children, committed by a male killer who tends to follow a distinct physical or psychological pattern. The FBI describes the serial killer as "someone who has murdered three or more victims with a cooling off period in between each of the homicides."

My own definition of serial murder is more precise, with seven major components that may serve as flags to alert investigators to the possibility that a serial murderer is operating in their jurisdiction. I define a serial murder as occurring when:

1. One or more individuals (in many cases, males) commit a second murder and/or subsequent murders.

2. There is generally no prior relationship between victim and attacker (if there is a relationship, it will be one that places the victim in a subjugated relationship to the killer).

3. Subsequent murders occur at different times and have no apparent connection to the initial murder.

4. Subsequent murders are usually committed in different geographical locations.

5. The motive is not for material gain; it is for the murderer's desire to have power or dominance over his victims.

6. Victims may have a symbolic value for the murderer and/or they may be perceived to lack prestige, to be unable to defend themselves or alert others to their plight, or to be powerless given their situation in time, place, or status within their immediate surroundings.

7. Victims typically include vagrants, the homeless, prostitutes, migrant workers, homosexuals, missing children, single women (out by themselves), elderly women, college students, and hospital patients.

SERIAL MURDER BY THE NUMBERS

What is the prevalence of serial murder? How many serial murderers are there? How many people do they kill?

Researcher Kim Egger has compiled what is perhaps the most comprehensive set of data regarding serial murders. According to Egger's data, which spans the years 1900 through 1999, there were 1,246 serial killers identified during this period worldwide. During the same period, 18,361 suspected victims were identified for an average of 14.735 victims per killer. There were 236 serial killers in the United States during this time, accounting for 3,130 victims, for an average of 13.262 victims per killer.

Another source of data on serial murderers is the FBI Behavioral Sciences and Investigative Support Unit at the National Center for the Analysis of Violent Crime. According to an official summary provided by this unit, there were 331 serial murderers and almost 2,000 confirmed victims of serial murder between January 1977 and April 1992.

But an independent examination of the FBI's supporting data, commissioned by CNN, found a very different picture. The FBI data had been collected from major newspaper wire services and other publications; after removing a number of duplicated cases, the total number of serial killers listed in the FBI's own supporting data was only 175. After adding in serial murderers missing from this data, the total number of known serial killers during this period was 191, and the actual number of confirmed victims totaled 1,007. This independent analysis reduced the number of serial killers by 140, or 42 percent, and reduced the number of victims by almost 1,000, or almost 50 percent.

(A spokesperson for the FBI admitted to CNN that the numbers were "[v]ery squishy. Very unreliable numbers. It's hard for anybody to come up with accurate numbers.")

WHO ARE THEY?

Who are these serial killers? To answer that question, let's look briefly at some of the better known serial killers in our society.

Jeffrey L. Dahmer's deadpan stare is known to most people who ever watch TV or glance at a copy of *Time, Newsweek,* or *People.* In July 1991, Dahmer was charged by Milwaukee police with the death of sixteen young men in that city; he was also charged with the death of one young man in Ohio. He confessed to killing and dismembering his victims and at his trial pled guilty but insane. The judge decided Dahmer was sane and sentenced him to fifteen consecutive life sentences in Wisconsin, a state that prohibits the death penalty. Dahmer was killed in prison in 1994; you can read more about him in Chapter 10.

Police in Des Plaines, Illinois found the bodies of most of the young men killed by **John Wayne Gacy, Jr.** in a crawlspace under Gacy's house. Gacy is discussed in detail in Chapter 4.

Shortly after his arrest on suspicion of killing an eighty-four-year-old woman, **Henry Lee Lucas**, discussed in Chapter 5, confessed to having killed sixty people.

"Hillside Stranglers" **Angelo Buono** and **Kenneth Bianchi** were accused of killing ten young women in the Los Angeles, California area. Bianchi was convicted of two killings in Bellingham, Washington after his claim of having a multiple personality was found to be a hoax. Bianchi is discussed in Chapter 6.

Between March and June 1990, a serial murderer calling himself the "Zodiac Killer" shot and seriously wounded four people in the Brooklyn and Queens boroughs of New York City. The fourth victim died three and a half weeks after he was shot in the back. Newspapers received letters signed "The Zodiac," in which the writer provided details about the killings that, according to police, only the killer could know. The writer claimed that he intended to kill one person for each of the twelve signs of the Zodiac, the chart used by astrologers to predict the future. The killer eventually shot nine victims, three of whom died. **Heriberto Seda,** later identified as the Zodiac killer, was arrested June 18, 1996 in his Brooklyn apartment, where he allegedly shot his sister, then held police at bay for three hours. He was convicted of three counts of murder and sentenced to eighty-three years' imprisonment. Prior to his conviction, Seda told the arresting detectives that he was envious of Ted Bundy and "wanted to be as good as [Bundy] was in getting victims."

Theodore Robert Bundy, of course, is well known to those with even the most casual interest in the phenomenon. He is discussed at length in Chapter 7.

Richard Ramirez, dubbed the "Night Stalker" by the press, claimed to worship Satan. He was convicted of thirteen murders and thirty felonies by a California jury and is currently incarcerated in San Quentin Prison in California.

Arthur Shawcross pled innocent to the murders of ten women. His lawyers argued that he was legally insane, but he was found guilty of second-degree murder and was sentenced to a minimum of 250 years in prison in New York. He also pled guilty to killing an eleventh victim.

Wayne Williams pled innocent to the killing of two black youths in Atlanta, Georgia but an Atlanta jury found him guilty of two counts of murder, and he was sentenced to two consecutive life terms in Georgia. At the time, police believed that Williams was responsible for killing twenty-four young people in what were referred to as the "Atlanta Child Killings." By linking Williams to these other murders, prosecutors effectively closed the files on twenty-nine young people who had been murdered or were missing.

Donald Harvey's co-workers called him the "Angel of Death." It seemed that whenever he was working as a nurse, someone died in the hospital. Harvey was charged with killing hospital patients in Ohio and Kentucky and was convicted of thirty-seven murders, seven aggravated murders, and one felonious assault. He pled guilty to avoid the death penalty. He claims to have killed eighty-seven people and is believed by others to have killed an additional twenty-three victims.

Patrick Wayne Kearney pled guilty to killing thirty-two young men between 1975 and 1978 in what were referred to as the "Trash Bag Murders" in the Los Angeles area. These victims were dismembered and dumped in trash bags. Kearney received two concurrent life sentences.

Over a thirteen-month period in 1976 and 1977, the "Son of Sam" shot thirteen young men and women in eight different incidents in New York City. Six of these victims died. **David Berkowitz**, a twenty-four-year-old postal worker, was charged with these crimes. Claiming that a dog told him to kill, he pled guilty to the murders of five women and one man, and was sentenced to twenty-five years to life.

Juan Corona was convicted in January 1973 of the slayings of twenty-five migrant farm workers in California. The prosecution argued that these were homosexual murders, but a motive for these killings was never firmly established. Corona was sentenced to twenty-five consecutive life terms. An appeals court ordered a new trial, and he was again convicted of all of these murders.

Albert DeSalvo claimed to be the "Boston Strangler," but police lacked evidence to bring him to trial for the murders of thirteen female victims killed between mid-1962 and early 1964. DeSalvo was tried and convicted for unrelated assaults and was sentenced to life imprisonment. He was stabbed to death in his cell in 1973.

Westley Allan Dodd was the first person in over thirty years to be executed by hanging in the United States. Dodd was convicted in 1993 of the kidnapping, rape, and murder of three small boys. Prior to these murders, he claimed, he molested young boys virtually nonstop for fifteen years. Dodd is quoted as saying that if he were ever freed, "I will kill and rape again and enjoy every minute of it."

Lawrence Bittaker and **Roy L. Norris** began committing a series of rapes, torture, and murder of teenage girls during the summer of 1979 in California; the two had met in prison the previous year. They dumped their last victim, naked and mutilated, on the lawn of a suburban house so they could see the reaction of the press. They were found guilty of five murders and twenty-one other felonies, including rape, torture, and kidnapping. Norris received forty-five years to life in prison, and Bittaker received the death penalty.

Known by the media as the "Sunset Slayer," **Douglas D. Clark**, together with his partner, **Carol Bundy**, abducted and murdered six young prostitutes and runaways from Hollywood's Sunset Boulevard during the summer of 1980. Clark was found guilty of all six murders and sentenced to death. Bundy, who testified for the prosecution, received two sentences, twenty-seven years to life and twenty-five years to life, to run consecutively. Clark continues to deny all involvement in the murders. He still claims that Bundy (no relation to Ted

Bundy) did all the killings and was attempting to duplicate Ted Bundy's crimes.

Jerome Brudos, at seventeen years of age, forced a young girl at knifepoint to pose in the nude. As a result, he spent nine months in a mental hospital. Nine years later, between 1968 and 1969, he began killing young women in his garage under a special mirror he had installed to feed his fantasies. He was convicted of three murders and is serving three consecutive life sentences at the Oregon State Prison.

On August 21, 1992, **Benjamin Thomas Atkins** confessed to killing eleven women in the Detroit, Michigan area. During his lengthy confession, he explained to police in detail how he raped and strangled the eleven women in Highland Park and Detroit from the fall of 1991 to the spring of 1992. The bodies of his victims, all black women suspected of drug use and prostitution, were found nude or partially clothed in abandoned buildings. Atkins was found guilty on eleven counts of murder and one count of rape, and was sentenced to life without parole.

Richard Angelo, referred to as the "Angel of Death" by the media, worked as a supervising nurse in the intensive care and coronary care units of Good Samaritan Hospital in Long Island, New York. He had conducted experiments on field mice with the drugs Pavulon and Anectine, and in 1987 he began using these drugs on patients to put them into cardiac arrest. In some cases, Angelo would revive these patients; in other cases, the patients would die. When a surviving patient complained, an investigation was initiated, and thirty-three bodies were exhumed. Angelo was convicted of second-degree murder and manslaughter for injecting four patients with a deadly drug and was sentenced to fifty years to life. He is suspected of having killed as many as twenty-five patients.

Florida law enforcement officials believe that **Christine Falling** murdered six young children. She was found guilty of murdering three children who were under her care as she worked as their babysitter. When she is released, she says, she wants to babysit for young children again. She told CNN, "I just love kids to death."

Gerald Gallego and his wife, Charlene, went on a killing spree, abducting young women in search of the perfect sex slave, then murdering them. Charlene lured the women to the car Gerald was driving and often held a gun on the women while Gerald raped them. This team of killers murdered at least ten young women between 1978 and 1980.

John Joseph Joubert, IV says that he had a fantasy of cannibalism from the time he was six or seven years old. He was convicted of killing three young boys near Omaha, Nebraska in 1983, and he is believed to have killed others. He is on death row at the Nebraska State Prison.

As part of a plea bargain to avoid the death penalty, Robert Berdella confessed to killing six men in Kansas City, Missouri in the late 1980s. All of his victims were killed by injections of an animal tranquilizer after he had tortured them and used them as his sex slaves for a number of days. Berdella then dismembered the bodies. One of his victims escaped, and police subsequently found skulls and a number of pictures of the victims in his apartment. Berdella died in prison of a heart attack in October 1992, following a lengthy series of interviews with British television journalists.

There are four serial killers who play bridge together on California's death row. They have been convicted of killing a total of forty-nine people. One of these card players is William Bonin, known as the "Freeway Killer," who killed fourteen young men and boys between August 1979 and June 1980. Another player, Randy Kraft, was convicted in 1989 of killing twenty-four young men. Authorities believe he may have killed as many as sixty-three people. The third card player is Lawrence Sigmund Bittaker, who, with Roy Norris, committed five murders. The fourth is Douglas Clark (the "Sunset Strip Killer"), who was convicted of killing six prostitutes and runaways during the summer of 1980.

Kenneth Allen McDuff was on death row for the murders of three teenagers in Fort Worth, Texas in 1966. His sentence was commuted to life in 1972, and in 1990 he was paroled. Less than two years later, he was suspected of killing at least six women in Texas. The body of one of McDuff's victims was discovered just three days after his release from prison. After he was profiled on the television program *America's Most Wanted* in May 1992, a viewer spotted him in Kansas City, Missouri, where he was arrested. He was convicted in 1993 of killing a pregnant convenience store clerk in Temple, Texas, and he is still a suspect in the disappearance of several women in the Temple, Texas area. He was sentenced to death and was executed in November 1998.

Ray and **Faye Copeland**, a farm couple from rural northern Missouri, celebrated their fiftieth wedding anniversary in separate jail cells shortly after they were arrested for killing five transient farm workers with a .22 caliber rifle and burying them on the farm. Ray died of natural causes in 1993 in a Missouri prison.

In 1964, when **Edmund Kemper** was fifteen years old, he killed his grandparents and was committed to a California state hospital for the criminally insane. In 1969, he was released as "cured." Then, in an eleven-month period, he murdered six young female hitchhikers, and he also murdered his mother. After murdering his mother, he drove to Pueblo, Colorado, where he called the local police and confessed to the murders.

After his arrest, **David Martin Long** told police: "I've got something inside my head that clicks sometimes. It just goes off." Four of these lethal "clicks" resulted in the violent deaths of five women whom Long killed with an ax.

Wayne Nance killed at least four people in Montana between 1974 and 1986, and is suspected by police of killing others. Nance was referred to as "Montana's baby-faced serial sex murderer." Unlike most of the killers described here, Nance was acquainted with his victims. One of them was the mother of one of his high school classmates.

Charles Ng, along with **Leonard Lake**, tortured and killed at least eleven women in Ng and Lake's survivalist bunker near Wilseyville, California between 1981 and 1983. They are believed to have killed at least fourteen additional women during this time. Lake committed suicide shortly after his arrest for theft in June 1985. Ng, who was with Lake at the time, escaped and fled to Canada. The car that Ng and Lake were driving led police to the killers' hideaway, a torture-murder bunker in Calaveras County. Ng was arrested in Canada in 1985 and, in September 1991, was finally extradited to California, where he was arraigned on eleven counts of murder. Police found Lake's diary in the bunker. He wrote, "God meant women for cooking, cleaning house, and sex and when they are not in use they should be locked up." In 1999, Ng was found guilty of eleven counts of murder for the killing of three women, six men, and two infants.

In 1997, **Andrew Cunanan** went on a killing spree that left five men dead in Minnesota, Illinois, New Jersey, and Florida. The media called him "a gay thrill-killer who committed random murders." Following the death of his fifth victim, the internationally famous clothes designer Gianni Versace, police finally tracked Cunanan to a houseboat in Miami. Before police could apprehend him, he committed suicide.

Once a month between April and December 1995, **Robert Silveria** killed someone riding the rails. He killed in Oregon, Kansas, and Florida. In addition to the eight killings in 1995, he is suspected of killing dozens more. Nicknamed "Sidetrack," Silveria was a heroin addict who belonged to the Freight Train Riders of America (FTRA), an organization formed by Vietnam veterans who wear lightning-bolt tattoos, are considered welfare outlaws, and have links to far-right militia and racist groups such as the Aryan Nations. Past and present members of this group are suspected by police of having committed some 300 murders nationwide. Silveria would wait until his victims were asleep, then would beat them to death with a blunt object or a baseball bat. He would then assume the identity of his victim in order to collect more public welfare. When he was arrested in Oregon, he had twenty-eight food stamp accounts around the country and was picking up $119 per month from each one.

The South Side of Chicago spawned at least four serial killers between 1992 and 1999. In June 1995, **Hubert Geralds, Jr.** was charged with the murder of six women, some of whom had children. Most of his victims were drug users, and some had turned to prostitution to finance their drug habits. Geralds's murders were particularly difficult for the police to solve because there was little indication of foul play. Geralds's method of killing his victims was to smother them by covering their noses while pressing his thumb on the victim's throat, leaving no marks associated with strangling.

Derrick Flewellen is accused of strangling two women during the same time period that Geralds was killing. **Ralph Harris**, a third suspected serial killer, was charged with killing five men, all believed to have been robbery victims. In May 1996, the fourth Chicagoan, **Gregory Clepper**, was charged with killing eight women who apparently objected when he refused to pay them for sex. His victims, according to police, had all been drug addicts and prostitutes; all had been sexually assaulted, strangled, and left in trash containers on the South Side.

Andre Crawford was arrested by Chicago police in January 2000 and charged with killing ten women and raping eleven other women on the South Side of the city between 1993 and June 1999. Crawford confessed these crimes on videotape to the police. A DNA sample from Crawford linked him to seven murder victims and to one woman who survived a brutal assault. Most of Crawford's victims were strangled or received blunt trauma injuries. Many victims had arrest records for drugs and prostitution.

Dana Gray lived to shop, and when the money ran out, other people paid for her spending sprees with their lives. Her first victim was sixty-eight-year-old June Roberts; Gray strapped her to a chair, strangled her with a telephone cord, then smashed her in the face with a wine bottle. Her second victim was fifty-eight-year-old Dorinda Hawkins, an antique store clerk whom Gray strangled and left for dead. Hawkins survived the attack. Gray's third victim was Dora Beebe, eighty-seven, whom Gray hit with an iron, then strangled. Within minutes of each murder or attack, Gray was indulging her "shopaholic" tendencies, running up bills of thousands of dollars with the money and credit cards of her victims. Gray was sentenced to life without parole for the two murders and one attempted murder; police believe she is also responsible for three more murders. Gray's only explanation for her crimes was, "I had this overwhelming need to shop."

In November 1998, **Wayne Adam Ford**, a truck driver, walked into the Humboldt County sheriff's station in Eureka, California, holding the severed breast of a woman. He proceeded to confess to four murders of women hitchhikers and prostitutes. He was convicted of these four murders.

Between 1978 and 1993, an individual known as the "Unabomber" detonated seventeen bombs around the United States, killing three persons and injuring twenty-three. In September 1995, the Unabomber mailed a 35,000-word manifesto to several major national newspapers, an act that proved to be his undoing. Both the *New York Times* and the *Washington Post* (after extensive soul-searching and a number of meetings with officials of the U.S. Justice Department) published the manifesto, drawing the attention of one David Kaczynski, who realized that it was very similar in nature to papers written by his long-absent brother, Ted. He notified authorities, and on April 3, 1996, after a nearly two-month stakeout, federal law enforcement agents arrested **Ted Kaczynski** as a suspect in the Unabomber case. Agents found explosive chemicals and bomb-making material in Kaczynski's remote mountain cabin in Stemple Pass, Montana, where he had lived for the previous twenty-five years. In 1998, Kaczynski was sentenced to life in prison without parole.

And the list goes on, and on, and on, and on.

NOT ALL KILLERS ARE CAUGHT

It doesn't end there.

A number of still-unsolved homicides are believed to be the work of serial killers. These unsolved murders can be found in almost every state of the United States, as well as in many foreign countries; unfortunately, the killers behind these crimes may never be caught.

CALIFORNIA

When the bodies of four women were found in the East San Gabriel Valley and nearby Chino, California in the fall of 1993, authorities said the killings did not appear to be linked. The victims were all black and in their thirties, they had been strangled, and their bodies had been thrown into business parks or along the roadside, but investigators said that these similarities were happenstance and that the murders were not the work of a serial killer. They said that the bodies of eight slain women had been found dumped in Los Angeles in November alone. The San Gabriel Valley murders, officials reasoned, were just part of an abnormally high monthly tally of dumped bodies. It was only after the body of a fifth woman was found in the San Gabriel Valley on December 30, 1993 that the Los Angeles County sheriff's department and the Pomona police department indicated that three of the deaths were considered to be linked—and that two other victims also might be connected.

In another instance in May 1993, Los Angeles police sought public help in finding a Jeep driver who, they said, had killed three black men and wounded a fourth in a series of shootings since January of that year. The attacks occurred within a three-block radius in the Harbor City area near San Pedro. The suspect was described as a white man, age twenty-five to thirty-five, with red hair, driving a Jeep that was possibly red in color. The killings occurred on January 31, February 14, and April 15, 1993. The last attack, in May, resulted in the wounding of a thirty-eight-year-old man. No one has ever been charged with these shootings.

TEXAS

Over the past twenty-nine years, more than thirty women and girls have been murdered and dumped in the bayous along the fifty-mile stretch of Highway I-45 between Houston and Galveston. In addition, six more girls disappeared from this area and were never found. Despite the work of a task force set up by the Houston FBI office and the surrounding police agencies whose jurisdictions were involved, not a single case has been solved. Don Clark, special agent of the FBI's Houston office, stated: "Clearly there is more than one deranged individual out there. We think we are dealing with two or possibly three serial killers. But we don't even know if they are local or transient." The only thread that apparently links all these crimes is the very busy I-45, which joins a national freeway network north of Houston. Anyone committing a crime in the Houston area could be more than 1,200 miles away within twenty-four hours without breaking the speed limit.

Within this group of unsolved I-45 homicides, it appears that four murders outside of League, Texas were committed by the same killer. The skeletal remains of Heidi Villareal Fye, age twenty-five, a waitress reported missing on October 10, 1983, were found on April 4, 1984. The body of Laura Lynn Miller, sixteen, reported missing September 14, 1984, was found on February 2, 1986. The remains of "Jane Doe" and another unidentified victim, "Janet Doe," were found on February 2, 1986 and September 8, 1991, respectively. Local police believe these four women were victims of an "organized serial sexual offender" but have not been able to link the murders to any suspects. Efforts to identify Jane Doe and Janet Doe have been unsuccessful.

NEW YORK

A number of unsolved killings of prostitutes and alleged drug addicts in Rochester, New York since 1989 raised fears that another serial killer was at work—just two years after mass murderer Arthur Shawcross was convicted in a series of slayings in that area. Beginning in September 1992, the bodies of four women with a history of prostitution and drug abuse were found within a few miles of one another near the Lake Ontario State Parkway in northwestern Monroe County. The bodies of another ten women with similar histories have been found elsewhere in the Rochester area since 1989. Police are searching for two other missing women.

Following the 1990 conviction of Shawcross, who killed primarily prostitutes, police and sheriffs set up a program to pursue all missing persons cases aggressively. "Now we chase every lead," said Captain Lynde Johnston. "We immediately get dental records and other things to help with identifications. We treat them all like potential homicides." Police still have no suspects in these murders.

LOUISIANA

The body of a thirty-year-old woman clad in nothing but pink socks was discovered by two crawfishermen shortly after dawn on Sunday, February 21, 1993 in a ditch alongside a two-lane blacktop road in a rural stretch of St. Charles Parish near New Orleans, Louisiana. The woman, whose body had been there for several days, had been strangled. The next morning, another strangled, naked female body was discovered 700 feet down the road. The St. Charles Parish sheriff's office determined that the second body had been there less than twelve hours. Both victims were known prostitutes. After these murders were linked to a murder in September, sheriff's investigators discovered that New Orleans had ten similar cases.

"We haven't linked all these murders to one suspect," Sergeant Sam Fradella of the New Orleans police said of the unsolved Louisiana cases. "The murders are similar; the victims are similar. But we can't call this a serial killing. We're handling each one as an independent murder." However, as of April 1996, the bodies of twenty-six women have been found along roadways and in swamps within a sixty- to seventy-five-mile radius in the greater New Orleans area.

INDIANA, KANSAS, MISSOURI, TEXAS

What are now referred to as the "I-70 Robbery-Murders" began on April 8, 1992 with the slaying of a shoe store clerk in Indianapolis. Three days later, the owner and a clerk at a Wichita, Kansas bridal shop were slain. The killings continued on April 27, 1992, with the slaying of a ceramics store clerk in Terre Haute, Indiana. Eight days later, a western footwear shop clerk in St. Charles, Missouri was killed. Another murder occurred May 7, 1992 in Raytown, Missouri, outside Kansas

City, where a curio shop clerk was killed. Five of the six victims in the Midwest were women; the sixth was a man with long hair tied in a ponytail. All were shot in the head. None of the stores involved had security alarms, and all were robbed of the little money available. Ballistics tests revealed that the same .22 caliber weapon had been used in all of these homicides. Authorities then began examining three killings in the Dallas-Fort Worth, Texas area that appear to be similar in nature.

WASHINGTON AND OREGON

Since 1982, King County, Washington authorities have sought the so-called Green River Killer, blamed for the deaths of up to forty-nine women in Washington and Oregon. In 1986, the following teletype was sent out to all U.S. law enforcement agencies:

```
ALL POLICE DEPARTMENTS
(CITY, COUNTY, STATE, NATIONWIDE)
MSG H22KING COUNTY POLICE OCTOBER 17, 1986
```

THE KING COUNTY POLICE DEPARTMENT-GREEN RIVER TASK FORCE, SEATTLE, WASHINGTON, HAS BEEN INVESTIGATING A SERIES OF FEMALE HOMICIDES WHICH OCCURRED FROM APPROXIMATELY JULY 1982 THROUGH MARCH 1984. IT IS THE OPINION OF THE FBI'S BEHAVIORAL SCIENCE UNIT, AS WELL AS OTHERS FAMILIAR WITH SERIAL MURDERS, THAT THIS KILLER WILL NOT STOP UNTIL HE IS CAUGHT, OR MOVES FROM THE AREA. SINCE THERE HAVE BEEN NO MURDERS IN KING COUNTY ATTRIBUTED TO THIS KILLER SINCE APPROXIMATELY MARCH 1984, IT IS HIGHLY PROBABLE HE HAS MOVED AND IS KILLING ELSEWHERE. IT HAS ALSO BEEN DOCUMENTED THAT SERIAL MURDERERS HAVE CHANGED THEIR MODUS OPERANDI TO AVOID DETECTION.

RECEIVING AGENCIES ARE REQUESTED TO ADVISE THE KING COUNTY POLICE DEPT-GREEN RIVER TASK FORCE OF ANY SERIAL MURDERERS AND THEIR MODUS OPERANDI WHO HAVE OPERATED IN THEIR JURISDICTION SINCE MARCH 1984. IT SHOULD BE EMPHASIZED THAT INFORMATION IS BEING SOLICITED ON SERIAL HOMICIDES IN YOUR AREA, NOT JUST THOSE WHOSE MODUS OPERANDI IS SIMILAR TO THAT OF THE SERIAL MURDERER WHO OPERATED IN KING COUNTY.

IN EVALUATING WHETHER A "SERIAL MURDERER" HAS OPER-
ATED IN YOUR AREA, IT MAY BE USEFUL TO NOTE THAT A
"SERIAL MURDERER" GENERALLY REFERS TO A NUMBER OF
MURDERS BY A SINGLE PERSON OVER A PERIOD OF MONTHS—
OR, OCCASIONALLY YEARS. EACH KILLING IS USUALLY A
DISCRETE EPISODE, BUT THERE IS USUALLY A COMMON
MOTIVE, METHOD, AND/OR TYPE OF VICTIM.

A REPLY IS REQUESTED REGARDLESS OF WHETHER THE
RESPONSE IS POSITIVE OR NEGATIVE.

In 1993, law enforcement officials gave the press a list of twenty-nine unsolved killings and twelve cases of disappearance of women since 1985 in King, Snohomish, and Pierce counties in the state of Washington. These murders were said to have been committed by a new killer—*not* the Green River Killer, who apparently stopped murdering young women in the Seattle area sometime in 1984. Many of these new cases involved prostitutes or young, street-wise teenagers. This was the first public acknowledgment that a killer or killers were killing in the Seattle area since the Green River Task Force was disbanded in 1990. These killings remain unsolved.

FLORIDA

It would appear that one or more serial murderers may have been at work in Florida. In January 1993, a Marion County sheriff's office spokesman reported that eighteen women had been killed and dumped in remote areas in Florida between late 1991 and January 1993. All of the victims were believed to be prostitutes, and no arrests have been made. In describing these murders, the spokesman indicated that nine victims were found in Brevard County, four in Volusia County, three in Lake County, and one each in Marion and Pasco Counties. He also reported that four of the victims had been found in the state of Indiana and three in Tennessee.

MASSACHUSETTS

In the New Bedford, Massachusetts area, the district attorney's office and the police spent years investigating the killings in the late 1980s of eleven women, all of whom had connections to drug use and prostitution in the Weld Square area. All of the victims had small children; most were strangled to death and abandoned along the major highways that ring New Bedford. Although a man was charged in one of those killings, the case was dismissed for lack of evidence. The killings did not continue and remain unsolved.

CONNECTICUT

In Connecticut, investigators created a task force in 1980 to seek the killer responsible for strangling two Waterbury prostitutes in 1988 and 1989. The task force was disbanded a few months later without a conviction.

PENNSYLVANIA, KENTUCKY, TENNESSEE, MISSISSIPPI, AND ARKANSAS

Between October 1983 and April 1985, eight female victims, some of them red-haired prostitutes, were found strangled and left along highways in five states bordering the Ohio and Mississippi Rivers. The case remains open, and no viable suspects were ever identified.

MICHIGAN

Michigan police have never been able to identify the "Oakland County Child Killer." The victims of this murderer were two young boys and two young girls killed in 1976 and 1977. A task force was formed to catch the killer but was finally disbanded when all leads had been exhausted.

CALIFORNIA

During the period from October 1966 through October 1969, California was the scene of a series of baffling murders committed by an unknown person who signed himself variously "r-h," "Z," "the Zodiac," "a friend," "A Citizen," and "Red Phantom." The "Zodiac Killer," as he became known in the press, killed six people and wounded two others; he also wrote to the San Francisco police, taunting them. The killer was never identified.

KANSAS

Between October 1989 and March 1990, four Native Americans were found murdered in Lawrence, Kansas. Leaders of the Arapaho and Cheyenne tribes, suspecting that these deaths were the work of a serial killer, asked the FBI to investigate. Local authorities, however, claimed that the homicides were unrelated.

MARYLAND

In Suitland, Maryland, a suburban community adjacent to the District of Columbia, five young black women were killed within a two-month period in December and January 1987. Their bodies were found in a wooded park in Suitland. All had been sexually assaulted and stabbed to death. No one was ever charged with these murders.

OUTSIDE THE UNITED STATES

Serial murder is definitely an international phenomenon. Although the United States has reported many more serial killers than other countries, more and more serial killers are being identified across the globe. Serial murders have been reported in the United Kingdom, Australia, South Africa, Germany, China, Japan, Austria, France, Russia, Nigeria, Bonsai, Italy, Hungary, and the former Soviet Union. Few countries have escaped the horror of the serial killer.

WHAT DO THEY LOOK LIKE?

Unlike the serial killer Hannibal Lecter in the film *Silence of the Lambs,* serial murderers do not look like killers, nor does their appearance reflect an ultimate evil. Unfortunately, serial killers simply do not stand out on our city streets, in suburban neighborhoods, or on our highways as anything other than the average person. Once a Ted Bundy, Henry Lee Lucas, or John Wayne Gacy is identified, some are quick to comment on the killer's appearance: "He has an evil eye." "He sure looks like a serial killer." "I wouldn't want to meet him in a dark alley late at night." Without a criminal identity, however, in most instances the serial killer looks just like anyone else.

Even though a number of people retrospectively reinterpret the background and appearance of a serial killer after he or she has been caught, many others marvel at the fact that these killers look like the "boy next door," your "average Joe," or "just like any other normal person." Jeffrey Dahmer certainly doesn't look like a killer, and neither do many of the other serial killers briefly described in this chapter. The normal outward appearance of the serial killer seems to dumbfound many people and remains a fascination for many more.

THEY MAY BE YOUR NEIGHBORS

Robert Hansen was considered a family man and a respected community member in Anchorage, Alaska, where he owned a bakery and was a member of the local chamber of commerce. Yet in early 1984, he entered a plea-bargaining agreement in which he admitted killing seventeen women and raping thirty more. Hansen tortured his victims in his home while his family was away; he then killed them with a high-powered rifle after releasing them in rural areas outside Anchorage, where he also buried his victims.

Like Hansen, **Robert Yates, Jr.** was considered an upstanding community member and a good neighbor in Spokane, Washington. Unlike his neighbors, however, Yates was a killer; at least eleven Spokane prostitutes lost their lives to his brutal assaults, which began in 1996. Before he was identified as a serial killer, this father of five appeared to all, including his wife and father, to be living the American dream.

After his arrest in April 2000, Yates pled guilty to three additional murders—two Walla Walla killings in 1975 and the killing of Stacy Hawn in 1988. The first case, the killing of a college couple, had remained unsolved for a quarter century;

the case of Stacy Hawn had also gone unsolved. Authorities suspect that the modus operandi of these crimes may have established Yates's future pattern of killings of Spokane prostitutes. In October 2000, Yates was taken to Tacoma, where he was found guilty of killing two additional women.

WATCH OUT FOR THE QUIET ONES

When **Joel Rifkin** confessed to having murdered seventeen prostitutes in the New York City area, a high school classmate described him as "quiet, shy, not the kind of guy who would do something like this." When David Berkowitz was convicted of six "Son of Sam" murders committed in 1976 and 1977 in New York City, a former friend from his army days stated, "He was quiet and reserved and kept pretty much to himself." Berkowitz's boss said, "That's the way he was here, nice—a quiet, shy fellow."

Juan Corona was convicted of twenty-five murders of itinerant farm workers in California in 1971. Following Corona's conviction, a friend described him as a very quiet person: "That's the kind of man he is—kept to himself and never said much, for the most part."

When Jeffrey Dahmer confessed to having killed and dismembered seventeen people in Milwaukee and Ohio in 1991, a friend of one of Dahmer's victims said, "He [Dahmer] didn't have much to say about anything, just 'Hi, nice to meet you.' He seemed quiet."

And when Westley Allan Dodd was arrested and eventually executed in 1993 for the kidnapping, rape, and murder of three small boys, one of his neighbors stated, "Wes seemed so harmless, such an all-around, basic good citizen."

Appearances can be deceiving.

PROFILING THE SERIAL KILLER

Although every serial killer is different, experts have noted some general similarities that might prove useful in the understanding of these criminals.

MOBILITY

One important characteristic of many serial killers is their mobility. Serial murderers are generally considered to be extremely mobile, often moving from city to city and state to state. Robert Keppel, the chief criminal investigator for the Washington State Attorney General's Office (he investigated the Theodore Bundy case, as well as the Green River Killings in the Seattle area), characterized serial murderers as ready to move quickly to another town after committing several killings that might lead to their detection. For example, Theodore Bundy is reported to have left victims across the country, from Seattle to Pensacola; killings by Henry Lee Lucas are suspected by law enforcement agencies in twenty-seven states.

Many serial murderers travel continually. Whereas the average person might put 10,000 to 20,000 miles a year on his car, some serial murderers have traveled 100,000 to 200,000 miles a year by automobile. However, not all serial murderers are so mobile; some commit their killings within a relatively small geographic area. For instance, John Wayne Gacy committed his killings in and around the suburbs of Chicago; Robert Hansen committed his killings within the Anchorage, Alaska area, even though he buried his victims in rural areas outside Anchorage.

FASCINATION WITH LAW ENFORCEMENT

A number of serial murderers appear to have been fascinated with law enforcement. Several have posed as law enforcement officers in order to lure their victims, some have held positions as security guards, and some have actually worked as auxiliary police.

Some serial murderers are so fascinated by detective work that they school themselves in police procedures and investigative techniques. For example, Theodore Bundy worked for the King County Crime Commission in Washington; Wayne Williams often photographed crime scenes; John Wayne Gacy had a police radio in his home; and Edmund Kemper frequented a bar near police headquarters and questioned off-duty officers about the murders he had committed.

STABILITY AND TRANSIENCE

Serial murderers can also be defined in geographic terms. Cecil Wingo, chief investigator for the Harris County, Texas medical examiner (retired), coined the terms *megastat* and *megamobile* to describe where serial killers commit their crimes. The megastat commits killings over time in a single, static urban environment. The megamobile killer is mobile, moving over great stretches of geography as he commits his killings.

Researchers R.M. Holmes and J. DeBurger prefer the terms *geographically stable* and *geographically transient*. They define the former as one who typically lives in a particular area and kills his victims within the general region of his residence and the latter as one who travels continually throughout his killing career. They further differentiate between these two types, stating that for the geographically stable serial murderer, "[v]ery frequently, the motive is sexual in nature and the predator may slaughter a selected group of victims."

Another researcher, E.W. Hickey, used geographic identifiers to describe three different types of serial killer: the "traveling or mobile," the "local," and the "place-specific." In Hickey's words:

> Mobile murderers are those individuals, almost exclusively male, who move from city to city and across state lines, killing victims at random, or seeking out a specific type of victim. These killers tend to appear friendly and helpful to their victims and usually take considerable precaution against being caught, i.e., Edmund Kemper....

> [T]he local serial murderer stays in close proximity to his city or community. Again, almost exclusively male, these killers usually have a specific type of victim, i.e., prostitutes in the Green River Killings or the young males in the Atlanta Child Murders....

[T]he place-specific serial murderer, or the killer who repeatedly murders in the same place. This type of killer usually operates in nursing homes, hospitals, or in private homes. Either male or female, these murderers kill for reasons of financial security, "mercy" killing, hatred of a particular group of people such as infants, handicapped, or the elderly as well as motives of violence and sex ... i.e., Ed Gein; John Gacy; ... Herman Webster Mudgett.

LUST-MURDERERS

The classification of murder according to its motive is also a useful way to categorize different types of serial murder. In her classic book, *Murder and Its Motive* (Knopf, 1924), F.T. Jesse provided six "natural" groups of motives:

1. Gain

2. Revenge

3. Elimination

4. Jealousy

5. Lust of killing

6. Conviction

The focus of many researchers of serial murder has been the fifth motive—the lust murder. R.R. Hazelwood and J.E. Douglas, early pioneers with the FBI who examined serial murder, described two types of lust-murderers. The "organized nonsocial" is seen as a totally egocentric, amoral individual who can be superficially charming and manipulative of others. His crimes are committed with method and expertise. The "disorganized asocial" type is described as a loner with feelings of rejection who has great difficulty in interpersonal relationships. His killings are less cunning and are done on impulse. These killers generally select female victims, although male victims are not unknown.

Note, however, that although some serial killers are lust-murderers, not all are—nor are all lust-murderers serial killers.

IT'S NOT A NEW PHENOMENON

Whatever their motives, serial killers have been with us for longer than some might think. While there is a general impression that serial murder has emerged only in the last few years, this perception cannot be supported.

Researcher E.W. Hickey analyzed reams of historical literature and discovered serial murderers as far back in U.S. history as the early 1800s. He reached the following conclusions:

> First, the data unequivocally contradicts the assumption that serial murderers are a recent phenomenon. Regardless of their typologies, serial murderers can be traced back 200 years. Secondly, the emergence of serial murderers to the public view is made possible by our advancing technology, but they probably have always existed and operated in the United States.

The killers have been among us for a long time.

2

WHY DO THEY KILL AND KILL AND KILL?

The killing of a stranger is the most frightening of crimes. It is an unexpected and seemingly random act, not motivated by previous friction in the killer-victim relationship. To the friends and family of the victim, it is a crime beyond understanding.

Yet understanding the motivation behind these crimes is a critical factor in finding and stopping serial killers. Although law enforcement is quite naturally focused on identifying and capturing these murderers, it is becoming increasingly important to understand why they behave as they do.

Was John Wayne Gacy like Ted Bundy? How is Andrew Cunanan, who killed five men from Minnesota to Florida, different from Arthur Shawcross, who killed eleven women in the Rochester, New York area? Was Herbert Richard Baumeister, who was considered to be a family man but who may have killed sixteen young gay men in the Indianapolis area, any different from Robert Yates, reportedly also a devoted family man, who killed at least eleven prostitutes in the Pacific Northwest?

Answering these questions will help us figure out why someone becomes a serial killer—and more readily identify the killers among us.

THE BUTCHER OF ST. PETERSBURG

Consider the case of the Russian serial killer Ilshat Kusikov. St. Petersburg police charged Kusikov with the murders of three men in November 1995; they fear he also killed many more victims, including women and children. On the day Kusikov was arrested, police found in his apartment two human legs severed below the knee and two forearms cut from the elbow. When he was arrested, Kusikov begged the police to take his jars of dried human ears and buckets of human bones—so they wouldn't go to waste, he said.

Little is known of Kusikov's childhood except that his father strangled his mother when he was eleven years old. Records from Tadjikistan, where Kusikov grew up, show that he had an intense interest in surgery. He is reported to have had an incestuous relationship with his brother following the death of his mother. Also at this time, he developed an obsession with human physiology and was able to have orgasms while watching surgical operations on television. In the early 1970s, Kusikov worked as a welder before he was diagnosed as schizophrenic and began receiving a disability pension from the government.

When Kusikov's killings began, his wife—who had been an outpatient at the same mental hospital where her husband was treated—walked out on their two-year marriage after he attacked her with a knife. By this time, Kusikov was drinking excessively, eating dogs, and leaving the rotting corpses of cats in his apartment. He also was drinking his own urine and becoming sexually aroused by the smell of human excrement.

In his confession to Dr. Valery Ivanov, a Russian psychiatrist and expert on serial killers, Kusikov stated that he always committed the murders on the day he received his disability pension check. He would invite one of his "friends" to his apartment to drink vodka. When he and his companion were very drunk, Kusikov would make homosexual advances to his friend. If these advances were refused, Kusikov would become very angry and would strike his "friend" in the back of the head with a knife handle before slitting the victim's throat. He would then strip himself and his victim and would dismember the victim with a meat cleaver. Finally, Kusikov would cook his victim's heart, liver, and other body parts.

What turned Kusikov into the butcher he became?

COMMON CHARACTERISTICS
OF SERIAL KILLERS

In 1988, researchers R.M. Holmes and J. DeBurger examined the behavioral backgrounds of serial killers and discovered three common characteristics:

1. "The basic sources of the repetitive homicide pattern are psychogenic." The serial killer's psyche includes the norms, values, beliefs, perceptions, and propensities that result in the killing. These psychogenic factors are in contrast to sociogenic factors, which provide context for these propensities but are not considered the immediate cause of the killing.
2. "Motives that impel and justify the repeated acts of homicide have an intrinsic locus; they are structured and rooted within the mind of the murderer." The killing is the expression of the killer's desire to kill; in most cases, the motive is not material gain, political power, or other external rewards.
3. "The serial killer's homicidal behavior is expressive of the interlocking motives and propensities that predominate in his mind and personality. His behavior is therefore oriented toward psychological gain." Given the killer's psychological drive to kill, the more murders committed, the greater the buildup of psychological gain.

Although noting that serial murder is psychogenic, Holmes and DeBurger argue that social and cultural elements in American society tend to enhance the probability of serial killings. They cite the emphasis on violence and thrills in our entertainment industry, the common view of violence as a normal way of dealing with problems, the anonymity and depersonalization of urban society, and the mobility of Americans as factors that all serve the homicidal propensities of the serial killer.

Another researcher, E.W. Hickey, found that most serial killers were not highly educated and generally did not hold professional or skilled jobs. Further, they did not commonly use firearms as their sole means of killing; mutilation was found in over half of the cases and strangulation or suffocation in one third. Hickey notes that the act of killing must be viewed as a process, given that a number of these serial killers have tortured, beaten, and mutilated their victims prior to death.

In terms of motivation, although sexual motivation was listed most frequently by offenders, only 9 percent gave it as their sole reason for killing; 46 percent listed it as their motivation "sometimes." "Enjoyment" was listed frequently, and "money only" was listed by only 7 percent of these killers. Rarely were these motives listed as the sole reason. Hickey noted that many of the stated motives of the killers in his study "may actually have been methods by which they achieved ultimate power and control over other human beings."

Hickey argued that solo killers who kill women can be referred to as *lust killers* because of the sexual nature of their criminal assaults; in his view, the primary motive of this group is control. In comparison with all other male serial killers, these lust killers were more prone to rape their victims or carry out bizarre sexual acts on the victims, to have a history of sex-related crimes, and to have spent time in prison or mental institutions. One third of this type of killer had experienced previous social or psychological problems, and two thirds of them had experienced prior incarceration in prison or a mental institution. Just over 30 percent of these offenders experienced some form of childhood trauma, ranging from rejection and an unstable home to poverty and a prostitute mother.

THE FEMALE SERIAL KILLER

Hickey also provided analysis of an interesting subset of serial murderers—the female serial killer. Hickey found that a number of them had histories of child abuse, extreme poverty, and unstable relationships. In a taxonomy of motives developed from his data, Hickey states that their motives "appear to center on financial security, revenge, enjoyment, and sexual stimulation."

Of the female killers he examined, Hickey listed the motive as "money sometimes" in 47 percent of cases. Because Holmes and DeBurger, among others, believe the primary motive of the serial killer is psychological, this could be seen as a drive to achieve creature comforts. However, the second most common motive among these female killers is listed as "money only" in 27 percent of cases. A number of researchers would exclude these cases because the motive is material. However, a number of these killers may be "black widows," women who kill their husbands or relatives for insurance compensation. Hickey notes that some of these killers' motivation for money may simply represent their attempt to meet an unfulfilled need; for others, psychological needs and economic needs are one and the same.

Also interesting was that very few of the female killers had a previous criminal history. Their primary method of killing was the use of poison, and almost half used poison exclusively.

SEX SLAVES IN PHILADELPHIA

One doesn't have to conduct a massive survey to study serial murder; researchers also learn from studying individual cases. One such researcher, J.A. Apsche, studied the case of serial killer Gary Heidnik to reach certain conclusions regarding serial murder.

Between November 1986 and March 1987, Heidnik kidnapped six women in Philadelphia and held them as sex slaves in the cellar of his home in order to have them produce his off-spring. One of these women died while hanging from the cellar rafters and was dismembered by Heidnik. A second victim was electrocuted by Heidnik, who then disposed of her body in New Jersey. Heidnik was found guilty on two counts of first-degree murder, five counts of rape, six counts of kidnapping, four counts of aggravated assault, and one count of deviate sexual intercourse.

Apsche interviewed Heidnik and analyzed other information presented during his criminal trial. In his analysis of Heidnik, Apsche argued that the characteristics found in Heidnik were very similar to those of other serial killers. He found an insatiable obsession, an almost instinctual drive, that pushes these killers to fill their empty lives with an overactive fantasy life leading to ritual murder.

In Apsche's view, serial killers are manipulative; they attempt to control the world around them. They also have a strong feeling of inadequacy and, as children, never felt the intimacy of bonding with their parents. Many serial killers attempt suicide, and all of them attempt to get help. Apsche stated that these killers "appear to want to stop what is about to happen yet they always regain control of themselves to prevent their discovery." Heidnik, as one example, attempted suicide a total of thirteen different times.

OTHER RESEARCHERS, OTHER ANALYSES

Other researchers have analyzed serial killers from a combination of sources and found similar behavioral characteristics. J. Paul de River categorized what we now refer to as lust killers, who suffer from "a deviation or perversion of the sexual impulse"; they are "cold, calculating, and egotistically sadistic." Researcher M. Guttmacher stated that many of these sadistic killers vent their hostile impulses through cruelty to animals; their real hatred, however, is not against animals but against their fellow humans.

Another researcher, D. Abrahamsen, interviewed David Berkowitz (the "Son of Sam") and described him as "a human being inexorably driven to destroy himself and others." Abrahamsen found Berkowitz to be totally indifferent to the fate of his victims and to have an urge to kill (and when the time was ripe, to confess). Berkowitz, as his own detective, became in a sense the victim as well as the victimizer through his confessions. Such a description could apply equally well to other well-known serial killers, such as Danny Rolling, John Wayne Gacy, or Dennis Nilsen.

In discussing these compulsive homicides, researchers E. Revitch and L.B. Schlesinger noted that the majority of these crimes have an underlying basis in sexual conflicts and that most sex murders belong to this group. Serial murderers, according to D.T. Lunde, are sadistic murderers who are apt to repeat their crimes. He describes the sadistic murderer as one who kills, mutilates, or abuses his victims to achieve sexual pleasure and who may choose victims having specific occupations or characteristics: "They usually have few normal social and sexual relationships. In fact, they often have had no experience of normal sexual intercourse." The sadistic murderer is one of the most common types of killers of strangers and, of all types of murderers, is the most likely to repeat his crime.

CHILDHOOD ROOTS

Many researchers cite inadequate socialization or childhood trauma as contributing to the makeup of a serial killer. The intense rage of the serial killer may mirror the horrors suffered in childhood; hatred bred in childhood can now be directed at his victims.

Researcher W.S. Willie found that the most common feature in the family backgrounds of these murderers was the violent punishment inflicted on the child and that there "appears to be no other factor which is as specific in the family backgrounds of homicidal offenders." This observation was reinforced by FBI agents Roy Hazelwood and J.E. Douglas, who wrote in the April 1980 issue of *FBI Law Enforcement Bulletin*:

> Seldom does the lust murderer come from an environment of love and understanding. It is more likely that he was an abused and neglected child who experienced a great deal of conflict in his early life and was unable to develop and use adequate coping devices (i.e., defense mechanisms).

Serial murderers are frequently found to have unusual or unnatural relationships with their mothers. As researcher D.T. Lunde wrote:

> Normally there is an intense relationship with the mother. Her death is often one of those fantasized during adolescence. Later on, she may become one of the victims.... Many serial murderers have had intense, smothering relationships with their mothers—relationships filled with both abuse and sexual attraction.

Norman Bates, anyone?

SEX AS A MOTIVE

The killer's sexual orientation is not a consistent factor in known serial murderers. For example, DeSalvo, Bundy, and Kemper preferred females as sexual partners and as prey, whereas Gacy, Nilsen, and **Dean Corll** preferred males in these roles.

Data indicates that sex is only an instrument used by the killer to obtain power and domination over his victim. Although the sexual component is frequently present in a serial murder, it is not the central motivating factor for the killer but merely an instrument used to dominate, control, and destroy the victim.

Dr. Helen Morrison, who has interviewed a number of serial killers, argues against a sexual theme in serial murder. She states: "The incidence of sadomasochistic sex is very high. The incidence of mass murders is not, at least in the sheer number of perpetrators." In other words, if sadomasochistic sex caused serial murder, there'd be a lot more killing than there actually is.

Fellow researcher A. Storr also discounted the sexual nature of sadomasochism or cruelty. He argued that "sadomasochism is less 'sexual' than is generally supposed and is really a 'pseudo-sexual' activity or preoccupation, much more concerned with power relations than with pleasure."

More than sex, it is the emphasis on power relations or control that is an important characteristic of serial murders. As researchers J. Levin and J.A. Fox wrote:

> Domination unmitigated by guilt is a crucial element in serial crimes with a sexual theme. Not only does sadistic sex—consensual or forcible—express the power of one person over another, but in serial homicides, murder enhances the killer's sense of control over his victims.

VARIATIONS ON POWER AND CONTROL

Levin and Fox believe that the serial murderer is trying to achieve a feeling of superiority over the victim and to triumph or conquer by destruction. They observed that as "the serial killer becomes more and more secure with his crime, however, he may also become increasingly more sadistic and inhumane.... [T]he pleasure and exhilaration that the serial killer derives from repeated murder stem from absolute control over other human beings."

Researcher J.D. Sewell analyzed the case of Ted Bundy and came to these conclusions:

> Bundy's overall violent response exemplified an instigation to aggression which was grounded in his rage against women and magnified by his need for excitement, attention, and ego gratification. His habit strength drew on his repeated successful acts of violence ... to obtain control of the victims and the unsuccessful attempts by a number of states to charge him with these crimes. A number of situational fac-

tors added to his predisposition towards violence as an acceptable response.

Sewell concluded that "it would appear that Bundy chose a violent response as an acceptable reaction to many situations." The grisly details of the Bundy case appear to bear this out.

SIMILARITIES TO RAPE

The motivational dynamics of serial murder seem to be consistent with the findings of research on the nature of rape. Power appears to be a vital component of both crimes. As researcher David Canter noted:

> [M]en I have spoken to who have admitted a series of rapes have often also admitted that they would have killed subsequent victims if they had not been caught. Rape has the same roots as murder. The difference between rape and murder lies in the form and degree of control the offender exerts over his victims.

The implication of Canter's statement is that the motivations of these two violent acts may be similar. However, the motivational dynamics of both violent acts are complex, and their similarities may explain only a certain level of action—in this case, the form and degree of control—and not necessarily the inner thoughts and drives of the violent actor.

It is certainly true that rape is part of the criminal histories of many serial murderers. In some cases, these rapes are found to have been committed months or even years before any act of murder is committed. In other cases, the killer may vary his crimes, raping some of his victims and killing others.

ROBBERY, RAPE, AND MURDER

To illustrate this point, we need only look at the crimes of **James Edward Wood**. Wood's crimes detail a varied serial pattern of rape and murder, as well as a number of robberies:

- 1961: Commits auto theft, Idaho Falls, Idaho.
- November 23, 1967: Stabs two women in Bossier City, Louisiana and rapes one of them.
- 1967–1971: Is imprisoned in Angola, Louisiana.
- 1971–1975: Is robbery suspect in Missouri, Arkansas, Texas, and Louisiana.
- December 24, 1976: Kills woman in Shreveport, Louisiana.
- July 1977: Commits armed robbery in Baton Rouge, Louisiana.
- 1979: Is suspected in two murders in Louisiana; convicted of rape in Ruston, Louisiana.
- 1979–1986: Is imprisoned in Angola, Louisiana.
- March 1987: Is robbery suspect in Oklahoma.
- October 24, 1992: Rapes Alton, Illinois, woman.
- October 25, 1992: Rapes and shoots Jamie Masengill in Bridgeton, Missouri.
- October 27, 1992: Robs restaurant in suburban Denver.
- November 28, 1992: Rapes fifteen-year-old girl in Pocatello, Idaho.
- March 13, 1993: Robs sandwich shop in Pocatello.
- March 27, 1993: Robs Tyhee County Store in Pocatello.
- June 9, 1993: Rapes fourteen-year-old girl in Pocatello.
- June 19, 1993: Rapes prostitute near Salt Lake City after robbing a restaurant.
- June 23, 1993: Robs restaurant in Idaho Falls.
- June 27, 1993: Robs Poppa Paul's Café in Pocatello.
- June 29, 1993: Kidnaps eleven-year-old Jeralee Underwood in Pocatello.
- June 30, 1993: Murders Jeralee Underwood in Idaho Falls.
- July 6, 1993: Is caught by police and confesses.

As you can see, over the course of his criminal career, Wood quickly escalated from robbery to rape to murder, demonstrating that rapists can turn into killers. Criminal psychologist Ronald Weiner, who specializes in treating sexual predators, found some rapists who "during the course of attacking a woman will wind up killing her. And like it! So their liking for rape escalates into murder."

BIOLOGICAL PREDISPOSITION

There is a developing body of literature that suggests certain biological characteristics may cause an individual to commit violent acts. These biological characteristics may be certain abnormalities in the brain—either genetic traits present from birth or abnormalities caused by trauma or brain damage.

For example, Adrian Raine, a professor of psychology at the University of Southern California, Los Angeles, recently completed a series of psychological studies that point to mild brain dysfunction in early life as playing a crucial role in determining whether a young boy turns into a violent man. Raine's research strongly implies that birth complications can lead to mild brain damage that may go unnoticed throughout childhood, yet may predispose a boy to violent behavior in adulthood.

Raine suggests that birth complications may have produced the prefrontal dysfunction that goes on to lead to low levels of arousal, which in turn results in a tendency to commit violent crime. As Raine states: "We suspect that under-aroused people seek out arousal to increase their levels back to normal. One way to do this as a kid is to join a gang, burgle a house, or beat somebody up."

But one can't fully explain the motivations of serial killers from biological factors. As Dr. Richard Restak, a neurologist and neuropsychiatrist, stated: "However much one might wish otherwise, neurology will never entirely solve the mystery of why some people kill others, much less explain why some murderers derive pleasure from their actions."

Dr. Jonathon Pincus, a noted neurologist, believes that a combination of factors, including brain damage and psychiatric impairment, produces illogical thinking and paranoia in the serial killer. The other factor that he believes is always present in these killers is physical and/or sexual abuse. Brain damage alone will not cause a person to be violent, but when brain damage, abuse, and psychiatric impairment are all present, "those factors interact and produce a very violent person."

THE SHAWCROSS REGRESSION

Consider the case of Arthur Shawcross, a serial killer who was convicted of killing eleven women in the Rochester, New York area between 1988 and 1989. Dr. Richard Kraus, a rural psychiatrist from New York, studied the Shawcross case and came to some interesting conclusions.

Shawcross had no predisposing family history of alcoholism, violence, criminality, or psychiatric disorder and no evidence of parental abuse, neglect, abandonment, or cruelty. However, at age seven, this "bright, well-dressed, neat" child (as he was then described) was beginning to exhibit solitary aggressive conduct disordered behaviors which set him apart from his family, alienated him from his peers, and probably contributed to his becoming a loner. In the years that followed, his lifestyle became that of repeated aggressive and antisocial behaviors, with convictions for burglary, arson, manslaughter, and finally, the serial homicides of eleven women.

In examining Shawcross's medical history, Kraus found a number of serious accidents. When he was nine, Shawcross suffered leg paralysis and was hospitalized for one week. At age sixteen, he suffered a skull fracture and a cerebral concussion. When he was twenty, he was accidentally struck in the head with a sledgehammer and in that same year was involved in an auto accident. In each of these instances, he suffered a cerebral concussion. The following year, Shawcross fell from a ladder. His prison records show numerous complaints of passing out, headaches, and similar problems. Shawcross also received a 10 percent medical disability for numbness in his left hand related to a military injury suffered when he was in Vietnam.

Shawcross stated that his homicides were due to an "uncontrollable rage ... it wasn't everyone, just certain ones [who] were more aggressive ... the first one, she bit me ... some tried to rob me ... some belittled me ... some didn't care ... one threatened to tell my wife [about his infidelities]."

Kraus found that Shawcross was not too impaired to understand the nature and consequences of his acts or to know that what he did was wrong. But Shawcross did have a "hair-trigger" temper and would lose control when provoked or under stress.

A battery of psychological tests on Shawcross revealed a primary diagnosis of antisocial personality disorder. Laboratory examinations revealed that Shawcross had a 47, XYY karyotype chromosome. There is a great deal of controversy in the research literature regarding this XYY chromosome condition and whether it is suggestive of abnormality in some men. Further lab tests also revealed that Shawcross had ten times the normal level of krytopyrroles, which "correlated with marked irritability, rages, terrible problems with stress control, diminished ability to control stress, inability to control anger once provoked, mood swings, poor memory, a preference for nighttime, violence, and antisocial behavior."

In summary, Kraus found that:

These clinical findings revealed a matrix ... of genetic, biochemical, neurological, and psychiatric impairments, which at least partially explain the '... actual inner workings...' of this serial killer.... Such a matrix of findings in one individual can reasonably be expected to result in behavioral disturbance. While biological influences do not control behavior or predetermine outcomes, this case demonstrates that criminal tendencies do have biological origins.

ARE THEY SIMPLY EVIL?

Is it sufficient to identify serial killers as evil persons? After all, such individuals are certainly not good persons. Are they followers of Satan? Vampires? Demons with superhuman powers? Do serial killers represent the dark side of humanity?

Philip Jenkins, writing in *The Journal of Criminal Justice,* provided an interesting commentary on evil and serial murder:

> When the 20th century began, it was obvious to all educated people that this would be a great age of science and enlightenment. As this black age slouches towards its conclusions, it is clear that science has failed either to understand or to subdue the beast within humanity and the highest form of enlightenment might be to admit this fact. At the very least, let us agree on the failure of language to offer an acceptable terminology for the beast, the darkness, or whatever metaphor we choose to employ for that intuitively obvious reality. If not 'evil,' what?

HOW TO CREATE A SERIAL KILLER

As you can see, there are a number of different theories claiming to explain the behavior of the serial killer. Unfortunately, many researchers are still locked into a single-factor approach—the belief that a common profile of the "serial killer" exists and that all serial killers have certain common characteristics.

The mass media tend to drive this approach by constantly asking for a "profile" of the serial killer. But when we fail to consider those characteristics of serial killers that do not distinguish these killers from other nonkillers with similar characteristics, we are missing an important, even critical, ingredient in the behavior of serial murder. It is likely that the presence of these nondistinguishing characteristics *in combination with* other factors is what drives these killers to kill and kill again.

Dr. Park Elliot Dietz is one who believes that serial killers are produced by a combination of factors—in particular, bad genes and bad parents. When asked to imagine what it would take to create another Ted Bundy, John Wayne Gacy, or Edmund Kemper, Dr. Dietz came up with the following recipe:

> Start with an abusive, criminal father and a hysterical, alcoholic mother; torture the boy as erotically as possible; have the naked mother spank him and sleep with him until age 12; bind and whip him regularly; have the mother sexually arouse him and punish him for his erections; let the mother appear promiscuous while condemning prostitutes; leave detective magazines around the house for him to find; and encourage him to watch R-rated slasher films and violence against glamorous women.

That said, the decision to become a serial killer is just that—a matter of choice. As the old saying goes: It's not the cards you're dealt, it's how you play them.

3

THE VICTIMS

With an unknown number of serial killers at large in our society, how much at risk of attack are you and your loved ones?

Although it's true that most serial killers choose their victims based solely on their presence at a particular point in time at a particular place, the average heterosexual male is not likely to be targeted at random. The child in the park, the prostitute on the street corner, the homosexual male prostituting his body in clubs, the hitchhiker trying to find a ride along a stretch of highway—these individuals seem to be more vulnerable than the housewife doing laundry.

But should that housewife feel secure from the threat of a serial killer? The simple answer is no.

WHO ARE THE VICTIMS?

According to data on 1,246 serial killers in the United States from 1900 to 1999, 65 percent of the victims of serial killers were female. Additionally, 89 percent of the victims were white, 10 percent were African American, and 1 percent were Asian or Native American.

Although prostitutes make up the majority of female victims, that does not mean they are the only women targeted. Elderly women and women who live alone are also routinely targeted. A growing number of victims are in their homes when they meet their deaths at the hands of serial killers who choose home invasion as their modus operandi. Women also often fall victim to their lovers or spouses, who may kill them for monetary gain. But men are not alone in killing for profit; women are quite capable killers in their own right.

Children are frequently targeted by serial killers because they are unaware of their vulnerability, easily lured away, and easily subdued. Some children are also at special risk of being murdered by their mothers, as the murderers **Marybeth Tinning**, **Gayle Savage**, and **Waneta Hoyt** have proved. Children are at special risk when parents are afraid to warn them of the real threat that adults and even other children can pose to their safety. The tragic James Bulger case in England, where a two-year-old boy was killed by two ten-year-old boys, and the case of nine-year-old **Hamisi Prince** in Rwanda, who killed several younger children with clubs, stones, and by drowning or strangling, serve to remind us that children can and do kill other children. And in the third world and developing nations, children are killed in large numbers.

Male homosexuals are also at special risk. When male serial killers target other males, 48 percent of the victims will be homosexuals. As seen earlier, the number of victims of a homosexual serial killer is large. Because homosexuals are often marginalized in the larger community, serial killers seem to be able to operate for long periods of time, abducting and killing large numbers of victims before law enforcement is forced to act.

Race plays a role in the selection of serial murder victims. Approximately 7 percent of victims are chosen simply because of their race. The white racist **Joseph Paul Franklin** attempted to kill and did kill black males, many of whom were with white females. Hubert Gerald, a black male, killed black females on the South Side of Chicago. Local police and even an FBI analysis failed to notice his activity until he confessed.

Physical health can play a role in victimization. Being hospitalized can put a person at risk if he or she is unlucky enough to be admitted where an "angel of mercy" is at work. With medical personnel continually moving through patient rooms and medications frequently being given, medical serial killers easily find victims. In England, the trial of **Dr. Harold Shipman**, who killed at least 15 women in the town of old Hyde, shook up the medical community. In the United States, the reaction to **Dr. Michael Swango's** conviction in 2000 led to the medical community's trying to excuse its behavior. Swango was suspected of administering lethal injections to as many as 35 people while serving at a hospital at Ohio State University and a VA hospital on Long Island. The American medical community has refused to acknowledge its responsibility in allowing doctors and nurses to kill by ignoring and discouraging personnel who report suspicious activities. The mere fact that Dr. Swango was allowed to keep his medical license after he was convicted of poisoning emergency medical personnel serves to warn the public of the tolerance given to doctors who commit crimes.

At least 2 percent of victims are chosen because of their location. They are in the right house, or working in the right shop, or living in the right alley, or shopping in the right mall, or working the right street corner. They are chosen simply because they happen to be in or live in the place where the serial killer is hunting—where he feels most comfortable and safe in killing. This means that despite the statistics describing the most frequent victims, we are all at risk. If we are in the path of a serial killer, we can easily become his next victim unless we are aware of our vulnerability.

EXPLOITING THE WEAK

Most victims of serial killers are persons who are vulnerable—those individuals who are perceived as powerless or lacking in prestige by most of society. A lack of power or prestige readily defines them as easy prey for the serial killer. A careful selection of vulnerable victims does not mean that the serial killer is a coward; it means only that the killer has the "street smarts" to select victims who will not resist, will be relatively easy to control, and will not be missed. Such a selection protects the killer from identification and apprehension.

As researchers Levin and Fox note:

> Serial killers almost without exception choose vulnerable victims—those who are easy to dominate.... The serial killer typically picks on innocent strangers who may possess a certain physical feature or may just be accessible.

Fellow researcher A. Karmen agrees:

> The vulnerability of an individual or group to criminal depredations depends upon an opportunity factor as well as an attractiveness factor. Extreme risks are run by people who appear at the "right time" and the "right place" from the offender's point of view. Hence certain lifestyles expose individuals and their possessions to greater threat and dangers than others.

Karmen provides examples of these high-risk lifestyles: homosexuals cruising downtown areas and public bathrooms, cult members soliciting funds on sidewalks and in bus stations, and released mental patients and skid row alcoholics wandering the streets at odd hours.

Society's Throwaways: The "Less Dead"

The victims of serial killers often come from a devalued stratum of humanity. As they fall prey to their hunters, they become "less dead"—because, for many, they were "less alive" before their death, ignored and devalued by their own neighbors and communities. Examples of these victims include prostitutes, the homeless, vagrants, migrant farm workers, homosexuals, the poor, elderly women, and runaways.

This attitude toward marginalized members of society is often reflected in conversations at the dinner table. I have heard, "They were asking for it," too many times and in too many places not to believe that this attitude is prevalent in American society.

Unfortunately, this attitude goes beyond mere "table talk." A great deal less pressure is on the police when the victims of a serial murderer come from the marginal elements of a community. The public is much less incensed over a serial murderer operating in their area when they feel little or no identification with the victims. In this case, the victims seem far from real, and little attention is paid to their demise.

In the United States, nearly 78 percent of female victims of serial murderers are prostitutes. It is probable that the serial killer selects prostitutes most frequently because they are easy to lure and control during the initial stages of an abduction. Potential witnesses to the abduction see only a pickup and transaction prior to paying for sex. They are programmed to see only what they expect to see when a woman gets into a car with a john.

And who will miss one less prostitute plying her trade on the streets? It becomes too easy to blame her for her own fate. As Michael Newton pointed out in his book, *Serial Slaughter* (Loompanics, 1992):

> Worse yet are cases where police or members of the general public blindly overlook—or actively applaud—a killer's work. Authorities in San Diego, California still reject Eddie Cole's confession to five local homicides, dismissing each case—including that of Cole's wife, found strangled to death in a closet, wrapped in a bedspread—as "death by natural causes." In Portland, Oregon, following the unsolved murders of several prostitutes, a police lieutenant voiced his opinion that violent death was an occupational hazard for streetwalkers. England's Yorkshire Ripper, Peter Sutcliffe, preferred to call himself "The Streetcleaner," purging his district of whores, and few complained about his crimes until Sutcliffe accidentally bagged an "innocent" girl on his fifth outing. Closer to home, similar feelings are echoed in Lake Elsinore, California, where some residents claim that a local

prostitute-killer—as yet unidentified—is merely "cleaning up the trash downtown." Small wonder, in the face of such an attitude, that women's groups and gay rights activists complain of being short-changed by a legal system that evaluates a human life in terms of income, social status, sex, or race.

In many cases, selection of a prostitute assures the serial murderer that his killings may never be revealed. Even if such a victim's remains are found, she will be difficult for the police to identify, given her lifestyle and lack of close ties to her family or the community.

It is unfortunate that to many, these "less-dead" victims become relatively unimportant over the course of a serial killing event. Instead, the multiple nature of the killer's acts and his ability to elude the police become the central focus of this phenomenon.

For many, the serial killer is a symbol of courage, individuality, and unique cleverness, a figure who allows them to fantasize rebellion or the lashing out at society's ills. For some, the serial killer may become a symbol of swift and effective justice, cleansing society of its crime-ridden vermin. The serial killer's skills in eluding police for long periods of time transcend the very reason he is being hunted: The killer's elusiveness overshadows his trail of grief and horror.

GAY KILLERS—AND VICTIMS

Homosexual killers most often prey on homosexual victims, although bisexual and heterosexual males become victims as well. Whereas Jeffrey Dahmer, **Larry Eyler**, and **Herbert Baumeister** preyed on males who were either homosexual or bisexual, John Wayne Gacy also victimized young heterosexual males who were seeking employment, who were employed by him at the time of their deaths, or who had been employed by him in the past, as well as young male hustlers.

Note, however, that homosexual serial killers appear to be feared out of proportion to their actual statistical threat.

Homosexuals who become serial killers represent less than 5 percent of all known serial killers—even though their ranks include some of the most prolific slayers in modern times. Notorious homosexual serial killers include Donald Harvey (37 convictions; confessed to over 50 victims), John Wayne Gacy (33 convictions), Dean Corll (27 deaths; died after arrest), Juan Corona (25 convictions), Patrick Kearney (21 convictions; confessed to 28), Jeffrey Dahmer (17 convictions), William Bonin (10 convictions), and Randy Kraft (16 convictions; suspected in the deaths of 51 more victims).

One of the latest killers to prey on homosexuals was Herbert Baumeister in Indiana. A local businessman and married with children, he was not suspected of leading a dual life. But while his family was out of town, he preyed on young homosexual males. Baumeister, who buried the violated corpses at his home in Hamilton County, went undetected for years. After committing sixteen murders, he committed suicide in Canada before he could be arrested. How many deaths did he cause? No one can say for sure.

FROM VICTIM TO VICTIMIZER

That said, heterosexual males are responsible for the majority of serial murders. The typical serial killer is a heterosexual male wrestling with his demons who chooses to work out his problems by torturing and murdering woman after woman. Many of these female victims are prostitutes, a group of women who are especially vulnerable to predation by serial killers.

But why?

Research indicates that many serial killers were abused, neglected, or otherwise victimized in their childhood. This suggests that these killers may have chosen victims like their earlier selves or from the same general lifestyle.

Psychiatrist Helen Morrison contends that the "look" of the victims is significant. She states, "If you take photos, or physical descriptions of the victims, what will strike you is the similarity in look." Morrison also theorizes that some nonverbal communication exists between victim and killer: "There's something unique in that interaction." She believes that the victims of serial murderers are symbolic of something or someone deeply significant in the murderers' lives. Some psychologists have specifically said that the victims represent cruel parents on whom some murderers feel they cannot directly take revenge.

But psychological explanations such as this do little to explain the carnage. Ted Bundy, for example, did prey on young coeds who looked like the woman who had dumped him. But Bundy had long been practicing sexually deviant behavior. The resemblance between victims and the former girlfriend may have been intentional, or it may have had little to do with their selection. Kimberley Leech, Bundy's final victim, certainly did not resemble his former girlfriend. The victims' selection may, rather, have been due to the fact that they were easily lured away and restrained.

DEHUMANIZING THE VICTIM

Dr. Morrison goes on to note that the typical serial murderer does not distinguish between human beings and inanimate objects. Researcher D.T. Lunde found that sexual sadist murderers often dehumanize their victims or perceive them as objects. He argued that this "prevents the killer from identifying with the victims as mothers, fathers, children, people who love and are loved, people whose lives have meaning."

Typically, the serial killer does not think much about his victims, have any empathy for the victims' loved ones, or reflect any feelings of remorse. When asked about his victims, Ted Bundy responded, "What's one less person on the face of the earth, anyway?" When the Australian serial killer **James Miller**, charged with the murder of seven young girls and women, was asked about his victims during his trial, he stated: "They weren't worth much. One of them even enjoyed it."

The depravity of the victims' deaths is ample evidence that the serial murderer objectifies his victims. Serial killers lack the normal capacity for feeling or conscience; their ability to compartmentalize their "normal" lives and their true selves is telling. Their lack of empathy or compassion for their victims is evidence of an absence of psychological development that is rooted firmly in their early development and experiences.

The developing serial killer may also be aware that certain segments of society are objectified by the general public so that when, for instance, a prostitute dies, the public is quick to blame her. How often does the serial killer hear that a dead prostitute "asked for it" by being out on the street or climbing into a john's car? Might this awareness help the budding serial killer rationalize and objectify his victims? Most likely it does.

THE KILLING FIELDS: WHERE DO SERIAL KILLERS HUNT?

The hunting grounds of the serial murderer vary a great deal among killers. However, serial killers tend to select their victims from the same general areas where they feel comfortable, have control over those frequenting the area, or are assured that the area is infrequently patrolled by local police.

RED LIGHT DISTRICTS

Many serial killers hunt in areas where they will not be noticed or appear different from others. They seek anonymity.

This makes the red light districts of larger urban areas the most favored hunting grounds, as evidenced by the large number of prostitutes who fall victim to serial murderers. Here the killer can blend in with all the other johns and have relatively little fear of drawing special attention from witnesses.

POINTS OF TRANSIT

In addition, many serial killers have lured and abducted their victims from business establishments providing short-term services to people in transit, such as convenience stores or service stations near interstate highways. These locations appear to provide attractive hunting grounds to the serial killer, given the almost guaranteed anonymity in places where stranger-to-stranger interaction is commonplace and witnesses remember little of their brief time spent there.

From the killer's perspective, one unique and attractive characteristic of these points of prey is that stranger-to-stranger interaction is the expected norm; no one takes any notice. The so-called I-70 Killer, for example, found businesses near interstate highways to be a perfect killing ground for all the same reasons. A similar environment can also be found on many large college campuses. **Danny Rolling**, Edmund Kemper, and Ted Bundy found these sites perfect.

PUBLIC VENUES

Shopping malls, city parks, pools, fairs, parking lots—all are locations with large numbers of people paying little attention to their personal safety, making them easy places for stalking and abducting victims. Adam Walsh, six-years-old, was abducted from a Florida department store in 1981 when he was out of his mother's sight for only a few moments. Westley Alan Dodd stalked his young victims in parks and attempted to abduct his final victim, a young boy, from a movie theater. We feel secure in these places, and we forget to be aware of our surroundings and the people around us.

HOMES AND NEIGHBORHOODS

Because of the methods serial killers adopt, we are all at risk. It's a disturbing fact that the home is not always the sanctuary that it seems to be. We've all seen the newspaper stories and television reports; every year dozens of children are abducted from their yards or from in front of their homes.

In addition, many small children have been killed by their caregivers or parents. The unexplained death of an infant is devastating, and all consideration must be extended to the grieving parents. More than one murderous mother has been able to kill her children as a result of a lack of vigilance by the medical community. These serial killers have been identified only when the number of deaths stretched the bounds of believability.

Home invasions committed by serial killers also seem to be on the rise. This is especially frightening because we all have a sense of security when we are in our homes. The Boston Strangler would gain entry, then rape and murder his victims. Richard Ramirez terrorized southern California with his night-time invasions of Los Angeles homes. In Sacramento, California, **Richard Chase** went from house to house during the day, looking for an unlocked door and killing whoever was home.

This trend seems to be increasing as the twenty-first century begins. The cases of children abducted from their neighborhoods and young women abducted from their homes and workplaces emphasize that none of us is truly immune to the threat of a serial killer.

We are all vulnerable.

WHO WILL BE NEXT?

How likely are you to be the victim of a serial killer's attack? Compare your lifestyle with the following statistics about the known victims of serial murder over the past hundred years:

- Serial killers are most likely to choose their next victim on the basis of sex alone. This is the primary factor in victim selection 40 percent of the time. Killers in this category overwhelmingly select women.
- Serial killers will change their victim criteria 13 percent of the time. Arthur Shawcross, as an example, first killed

two children and after his release from prison began killing women.

- It is impossible to determine the victim criteria in 12 percent of the known cases.
- For-profit killing is a primary motive in victim selection 7 percent of the time. **Margie Barfield**, **Rhonda Bell Martin**, **Herman Drenth**, and **Herman Mudgett** all found ready sources of money by killing family members.
- Victims selected on the basis of their age (6 percent) include not only children but also the elderly. Killers such as Westley Alan Dodd specifically targeted children, whereas the killers **Carlton Gary** and **Edward Kaprat**, and the French team of killers **Thierry Paulin** and **Jean-Thierry Mathurin** have targeted the elderly.
- Victims who are chosen because of their health or physical condition (3 percent) most often fall prey to medical serial killers. Britain's Dr. Shipman is believed to have killed over two hundred of his patients. The American nurses Donald Harvey, **Lynn Majors**, and Richard Angelo all found their patients perfect victims for their murderous cravings. Other serial killers have targeted the physically handicapped.
- Race is another characteristic that can lead to being targeted by a serial killer. In 2 percent of cases, race is the primary reason for being victimized. White racist killers such as Joseph Paul Franklin and **Richard Clarey** randomly targeted African American males. The **De Mau Mau** gang consisted of African American males who targeted solely white victims. Other serial killers prefer to prey on their own race.
- Where a victim lives is the primary criterion in 2 percent of cases of serial killers. The homeless have been repeatedly victimized by men such as **Charles Sears**, **Vaughn Greenwood**, and **Bobby Joe Maxwell**. **Calvin Perry**, **Henry Lee Moore**, and **Sylvester Mofokeng** of South Africa based their victim selection on the location of their victim's residence.
- A victim's occupation is the primary concern in only 1 percent of serial killings. Prostitutes are specifically tar-

geted, as are topless dancers and female college students. Victims targeted by occupation are overwhelmingly female, although male prostitutes are just as likely to be targeted by these serial killers.

Little else is known about the victims of serial murderers other than that they are commonly murdered by a stranger—unless the murder takes place inside the family, of course. In a preponderance of known cases, the victims seem to be young females, presumably chosen to satisfy craving for dominance of the mostly male serial murderers. The victims are sometimes young males, as in the cases of John Wayne Gacy, **Elmer Wayne Henley**, and Jeffrey Dahmer. (It has been estimated that 50 percent of unidentified bodies in county morgues or medical examiners' offices across the country are those of young children or adolescents; unfortunately, we do not know how many of these bodies represent victims of serial murder.)

In a number of cases, it appears that the victims were selected solely because they crossed the path of the serial murderer and became a vehicle for his arousal and pleasure. Some victims may be self-selecting only because of their presence at a certain place and time. This and possibly the physical appearance of the victim, which may hold some symbolic significance for the killer, are apparently the only known precipitating factors for their selection.

REDUCING YOUR RISK

None of the statistics and research answer the question that is most immediate for most of us: How do we avoid becoming the victim of a predatory serial killer?

The simplest answer is to avoid being out alone in parking lots, malls, public parks, and the other usual hunting grounds of the serial killer. We need to be aware at all times that there is a legitimate threat out there, not only from serial killers but also from other predators, such as rapists, pedophiles, and robbers. We also need to be aware that our home is not a sanctuary but is another common target of predators and of a growing number of serial killers. Home invasions have increased over the past decade as a way of satisfying the serial killers' needs. And above all, we need to keep in mind that although the "less dead" are the most common targets of a serial killer, more and more serial killers are targeting mainstream victims.

But the best answer to the question is simply to cease creating these monsters so that succeeding generations do not have to deal with them. How do we do this? We need to ensure the safety of all children, not only from outsiders but from their own families as well. We have seen that children are especially vulnerable to the murderous desires of a parent. We as a society need to recognize that children deserve special protection from physical, emotional, and sexual abuse by adults, including their parents. We need to remember that serial killers were once children who needed protection, help, and comfort but didn't get it.

If we want to avoid victimization, we need to protect the next generation from being victimized. We can do that by providing economic, academic, and social support for all children, regardless of their socioeconomic standing; we also need to be aware of the social environment in which our children are growing up. Only by breaking the cycle of victimization can we reduce the number of serial killers in our midst.

STUDYING THE KILLERS

The next section of this book presents case studies of seven of history's most notorious serial killers:

- John Wayne Gacy
- Henry Lee Lucas
- Kenneth Bianchi
- Ted Bundy
- Jerry Marcus
- Joseph Miller
- Jeffrey Dahmer

These particular cases were selected based on four criteria:

1. Ease of access to information
2. Currency of the murderer's arrest or conviction
3. Geographical representation
4. Murderer's mobility

These killers are good examples of the overall serial murder phenomenon and can help you better understand those monsters who choose to make victims out of strangers.

2

THE KILLERS

4

JOHN WAYNE GACY

John Wayne Gacy killed thirty-three young men in the Chicago area between 1972 and 1978. He preyed on homosexuals, male prostitutes, and his own employees; he often convinced his victims that he was a policeman. He buried most of the bodies in the crawlspace under his house after soaking them in acid or lime.

THE KILLER AS A YOUTH

John Wayne Gacy was born on March 17, 1942 at Edgewater Hospital in Chicago, Illinois. His parents, John and Marian Gacy, were both factory workers. He grew up in a working-class neighborhood in northwest Chicago. He had two sisters, one two years older and one two years younger.

Gacy was strongly influenced by his mother. When he was a newborn, she gave him daily enemas for no apparent reason. After she found a bag full of her underpants under the porch where John played, she made him wear a pair of her underpants to embarrass him. When his father learned of this, he whipped John with a leather strap.

Although Gacy was reportedly a hard worker, he rarely succeeded in pleasing his father. When he failed to meet his father's standards, his father called him stupid. The elder Gacy was of Polish ancestry, a hard worker, a perfectionist, a stern parent, and a good provider; he was also a drunkard who beat his wife and had a Jekyll and Hyde personality, according to his children. When young John tried to defend his mother against his father's beatings, his father called him a mama's boy or a sissy. His father reportedly never showed his own emotions—except once, when Gacy was sentenced to prison in Iowa on a sodomy conviction. At that time, his father cried.

During grade school, young John daydreamed a lot and was resistant to his teachers. He wanted to be a police officer when he grew up and as a boy often played policeman.

BLACKOUTS

One unusual aspect of Gacy's childhood is that he occasionally experienced blackouts. The problem, diagnosed when he was sixteen years old, was a blood clot on the brain, which was thought to have resulted from a playground accident five years earlier. The boy was treated and apparently cured.

However, episodic blackouts continued into Gacy's adult life. He sometimes complained of shortness of breath and pains in his chest. His childhood problem had been diagnosed as syncope, a brief loss of consciousness caused by transient anemia, leading to probable psychomotor epilepsy later on. Once, after a seizure, he was hurriedly given last rites by a priest. But the cause of his malady was never determined with certainty, and his friends tended to regard it as heart trouble.

HIGH SCHOOL

Gacy attended a vocational high school, where he took business courses. His grades ranged from good to excellent. He began dating at age sixteen and had his first experience with sexual intercourse at age eighteen. He was enamored of uniforms, and he became active in a civil defense organization, which enabled him to go to accidents and fires with a flashing blue light on his car.

Gacy left home during his second year of high school. His departure was prompted by a specific incident: His father, who had loaned him money to buy his first car, was tired of all John's driving around and removed the distributor cap. Gacy became angry, left home, and moved to Las Vegas, where he worked for a brief time for a mortuary.

MARRIAGE

Gacy returned to Chicago in 1964 and got a job with a shoe company. Shortly after, his employer transferred him to Springfield, Illinois to run the company's retail clothing store. He was viewed as a hard worker and became heavily involved in the Junior Chamber of Commerce; he even received a nomination as the group's Man of the Year.

Later, Gacy met a woman, whom he dated for nine months, then married in 1965. The couple had a boy, then a girl. Gacy claimed that his first homosexual experience occurred after his wife's first pregnancy, when he got drunk with a friend who then performed fellatio on him.

According to neighbors, Gacy was a loving and attentive father.

For her part, Gacy's wife described her husband as a "police freak." He had an intense curiosity about emergency vehicles, which he sometimes followed at high speeds with his portable red light flashing. He liked to be known as having influence with the police; in fact, several times a month he would take free fried chicken to local police and firemen.

WATERLOO

In 1966, Gacy and his family moved to Waterloo, Iowa, where he managed three fried chicken restaurant franchises owned by his father-in-law. His father-in-law considered him a "braggart and a liar" but encouraged the move so that his daughter and grandson would be nearby. Gacy's falsified résumé at the time indicated that he had managed several stores in Springfield and that he held a college degree in accounting and business.

Just as he had in Springfield, Gacy became active in the Waterloo Junior Chamber of Commerce. He recruited many new members and served as chaplain for the organization. After the local paper referred to him as "Colonel" in a story about his organizational activities, Gacy liked to be called "Colonel."

His friends in the Jaycees said that Gacy was a real go-getter, did a good job, and was an excellent member. Others described him as a glad-hander type who showered people with affection as a way of getting more attention himself. A man who defeated Gacy for presidency of the Junior Chamber of Commerce stated, "He was not a man tempered by truth. He seemed unaffected when caught in lies."

Gacy frequented the bar at a local motel, as well as a Waterloo nightspot that featured strippers. According to his friends, he constantly bragged about his sexual prowess with women. Yet Gacy never showed any affection in public toward his wife and on several occasions reportedly offered her as a sexual favor to other men in return for their performing fellatio on him.

FIRST OFFENSES

Gacy's first known criminal offenses occurred when he was twenty-four years old. He was a member of Waterloo's Merchants Patrol, a cooperative security force whose members guarded their own business establishments at night against break-ins. Male employees from the restaurants he managed went on patrol with Gacy and broke into businesses, stealing auto parts and funds from vending machines. Gacy would monitor the police radio to determine whether police patrols were nearby.

Gacy also organized a social club in the basement of his home, where young boys employed at the restaurants he managed were allowed to play pool and drink alcoholic beverages in exchange for monthly dues. Gacy had many of the boys perform fellatio on him when they won at pool; he intimidated and coerced them or convinced them that he was conducting scientific experiments for an Illinois commission on sexual behavior.

In the summer of 1967, Gacy took a sixteen-year-old boy to his home to watch some films, shoot pool, and have a few drinks. Gacy's wife was in the hospital after giving birth to their second child. When the boy refused to perform fellatio on him, Gacy attacked him with a knife and cut the boy on the arm. Gacy quickly apologized and insisted the boy stay and watch some pornographic films. After showing the films, Gacy chained the boy's hands behind his back and tried to sexually attack him. When the boy resisted, Gacy began choking him. The boy pretended to black out. Gacy revived him and agreed to take the boy home.

During 1967 and early 1968, Gacy frequently forced a fifteen-year-old boy who was a part-time employee to submit to oral sex. Gacy often got the boy intoxicated on alcohol before performing these acts. He told the boy that he was conducting experiments, and he usually paid the boy.

In the spring of 1968, the two boys told their parents about Gacy's sexual assaults; they took their accusations to the Waterloo police. On May 2, in response to these accusations, Gacy was given a polygraph examination. The polygraph examiner found indications of deception in the tests, although Gacy continued to deny any guilt. He was indicted by a grand jury later that month. In July 1968, Gacy took another polygraph examination with the same results, after which he admitted having had homosexual relationships with one of the boys but claimed that he had paid the boy.

In September 1968, Gacy was arrested for paying a boy to beat up one of the youths who had accused him of sexual assault and for being implicated in a lumberyard break-in. On September 12, at his court appearance, he was ordered by the court to submit to a psychiatric evaluation at the Psychiatric Hospital of the State University of Iowa.

During Gacy's seventeen days at the psychiatric hospital, he was observed by the staff, was given psychiatric interviews, and underwent physical and psychological tests. In his report to the court, Dr. Eugene F. Gauron stated:

> Gacy would twist the truth in such a way that he would not be made to look bad and would admit to socially unacceptable actions only when directly confronted. He is a smooth talker and an obscurer who was trying to whitewash himself of any wrongdoing. He had a high degree of social intelligence or awareness of the proper way to behave in order to influence people.
>
> The most striking aspect of the test results is the patient's total denial of responsibility for anything that has happened to him. He can produce an "alibi" for everything. He alternately blames the environment while presenting himself as the victim of circumstances and blames other people while presenting himself as a victim of others who are out to get him. Although this could be construed as paranoid, I do not regard it that way. Rather, the patient attempts to assure [sic] a sympathetic response by depicting himself as being at the mercy of a hostile environment. To his way of thinking, a major objective is to outwit the other fellow and take advantage of him before being taken advantage of himself. He does things without thinking through the consequences and exercises poor judgment.

According to Gacy's discharge summary, he did not seem to feel remorse for his actions. He was evaluated as competent to stand trial. The psychiatrists' diagnosis was that Gacy had an antisocial personality and was unlikely to benefit from medical treatment.

Gacy pled guilty to the charge. The probation officer's presentence investigative report recommended that Gacy be placed on probation. The judge disagreed and, on December 3, 1968, sentenced Gacy to ten years' imprisonment.

LIFE IN PRISON

While he was in prison, Gacy told other inmates he had been charged with showing pornographic films to teenagers. In September 1969, Gacy's wife divorced him; Gacy subsequently told his prison friends that as far as he was concerned, his children were dead.

During his incarceration, he was assigned to food service; reportedly, the prison food improved and the kitchen was kept spotless. Gacy also became involved in the Jaycees as director of the prison chapter, served as chaplain, and played Santa Claus at Christmas. He was awarded the chapter's Sound Citizen Award and helped build a miniature golf course on the prison grounds. Subsequently, Gacy applied for early release under supervision, but the parole board denied his request.

Following the denial of parole, Gacy completed his high school education, began taking college-level classes, and became more involved in the Jaycees. In March 1970, a psychiatric evaluation of Gacy was ordered by the parole committee. The prison psychiatrist diagnosed him as a "passive aggressive personality" and recommended parole, stating, "The likelihood of his again being charged with and being convicted of antisocial conduct appears to be small." After twenty-one months in prison, Gacy was paroled on June 18, 1970.

PAROLE

Upon his release from prison, Gacy returned to Chicago to live with his mother in an apartment on the northwest side of the city. He tried to arrange visitation rights with his children, but his former wife never answered his letters. Gacy told his mother to get rid of the pictures of his former wife and children and to consider them dead.

Through a family friend, Gacy got a job as a cook in a downtown Chicago restaurant that was a gathering spot for city policemen and politicians. It was here that he met Chicago policeman James Hanley, whose name Gacy later modified as his street alias.

Gacy briefly dated a waitress from the restaurant but was soon seen associating with homosexuals. In November 1970, he had a homosexual encounter with a twenty-year-old male in his mother's apartment. In February 1971, Gacy was arrested on a complaint of disorderly conduct filed by a nineteen-year-old male who claimed Gacy had sexually attacked him. However, Gacy filed a similar complaint against the boy, and the charges were dismissed.

NORWOOD PARK

Four months after his return to Chicago, Gacy borrowed money from his mother and bought a house in Norwood Park Township, an unincorporated area northwest of Chicago. Gacy moved there with his mother in 1971.

According to a former employee of Gacy's, he, as well as several other men, lived with the Gacys in 1970 and 1971. The former employee admitted that he had slept in John Gacy's bedroom.

John Gacy was described as a good, friendly, and generous man by his neighbors in Norwood Park. At Christmas, Gacy gave his neighbors hams or baskets of fruit. He also showed genuine kindness toward their children. However, his boastful personality turned many away. They were invited to the huge parties he held but many chose not to attend. To some, it seemed that John Gacy was striving for a social status that he would never attain.

SECOND MARRIAGE

In May 1971, Gacy became reacquainted with a high school girlfriend who had two children and was going through a divorce. They were married in July 1972, after Gacy's mother moved to an apartment.

While his mother shared the house, Gacy reportedly didn't like her answering the telephone and talking to his potential business clients as "John's mother." After his mother left, Gacy invited his wife's mother to move in with them. A year later, Gacy subsequently complained, he needed a court order to evict his mother-in-law.

Gacy's relationship with his second wife deteriorated rapidly when, shortly after their marriage, he began to associate more and more with young boys. His wife frequently found her bikini underpants in the garage; Gacy had begun bringing young men to the garage late at night, sometimes spending hours there with them.

In 1972, Gacy told his wife that he was bisexual, but she was convinced that he was rapidly becoming homosexual. On Mother's Day of 1974, less than two years after they were married, Gacy announced to her that this would be the last time they had sex together.

It was.

DIVORCE AND DRUGS

From that point on, Gacy and his wife lived separately in the same residence. They were divorced on February 11, 1975. The next day, one of Gacy's male employees moved into the house.

Gacy was known to have marijuana in his home. He used the drug frequently and often provided some to his employees. He also reportedly abused alcohol but was not habituated to either marijuana or alcohol.

ENTREPRENEUR

Gacy had formed his own construction company in 1971, which he operated out of his home. The company specialized in remodeling work at retail stores and subcontracting work on larger construction projects.

To all appearances, Gacy was a civic-minded building contractor. He claimed he had made $200,000 a year prior to his arrest in 1978 for murder. He was known as an excellent cook but as an untalented construction worker.

Gacy was described by those who employed him as a very gregarious man who put a lot of energy into getting the job done. He was obsessed about keeping track of his time and kept notebooks that recorded what he did minute by minute, even logging such trivia as the precise moment he mailed a letter. He kept an extremely neat and clean house, even doing his own housekeeping.

An associate in the construction business characterized Gacy as a workaholic who talked a big line. One of his employees stated that a lot of Gacy's workers quit because "[t]hey don't like the aggravation. John is so much of a perfectionist, it gets to where he's nitpicking."

Moreover, Gacy developed a reputation among some of his associates, friends, and employees as a man who did not always tell the truth. An employee commented, "John is a funny person. He's a bit of a bragger, and he lives in a fantasy world. Now, how much is fact and how much is fiction is up to the individual to decide, but he claims that he does work for the syndicate. He's said he has set up people before."

POLITICS

After his divorce, Gacy became active in Chicago-area politics, achieving the position of Democratic party precinct captain. In 1976, he organized a fundraiser for President Carter's reelection campaign; the event was attended by over five hundred people. Gacy was also involved in organizing the annual Polish Constitution Day Parade in Chicago. His second wife subsequently stated she felt that Gacy often used his local political involvement to buy his way out of trouble.

Gacy's neighbors described him as a likable man who frequently volunteered to perform as a clown for children at charitable events. One neighbor stated that he seemed short-tempered at times and that he often threw large parties. His former babysitter said many people, mostly teenagers who worked with him, were "always going in and out of the house." The head of the Norwood Park Democratic organization stated:

> The John Gacy I'm reading about in the newspapers is not the same John Gacy I knew. He was always available for any job: washing windows, setting up chairs for meetings, playing clown for the kids at picnics and Christmas parties, even fixing somebody's leaky faucet or rehanging a crooked door. I don't know anyone who didn't like him.

VIOLENT TENDENCIES

But Gacy's friends and associates didn't know about his violent dark side, which manifested itself almost immediately on his release from prison. In the late fall of 1971, shortly after starting up his contracting business, Gacy struck an employee on the head with a hammer. When the employee asked why Gacy had hit him, he replied that he didn't know but that he had had a sudden urge to kill the man.

In June 1972, a twenty-four-year-old man told police that he had been picked up by Gacy, who offered him a ride. Gacy identified himself as a county police officer, showing the young man a badge and telling him he was under arrest. Gacy then told the young man that if the youth performed oral sex on him, Gacy would let him go. Gacy drove the man to a building in Northbrook, Illinois, where the man resisted. Gacy then clubbed him and pursued him in his car, knocking the man down. The man finally escaped to a nearby gas station. The complainant later identified Gacy as his assailant, and police arrested Gacy on June 22, 1972. Gacy told the police that the complainant was threatening him and trying to extort money from him. After finding marked money given by Gacy on the complainant, the police dropped the charges against Gacy.

An employee who lived with Gacy for two months in the 1970s later stated that he had to sleep with his pants on because Gacy often entered the bedroom in the middle of the night and tried to have sex with him. On one occasion when Gacy and he were celebrating Gacy's birthday, John locked him in handcuffs to show him a trick. Gacy then stated, "The trick is you gotta have the key." He then began to swing the man around the room on the handcuff chain. They fought, and the man ultimately recovered the key and freed himself.

On July 15, 1978, Gacy was arrested by the Chicago police on charges of battery. The victim, a twenty-seven-year-old male, had been walking at 1:30 A.M. when a man driving a black car stopped and asked him whether he wanted to smoke some marijuana. The victim got into the car. Shortly thereafter, the man held a rag over his mouth and he lost consciousness. The victim awoke at 4:30 A.M. with burns on his face and rectal bleeding. He later identified the car and gave police the license number; it was Gacy's.

Meanwhile, Gacy's employees began to disappear, one after another. One boy went missing after only a week in Gacy's employ. Another boy was found drowned in a river sixty miles south of Chicago. Gacy sold the car of one former employee to another employee, stating that the owner had left for California.

When asked about the constant turnover of employees, Gacy would respond that the boy had gone back home or had been fired. The transitional nature of his business meant that victims would appear and disappear with little notice. It was reportedly very common for Gacy to offer money to his former employees in exchange for oral sex.

ENTER THE POLICE

In August 1975 and December 1976, Chicago police questioned Gacy about the disappearance of two young men. Then in January 1976, police officers placed Gacy's home under surveillance for two weeks during the investigation of the disappearance of a nine-year-old boy. Accusations of kidnap and rape were also placed against Gacy in December 1977 and March 1978.

On December 12, 1978, Gacy was contacted by telephone by the Des Plaines Police Department regarding the disappearance of a fifteen-year-old boy from outside a pharmacy in that city the day before. Gacy had been to the pharmacy twice on the previous evening, giving the owner advice on rearranging his display shelves. After leaving his notebook at the pharmacy, he had returned a second time to pick it up. The missing boy worked at the pharmacy; shortly after Gacy left the pharmacy the second time, the boy told another employee he was going outside to talk to a contractor about a job. He never returned.

The Des Plaines police pursued the missing persons report on the boy in a nonroutine fashion after a preliminary investigation indicated that he was probably not a runaway. Gacy became a suspect in the disappearance after the police examined his record and learned of his sodomy conviction in Iowa, his charge of battery in Chicago in 1978, and his charge of aggravated battery and reckless conduct in a Chicago suburb in 1972.

Gacy was interviewed at his home on December 12. He was then asked to come to the police station to fill out a witness form because he admitted seeing but not talking to the missing boy at the pharmacy. Gacy stated he would come to the station later that evening.

Gacy was then put under surveillance but eluded the officers. At 11:00 P.M., he called the Des Plaines police, asking whether they still wanted to see him. When they replied in the affirmative, he said he would be there in an hour. However, a vehicle registered to Gacy was reported by the Illinois State Police to have been stuck in a ditch alongside the northbound lane of the Tri-State Tollway approximately thirteen miles south of Des Plaines at 2:29 A.M. the next day. Gacy arrived at the police station at 3:20 A.M., but the officer he was supposed to see had left. He was told to come back later that morning.

Subsequently, Gacy returned to the station and was interviewed. When he was asked to make a written statement regarding his activities at the pharmacy, he complied. He was then asked to wait for the police lieutenant's return. In the meantime, the police and the Cook County state's attorney's office obtained a search warrant for his house based on probable cause of unlawful restraint. Gacy remained at the police station while the police searched his house, looking for evidence of the missing boy.

SEARCH AND SURVEILLANCE

The search of Gacy's house revealed a high school ring; a number of erotic films and pornographic books; a switchblade; a starter pistol; handcuffs; a wooden two-by-four that was three feet long with holes cut in each end; a hypodermic syringe; an empty, small brown bottle believed to have contained chloroform; and a customer photo receipt from the pharmacy where the missing boy had disappeared. Two driver's licenses were also found.

As they were taking up a section of carpeting believed to be stained with blood, the police discovered a trap door in a closet that led to a crawlspace under the house. The ground in the crawlspace was covered with something that appeared to be lime, and it showed no evidence of recent digging. The officers noticed a strong odor in the house but could not determine its origin.

Thereafter, Gacy's pickup truck and car were confiscated. He signed a Miranda waiver form on his lawyer's advice and was released by the Des Plaines police at 9:30 that evening. Although he was placed under twenty-four-hour surveillance by the police, he managed to elude surveillance officers on three separate occasions on December 15, 1978. He drove at high speeds and often in a reckless manner. During this time, officers arrested a friend of Gacy's in Chicago for reckless driving. It turned out that Gacy and another friend were passengers in the vehicle.

On December 16, Gacy began to converse with the police surveillance team as they followed him around the Chicago area. The officers ate with Gacy at restaurants where he stopped. On one occasion at a Chicago restaurant, Gacy said to the officers, "You know, clowns can get away with murder." He repeated this statement to another police surveillance team on the same day.

Before long, the police began to see a pattern in Gacy's travels around the Chicago area. He was leading his surveillants to places that the Des Plaines detectives had just checked out, apparently to learn what the investigators had found out.

On December 17, Gacy invited the surveillance team to his house for dinner. After dinner, he tried to elude the officers. On December 19, he accused the surveillance officers of trying to tape-record their conversations. Gacy also told the officers that he was prepared with bond money and that he expected to be allowed to call his attorney if they arrested him. Later that day, a surveillance team was invited by Gacy to his house for a drink. While there, they attempted to read the serial numbers on Gacy's television, which they suspected belonged to a missing boy. They again detected a strong unidentified odor in the house. On December 20, Des Plaines police and the state's attorney's office learned that on December 22, Gacy's lawyer would be filing a lawsuit against the police for harassment.

ARREST AND DISCOVERY

On December 21, 1978, Gacy had a late-night conference with his lawyers that lasted until 8:00 A.M. the next day. He was then followed around Chicago while he met with various friends, who later told the officers that Gacy was saying good-bye to them. Police observed Gacy giving one of his friends a plastic bag; they suspected it contained marijuana. Gacy was arrested on the same day on a marijuana charge.

Also on that day, one of the officers who had been in Gacy's house before determined that the strong odor he smelled in the house was the same odor he had smelled many times at the county morgue. That evening, another search warrant was obtained to search Gacy's house again.

During this search, police discovered several human bodies buried in the crawlspace. They also found other evidence of Gacy's criminality: a television and radio belonging to one of the missing boys, a foot-long vibrator with fecal matter on it, and pieces of plywood stained with blood.

CONFESSION

Early the following morning, on December 22, 1978, Gacy began confessing to a number of murders of young boys. He stated that the body of the missing boy they were searching for had been in the attic of his house when the police first interviewed him at home. Gacy had taken the body in his car later that evening to the Des Plaines River bridge of the Tri-State Tollway and dumped it into the river. This is why he had been late in coming to the Des Plaines police station on the following morning.

After hearing this, the officers took Gacy to the Des Plaines River bridge, and he showed them where he had dumped the body of the missing boy and four other boys he had killed. Gacy was then taken to his home, where he showed the officers where he had buried one of his victims in the garage. On December 22, 1978, Gacy was charged with the murder of the missing boy for whom the Des Plaines police had been searching. Gacy was denied bail and was transferred to the medical wing of the Cook County jail.

By December 29, 1978, police had recovered twenty-six bodies from under Gacy's house and one from his garage. On January 3, 1979, Gacy was interviewed by the police and the state's attorney's lawyers in the Cook County jail. At this time, he elaborated on his earlier confessions and was questioned regarding the identification of his victims.

The following week, Gacy was indicted by a Cook County grand jury on seven counts of murder and one count each of deviate sexual assault, aggravated kidnapping, and taking indecent liberties with a child. At his arraignment on January 10, Gacy entered pleas of not guilty to all charges and was ordered to undergo a behavioral-clinical examination to determine his fitness to stand trial.

"PSYCHOPATHIC PERSONALITY"

On February 16, 1978, the examining psychologist found Gacy mentally fit to stand trial. The psychologist, A. Arthur Hartman of the Cook County Court forensic unit, stated that Gacy was:

> [v]ery egocentric and narcissistic with a basically antisocial, exploitative orientation. One reflection of this is his development of a technique of "conning" (his own term) or misleading others in his business or personal dealings. He has a severe underlying psychosexual conflict and confusion of sexual identity.

Hartman's diagnostic impression of Gacy was of a "psychopathic (antisocial) personality, with sexual deviation and a hysterical personality and minor compulsive and paranoid personality elements."

The Cook County state's attorney's office also requested an evaluation of Gacy by Professor Frank Osanka, a sociologist from Lewis University in Glen Ellyn, Illinois. Professor Osanka reviewed all the files on Gacy, including taped interviews, but did not interview Gacy. He concluded:

The explanation of episodic psychotic states simply cannot explain multiple murders, committed essentially at the same location, in essentially the same methodological manner, hiding the remains in essentially the same methodological manner, over a period of eight years by a man labeled acceptable and successful by his neighbors and in his business. [Gacy] suffered neither with a mental illness nor mental defect which prevented him from appreciating the criminality of his behavior or from conforming his conduct to the requirements of the law.

Meanwhile, Gacy's defense lawyers employed a psychiatrist, who concluded that Gacy was insane at the time of his alleged crime. The psychiatrist, Dr. R.G. Rappaport, stated that Gacy had a "borderline personality organization with the subtype of psychopathic personality and with episodes of an underlying paranoid schizophrenia."

Rappaport supported his diagnosis of psychopathic personality by attributing the following characteristics to Gacy: "Unusual degree of self-reference, great need to be loved and admired, exploitative, charming on the surface and cold and ruthless underneath, noticeable absence of feeling of remorse and guilt, and a history of chronic antisocial behavior."

The state's attorney's office of Cook County employed psychiatrists from the Issac Ray Center at St. Luke's Medical Center in Chicago to examine Gacy. The psychiatrists found the following:

For at least the last fifteen years, Gacy had demonstrated a mixed personality disorder, which included obsessive-compulsive, antisocial, narcissistic, and hypo-manic features. He abused both alcohol and drugs. The crimes he committed resulted from an increasingly more apparent personality disorder dysfunction, coupled with sexual preoccupations within an increasingly primary homosexual orientation.

Narcissistically wounded in childhood, by a domineering and at times brutal father figure and [by an] inability to physically participate in athletics, Gacy continued to fail to master psychosocial milestones, in part because of a series of apparent psychosomatic disorders. Increasingly obsessed with his sense of failure (constantly emphasized by his father), he dedicated himself to a career of productive work, which brought him positive feedback. Simultaneously, however, his rage at his presumed powerlessness, due to a pervasive, defective self-image, began to merge with sadistic elements in a slowly unfolding homosexual orientation. This began to center upon young men with whom he re-enacted the projected helplessness and sense of failure that he himself continued to experience. His sadistic, homosexual conquests were much more gratifications through the exercise of power than erotic experiences motivated by unmet sexual needs. Murderous behavior became the ultimate expression of power over victims rendered helpless. With each murder victim he was presented with undeniable evidence of his crimes (a dead body), yet he continued with the same patterns of behavior. Ultimately he came to justify murder as socially acceptable because of the degraded nature of his victims (human trash) and his increasingly egocentric conviction that he would never be apprehended because of his own cleverness in concealment and a disordered belief that his murderous behavior was of assistance to society.

INVESTIGATION

During the ensuing investigation, police interviewed one of Gacy's employees, who told them that he had been down in the crawlspace under Gacy's house on two occasions. Once he helped Gacy spread lime. On another occasion, he dug some trenches. Gacy had told him he was going to lay some tile because of all the moisture. When the employee started digging away from the area Gacy had plotted out, Gacy became very upset.

On the basis of autopsies and the examination of bodily remains, forensic pathologists deduced that most of Gacy's victims were Caucasian males in their teens or twenties. In most cases, it was impossible to determine the cause of death. Clothing and clothlike material were found in the throats of some of the victims, indicating they had been suffocated. Gacy claimed that none of his victims had been tortured and that they all had been strangled.

He stated that he killed all but one of his victims by looping a rope around the victim's neck, knotting it twice, and then tightening it, like a tourniquet, with a stick. Many of the victims were handcuffed at the time. He stated that others put the rope around their neck themselves, anticipating that Gacy would show them an interesting trick. On more than one occasion, Gacy claimed, he had killed two boys in one night. He reportedly read the Twenty-third Psalm to one of his victims as the boy died. Gacy also stated that one of his victims was a masochist, so he chained the youth to a two-by-four with his wrists and ankles together. Gacy stated, "Since he liked pain, I did the ultimate number on him." When asked how he got the idea for the restraint board, he answered, "From Elmer Wayne Henley, the guy in Texas."

Gacy claimed he lost count of the number of victims buried in the crawlspace under his house. He either soaked the bodies in acid or put lime on them and buried them under a foot of earth. He told the police that one of his victims was buried in the garage and that the last five victims had been dropped into the Des Plaines River off a bridge southwest of Chicago.

In addition to his male employees, Gacy preyed on homosexuals and male prostitutes who frequented Bughouse Square, a park in north Chicago. He would cruise the area in his car late at night picking up youths. Gacy often convinced boys whom he picked up that he was a policeman.

He stated that he had had sex with one hundred people he had picked up in this area and that he had paid all of them. He had a schedule: Between 1:00 A.M. and 3:00 A.M. he had sex. All but two of his victims had died between 3:00 A.M. and 6:00 A.M., according to Gacy. He referred to most of his killings as involving the "rope trick." One of Gacy's intended victims survived the "rope trick" by physically forcing Gacy to release the stick. The survivor did not report the incident because he thought Gacy was a police officer.

Gacy told the police that his first killing took place in January 1972 and that his second occurred in January 1974. He said he had killed no one while his mother-in-law lived with him. Police determined that Gacy had killed five people in less than a month in June 1976. He stated that he had killed for two reasons: Either the victim raised the originally agreed-upon price for sex, or he posed some sort of threat—such as telling Gacy's neighbors about his sexual activities.

Gacy's murders appeared to have been well planned and thought out in advance. He eliminated most traces of his victims and disposed of their remains in a methodical manner. He even prepared the graves of his future victims in advance.

Sex and Control

Gacy was very concerned about other people's perception of his sexual identity. Although he had engaged in homosexual relationships since his early twenties and probably prior to that, he always talked about being bisexual because he did not want anyone to consider him a homosexual. He was certainly aware of his homosexual desires when he told his second wife that they would no longer engage in sexual intercourse. After his arrest in Des Plaines and during his confession, he wanted his captors to know that he was bisexual, not homosexual. He stated, "After all, I do have some pride."

Gacy also told police that the pornographic books taken from his house were not his. He claimed he would not spend money on that type of reading material and only used the books to stimulate some of his victims.

Gacy seemed to rationalize everything he did. After the fact, his actions were always inflated when he described them to others; or if his actions could be seen in a negative light, he would twist the truth so that he would be viewed as having committed no wrongdoing. He seemed to have an excuse and a ready explanation for everything; after his arrest, he told his family he had been mentally ill. On Christmas Eve, 1978, he wrote to his family, "Please forgive me for what I am about to tell you. I have been very sick for a long time (both mentally and physically). I wish I had help sooner. May God forgive me."

Whether he truly viewed himself as he portrayed John Gacy to others is difficult to determine. His psychological and psychiatric evaluations indicate that he did.

Gacy appears to have regarded himself as an important person and a good businessman. He always discussed his management and sales experience in Iowa in glowing terms. He also frequently exaggerated his actual experiences in business.

Gacy had always wanted to be in control of a social situation or an organized activity. He was the boss of his business and frequently mentioned this in conversation. While he was a member of the Junior Chamber of Commerce in both Springfield, Illinois and Waterloo, Iowa, he sought leadership roles and always held some sort of official position. He was later characterized by friends and others as a person who manipulated situations and people to his advantage and tried to place them under his control. The county attorney in Waterloo attributed Gacy's prominence in the community to a "[u]nique ability to manipulate people and ingratiate himself."

Gacy also wanted to be considered a celebrity. Whenever he felt it was appropriate, he claimed to be part of a criminal syndicate in Chicago. In Iowa, he seemed to enjoy being addressed by his friends as "Colonel." He is remembered by many in Iowa as always talking about his money and connections. And he was proud of his political activities. According to his first wife, his political work was extremely important to Gacy. In his home, he prominently displayed his political trophies, including an autographed picture from President Carter's wife.

Even after being arrested and jailed for murder, he acted important. For example, he asked the jail chaplain to have the Chicago archbishop visit him. He also falsely claimed to have received a social visit from the Cook County sheriff. People later realized he frequently lied about his previous status and accomplishments. However, he seemed to believe his own falsehoods.

ATTITUDES

Following his arrest, Gacy seemed to feel no remorse or concern for his victims. During his confession, he showed no emotion while speaking continuously about his murderous actions. Indeed, he discussed his victims with the police in an almost clinical fashion. He stated that he killed his victims "[b]ecause the boys sold their bodies for twenty dollars." Gacy gave his police audience the impression that he felt he was ridding the world of some bad kids. Dr. Helen Morrison, a psychiatrist who examined Gacy, quoted him as saying, "All the police are going to get me for is running a funeral parlor without a license."

John Gacy enjoyed the limelight that his crimes brought to him. In his first formal confession to a group of police officers, Gacy spoke as though holding court, frequently leaning back in his chair and talking with his eyes closed. He had overcome his fatigue and spoke with a renewed air of confidence. Just as he wanted, the room belonged to him.

Following his arrest, Gacy kept a scrapbook on his case. He complained about how his former friends were now treating him and how the press was libeling him. However, to those around him, he appeared to be enjoying all the attention. Regarding his former associates and friends, he wrote:

> When things were good and I was giving, everyone was on my bandwagon, but as soon as I am accused and suspected, they run and hide. May God have mercy on them. If it wasn't for God's will, I would have never given or helped so many people. Oh, I am no saint or anything like that, just one of God's children. I do not take the right to sit in judgment on others or myself.

THE TRIAL

On April 23, 1978, a Cook County grand jury indicted Gacy on an additional twenty-six murders, making a total of thirty-three. All charges against Gacy were consolidated for the purposes of the criminal trial, and a compromise on a change of venue for the trial was reached between the prosecution and the defense. Jurors were selected from the community of Rockford, Illinois in late January 1980, and the trial was held in Chicago beginning on February 6, 1980.

Gacy's criminal trial lasted six weeks. His lawyers' strategy and defense, as well as the major issue at the trial, was that John Wayne Gacy had been insane when he committed the crimes and could not control his conduct. The final rebuttal witness for the defense, Dr. Helen Morrison, diagnosed Gacy as having mixed or atypical psychosis. Despite his high IQ, she said, Gacy had not developed emotionally; his entire emotional makeup was that of an infant. She concluded that Gacy had been suffering from mixed psychoses since at least 1958. When asked under cross-examination whether she thought that Gacy would have killed his victim if there were a uniformed officer in the home with him at the time, she replied that she did.

On March 11, 1980, Gacy was found guilty on all indicted charges. Two days later, he was sentenced to death.

THE DEMISE OF JOHN WAYNE GACY

John Wayne Gacy's father died on December 25, 1985, while Gacy was in prison in Chicago. In subsequent years, Gacy sometimes cried on Christmas Day, remembering him.

During his time on death row, Gacy kept busy maintaining his innocence. He continually referred to himself as another victim. In personal correspondence to this author, Gacy wrote that "[n]early 80 percent of what is known about me is from the media, it is they who made this infamous celebrity fantasy monster image, and now they have to live with that as I have not granted any interviews in over ten years to media people."

Gacy's obsession was published in book form in 1991. *A Question of Doubt: The John Wayne Gacy Story* was a 216-

page book, spiral bound on $8\frac{1}{2}$-inch by 11-inch paper. The preface to this first-person account states: "These are the first words that John Gacy has spoken. This is *my side of the story*—the story of THE THIRTY-FOURTH VICTIM." But it is hard to imagine that anyone would consider John Wayne Gacy a victim.

On May 10, 1994, John Wayne Gacy was executed by the State of Illinois.

5

HENRY LEE LUCAS

Henry Lee Lucas
From the author's files

Some might say that Henry Lee Lucas was born to kill. He killed his first victim at age fourteen. He killed his mother; he killed his wife. He was convicted of eleven different murders, suspected in another hundred or so, and at one point admitted to killing 360 people in 27 states.

THE KILLER AS A YOUTH

Henry Lee Lucas grew up living at a very low economic level. The house he lived in until age fourteen was a two-room shack with dirt floors, located in a mountainous area of Montgomery County, Virginia. It had no flooring or electricity and was furnished with only the bare necessities.

Lucas has been described by a psychiatrist as having a poorly developed moral sense, owing to undesirable ancestry. Lucas's family consisted of his mother, the man he remembered as his father (records indicate the man was not his real father), a brother, three half brothers, and four half sisters. He was closest to one of his half sisters who lived in Tecumseh, Michigan.

According to Lucas, his parents "lived together, but my father didn't have no legs and he stayed drunk and my mother, she drank and was a prostitute. And that's the way I growed up, until it was time to get out on my own." Lucas remembered that his father usually was either drinking or trying to sell pencils, his mother was either not around or having sex with different men, and his brother was gone most of the time. His mother, the head of the family, dominated everyone.

He described his mother as a Cherokee Indian of muscular build, weighing 150 to 160 pounds. His mother "didn't work, she'd rather sell her body. [She] believed just in sex. Didn't try to provide for anyone." Lucas said the worst thing he remembered about his family was being forced to watch his mother have sexual intercourse with various men.

Authorities describe Lucas's mother as a bootlegger who drank heavily. According to her daughters, she cleaned homes and restaurants to support them. She was fifty-one years old when she gave birth to Lucas. Her granddaughter remembers her as a dirty old woman who was not nice to be around.

The man Lucas called his father, Anderson Lucas, had worked for the railroad and lost his legs when he reportedly fell under a train. He was described by one caseworker as being illiterate and as having a bad reputation as a bootlegger.

Lucas claimed his father never argued with anyone and that he had a good relationship with him. Lucas remembered his grief at his father's death in 1949 and his mother saying, "Good riddance."

ABUSE AND NEGLECT

From as early as he can remember, Lucas was apparently confused as to his own gender. "I grew up from four years old, best I can remember, 'til about seven years old as a girl. I lived as a girl. I was dressed as a girl. I had long hair as a girl. I wore girl's clothes." His half sister in Maryland still keeps a childhood picture of Lucas with long curls and dressed in girl's clothing.

In the first grade, at age seven, Lucas had his hair cut after his schoolteacher complained about its length. Lucas claims that his mother's attitude toward him changed after this; she beat him and forced him to carry heavy objects, steal, cut wood, carry water, and take care of the hog.

Lucas recalled no good times in his childhood because if he had fun, he "would get beat for it." In fact, he said that a scar on the back of his head resulted from his mother striking him with a two-by-four. He reported that he was unconscious for eleven hours following this beating and that his skull was fractured.

Lucas referred to his childhood as one of constant abuse or neglect:

> I don't think a human being alive that can say he had the childhood I had. Bein' beaten ever day. Bein' misused ever day. Havin' to cook my own food, havin' to steal my own food. Eatin' on the floor instead of the table. Bein treated like what I call the hog of the family. It's a lot harder than what people can imagine. Growing up with hatred, without any kind of friendship, without any kind of companion to be around or anything. The best thing was leavin' home.

CHILDHOOD RELATIONSHIPS

Lucas's half sister, in describing her brother, stated, "He always seemed like he wanted someone to love. He never seemed to be able to keep a friend for some reason." He was reluctant to initiate any conversation with other boys and girls while in school. In retrospect, those who knew Lucas as a boy characterize him as either socially inept or hostile.

His appearance, owing to an empty eye socket and the subsequent artificial eye, caused children to shun him or avoid direct contact with him. This restriction of peer relationships was intensified by his mother, who Lucas claimed would not allow him to play with other children, including his own brother.

The lack of any significant peer relationships combined with his treatment at home resulted in an overwhelming hatred. Lucas referred to it frequently. For example:

> I've hated since I can first remember, uh, back when I was a little kid I've hated my family and anything. Anytime I went out, uh, to go play [with other children] or some show, or something, I never could get anybody to go with me. I never could make friends and I just hated people. Nobody would accept me 'cause of my left eye. [I] looked like garbage! No girls would go out with me. No boys would have anything to do with me. They just wanted to stay away from me.

Lucas was in the first grade for the first three years of his schooling. His first-grade teacher remembers him as "a very humble little boy who was a little slow and a little dirty." He finished the fourth grade at age fourteen but never finished the fifth grade. His last known exposure to formal education involved vocational training while in prison.

"I Ain't Got No Roots"

Lucas's goal in life was to travel and have adventure. He made numerous attempts to run away from home and at age fourteen was successful. In fact, he traveled thousands of miles and never returned. He stated, "I ain't got no roots."

Lucas was always on the move when not incarcerated. "Remaining in one place causes me to have thoughts of escape. It becomes more of a pressure—not bein' able to get up and go."

He boasted of sometimes traveling twenty-four hours a day, keeping himself awake with amphetamines, marijuana, and PCP. For years he lived among the rootless, the searching, the homeless, and the roamers of this country, living out of his car, stealing, and murdering hitchhikers and stranded travelers.

His main concern in life was survival. And in order to survive, he kept moving—and he kept killing.

A LIFE OF VIOLENT CRIME

Although his first act to be labeled as deviant was theft, Lucas killed animals for his own sexual gratification in his early teens and began using alcohol at age nine. He also became fascinated with knives in the first grade. In fact, they became one of the tools of his "trade." The knife was his favorite weapon because it was silent and quick, its target the throat and chest area of his victims.

His criminal career was diffuse and intermittent, yet involving ever-increasing forms of aggression. His first homicide victim was a seventeen-year-old girl in Virginia in 1951. His second was his mother, nine years later.

> It was just an impulse thing that if I wanted to kill somebody, I'd go and kill 'em. I wouldn't plan it, how I was gonna do that. Then I would sit and plan how to get rid of the body. Whether I would just dump it out on the road or whether I would leave it partially clothed or would leave anything around the body or whether I'd leave the body cut up, how I would leave the body, ya know.

Many of his killings were the result of burglary, theft, and armed robbery. His most frequent target for robbery was the twenty-four-hour convenience store.

In describing his acts of killing, Lucas stated:

> We killed them every way there is except one. I haven't poisoned anyone .... We cut 'em up. We hanged 'em. We ran 'em down in cars. We stabbed 'em. We beat 'em, we drowned 'em. There's crucifixion—there's people we filleted like fish. There's people we burnt. There's people we shot in cars .... We strangled them by hand. We strangled them by rope. We strangled them by telephone cord. We even stabbed them when we strangled them. We even tied them so they would strangle themselves.

Lucas talked about some of his victims being used for target practice. A synopsis of two confirmed homicides reveals one victim being shot while standing at a car wash and another being shot while hanging up clothes in her back yard. Both were shot as Lucas and his accomplices drove by in a car.

Lucas admitted to being a necrophiliac, although the term itself had to be explained to him. "In most of my cases, I think you'll find that I had sex with them after death; uh, the other way I'm not satisfied."

Lucas stated, "I've had people in houses, I've had people in stores, I've had people in banks." During his confinement in the Williamson County jail in Texas, he claimed to have killed a total of 360 victims.

One reason Lucas gave for his killings was, "I didn't leave no witnesses. I've never left witnesses." In his opinion, in addition to his felony murders, a witness was whoever was on the street or in the area. "After the first few, ya know, I just felt the next one was covered. I'd just kill that one so they couldn't say I was there. If I came into contact with somebody, I couldn't afford to let 'em live."

Lucas claimed to have been drinking prior to most of his killings. Indeed, an argument with his mother in 1960 that led to her death began in a tavern. Also, he reportedly used amphetamines, PCP, LSD, and marijuana. He stated that the drugs kept him relaxed and kept him awake so he could travel a lot. "Drugs allowed me to stay on the road, to get out of the victim's neighborhood." For Lucas, being on drugs increased his degree of awareness.

He was constantly moving around the country, taking care not to be seen, not to leave behind clues, and rarely repeating in the same area the ways in which he murdered. Lucas talked of a "force" that kept him moving and traveling with no specific destination.

Many of his victims were subjected to what law enforcement referred to as "overkill." Lucas explained this by referring to the "force," which caused him to mutilate and frequently dissect the bodies of his victims. He and his accomplices claimed to have carried the head of one victim through two states.

Lucas contended that he constantly changed the way he killed in order to confuse law enforcement personnel. By the time one of his murders was discovered, he might be two or three counties away, killing in a different way. Sergeant Bob Prince, a Texas Ranger in charge of the task force, states, "Lucas has sixteen homicides within a fifty-mile radius of Georgetown [Texas]. If you laid these cases out on a table and asked investigators not familiar with Lucas to evaluate them, the officers would undoubtedly talk about numerous different killers instead of just one."

OTTIS AND BECKY

He was assisted in most of his killings by Ottis Toole, his homosexual partner. Toole had been a pyromaniac as a child and later became an admittedly sexually sadistic killer. Lucas stated that in their sexual relationship Toole was the passive participant.

Lucas originally treated Toole's niece and nephew, Becky and Frank Powell, like his own children. Ironically, he exposed these two children to his killings, just as his mother had allegedly exposed him to her sexual relationships. Lucas stated, "I would avoid actually killing anyone in front of them, and a lot of times they would sneak around to see what I was doin' and I would catch 'em and I would scold 'em for it." For Lucas, the fact that these young children witnessed some of his horrific deeds was not particularly important.

Lucas later married fifteen-year-old Becky; they lived together as man and wife in a trailer in Stoneburg, Texas. According to Lucas, Becky "more fit into my kind of life. She accepted everything I done. I could tell her things. She understood. This took off the pressure that was there. Before, I had the urge to destroy anything within my reach. Becky took some of the pressure away."

In describing his relationship with her, he said, "Yeah, uh, it's, uh, weird. My love for her was like a daughter—you know, a father to daughter. I never thought of her as sexual." He had sexual intercourse with her only three times, in order to satisfy her. "I loved her, but I don't think she felt love."

Lucas killed Becky the day after his forty-sixth birthday in 1982. He dissected her body in a nearby farmer's field. Lucas's partner in death, Ottis Toole, died of AIDS in a Florida prison on September 15, 1996.

PRISON LIFE

From January 1, 1952, when he was incarcerated in juvenile detention in Richmond, Virginia to June 11, 1983, when he was arrested in Stoneburg, Texas, Henry Lee Lucas spent over twenty-one years living under the control of various correctional authorities. In other words, 70 percent of his life during these thirty-plus years was spent under someone else's control.

Although he did not talk kindly of his keepers in prison, his discussions of prison life never conveyed the intensity of hatred with which he described his home life. Because Lucas spent most of his life in institutions of correction, he never learned to live by the rules of society. If the rules benefited him, he followed them. If they did not, he broke them.

For Lucas, prison was where he got his degree in criminality. He stated, "It was a learnin' to do crime." He spent many years in the Michigan prison as a records clerk. During this time, Lucas studied crimes committed by the inmates and learned how to commit them himself. He described living at Jackson Prison in Michigan as being like living in a big city.

Lucas consistently maintained that he requested not to be released from prison when he was paroled in 1975. He claimed he killed four people on the day he was discharged. In fact, five murders committed by Lucas have been confirmed by the Texas Rangers during the remainder of 1975. One of those murders was committed on the same day Lucas was married.

REMEMBERING HIS CRIMES

Although Lucas enjoyed playing detective in "solving" his crimes, which he refers to as "my cases," he appeared to have little regard for law enforcement in general. He stated, "The police didn't know who done it. They never would have knowed who done it. They'd never know who done it unless I'd told 'em." He frequently reiterated, "Unless I tell 'em, they'd never clear these cases." He characterized many of the hundreds of law enforcement officers who had interviewed him by stating, "I've seen better kids play cops than that!".

All officers who traveled to Georgetown, Texas to interview Lucas about his suspected homicides were thoroughly briefed by the Texas Rangers on ways to handle Lucas and specific procedures to follow. Lucas was either shown a picture of the victim when alive or a number of pictures including the victims. He was told the state, jurisdiction, and date of the incident. If Lucas remembered the victim, he would describe the crime in great detail. He had a phenomenal memory for details. In 113 separate instances, Lucas led law enforcement officers back to the scenes of his homicides, unassisted.

Lucas described his interviews with police officers:

I have to give 'em every detail ... how it happened, where it happened at, the description of the person, what was used, uh, every type of, uh, where the body was left, parts of bodies missing. I have to tell them what parts are missing, if they've been shot, I have to tell them that. If they were stabbed, cut, whatever. They don't give me no details.

Law enforcement authorities found that Lucas had a remarkable recall for road numbers, mileages, and landmarks. They frequently took Lucas into the countryside and let him direct them to the crime scene. In one instance in Texas, Lucas was being driven past a commercial building when he said that he and an accomplice had killed a man and woman in an armed robbery of "that liquor store over there." The officer noted that the building was not a liquor store, but later he learned that it had been one when the proprietors were killed in a robbery. In another instance, a rural crime scene was so remote that the officer could not find his way back to it. Lucas led the officers directly to the crime scene.

When questioned about his memory, Lucas stated, "Yeah, I can't recall how I do it, really … there's so many of 'em, they just seem to come back clear as crystal. It's like something in a movie, like watching a movie over and over."

Lucas said he confessed to his murders because "The Lord told me to." As for his phenomenal memory, "That was done by Jesus Himself. That was from a light comin' into my cell and, uh, asking me to come forth with my confessions. And, uh, I have been able to uh, go back to the bodies and give complete descriptions of the bodies through Him. And that's the only way I can do it."

It is possible that Lucas was suffering from delirium tremors from alcohol withdrawal and was hallucinating. Another explanation of his recall ability is referred to by psychologists as "hypernesia," that is, an unusually exact or vivid memory. Lucas's ability to remember his victims could also be attributed to an "eidetic" memory, which causes mental images that are unusually vivid and almost photographically exact.

ATTITUDES

Although frequently claiming to the contrary, Lucas seemed to enjoy his "celebrity" status. He knew he had something others wanted—information. Lucas was now in the limelight, no longer going unnoticed. When he spoke, a great many people were willing to listen.

Lucas later claimed remorse for killing his victims. However, a big smile crossed his face whenever he was identified as having committed a homicide and he cleared another of his "cases." This might indicate pride that he got away with a murder for so long, or it might indicate pleasure that he had, as he called it, "solved his case."

To value human life seemed beyond his capability. When asked why more of his victims weren't males, he replied, "That's somethin' I very seldom do, unless it's an emergency and [I] have to do it." For him, the victim was an object: "Only one that ever bothered me was Becky." As for his mother, "No, 'cause I didn't kill her, she died of a heart attack after I hit her with the knife." He didn't take any responsibility for his mother's death because she was beating him with a broom when she was killed. He viewed it as self-defense.

Lucas did not like to admit that some of his victims were young children. He blamed most of these deaths on his accomplice, Toole. He claimed to have believed that one four-year-old victim was fifteen years old.

He seems to have traveled from one victim to the next. "I'd go from one to the other and wouldn't think about the last one I'd killed. I never had no feeling for that person at all."

Most of his female victims were, in his opinion, prostitutes. "Most of the girls I've met on the highway has turned out to be prostitutes. [They] has been either out sellin' theirselves to truckers or people on the highway and I, uh, have always since I was a little kid hated prostitutes."

Lucas claimed to have studied law enforcement. On the one hand, he showed concern for law enforcement problems; on the other, he showed disdain for law enforcement agencies. "I've turned a lot of law enforcement, as far as people know it today, upside down. It took years of practice, years of understanding criminal law."

When asked how he had changed since his arrest in 1983, he responded, "I've changed from what I used to be. I was a killer. Let's put it plain out. The type of life I lived. I mean that thing was nothin' but crime. I didn't do nothin' else. It got so killin' somebody meant nothin' to me."

When asked why he had changed, he responded:

Seein' what I've done. It's my own personal feelin's. What I've seen what I've done. Stuff like 'at. That's caused me ta change. Since I've learned about the families. I've learned about the sufferin' they went through. How much sufferin'

I've caused. It hurts! It would cause anybody to change. Seein' the misery 'cause of what I've done. I'd never dreamt of that before.

PSYCHIATRIC ANALYSIS

The results of psychological testing conducted while Lucas was incarcerated reveal that he read at the sixth-grade level, spelled at the fifth-grade level, and understood mathematics at the fourth-grade level. Institutional psychological examinations conducted in Michigan show Lucas to have a total average of 65 on the Standard Achievement Test and an IQ of 89, as determined by the Army General Classification Test. He placed in the 60th percentile on the Revised Minnesota Paper Form Board.

Lucas was also administered the Minnesota Multiphasic Personality Inventory, the Figure Drawing Test, and the Rosenzweig P.H. Study. A summary of the interpretation of Lucas's performance on these tests, written by psychologists on July 14, 1961, is as follows:

> While contraindicating any underlying psychotic process as well as incapacitating neurotic qualities, test results are suggestive of a basically insecure individual who has a relatively well crystallized inferiority complex and who is grossly lacking in self-confidence, self-reliance, will power, and general stamina. There is also some evidence of a preoccupation with sexual impotence, the same which is believed to exist as only another reflection of his deflated impression of personal qualities in general. According to the Rosenzweig P.H. Study he was found more value oriented than he is need oriented, but due to his lack of will power and self-confidence he does not characteristically engage in behavior which is aimed at an implementation of his values. The anxiety and hostility caused by threats to the ego are usually directed intropunitively toward himself or inpunitively toward the frustrating situation. *He does not have the courage to blame others for mistakes or misfortunes or to engage in aggressive social behavior* aimed at alleviating some of his discomfort [emphasis added].

The following psychiatric diagnoses were made during Lucas' various periods of incarceration:

> **July 14, 1961**—Psychiatric Clinic Ward, Jackson Prison (second admission): *Passive-aggressive personality* with a significant inferiority complex and general lack of confidence, self-reliance, will power, and perseverance. *Schizophrenia, simple type, chronic, severe.* Transfer to Ionia State Hospital recommended, prognosis fair.
>
> **August 10, 1961**—Ionia State Hospital: *Schizophrenia, chronic undifferentiated type,* sex deviate, sadist.
>
> **January 28, 1965**—Ionia Staff Conference on Lucas: "The patient's affect during the staff interview was definitely inappropriate. He is *potentially dangerous* [emphasis added]."
>
> **November 17, 1971**—Center for Forensic Psychiatry: *Passive-aggressive personality.* Found competent to stand criminal trial for kidnapping. "It is not felt that there is much outside an incarceration setting which would be effective in modifying the defendant's presently erratic social behavior."

At Lucas's murder trial in San Angelo, Texas, a psychologist for the defense testified that Lucas was a chronic schizophrenic who belonged in an institution. Three other psychiatrists for the prosecution disagreed, finding Lucas sane enough to stand trial.

Lucas offered his own layman's diagnosis: "I need medical help, there's no doubt about it."

MASS MURDERER—OR MASSIVE HOAX?

On April 12, 1985, by authority of the state attorney general and the McLennan County district attorney, Henry Lee Lucas was transferred to the McLennan County jail in Waco, Texas. A grand jury had been convened to investigate two homicides Lucas had confessed to in the county and the conduct of the Lucas Task Force coordinated by the Texas Rangers.

Two days following the trip to Waco, on Sunday, April 14, the *Dallas Times Herald*'s front-page headline asked, "Mass Murderer or Massive Hoax?" The *Herald* devoted five full pages to the story, which charged that Lucas had perpetrated a hoax to embarrass authorities and keep himself off death row. The article claimed that law enforcement agencies across the country had provided Lucas with information on homicide cases so that he could confess to them. The paper also charged that in many instances the Lucas Task Force was aware that Lucas was confessing to murders he did not commit.

As a result of the Texas attorney general's staff investigation, a report was issued on the task force and alleged homicides committed by Lucas. The *Lucas Report,* issued in April 1986, was in effect an indictment of law enforcement investigators in thirty states and, more directly, an attack on the various judicial systems that found Lucas guilty of ten or eleven homicides. Note these excerpts from the report:

> "Questions about Henry Lee Lucas will be debated for decades. This report is not offered as a final answer. There may never be a final answer."

> "[W]e find numerous discrepancies between Lucas's confession and obtainable evidence regarding his whereabouts."

> "[T]here is a notable lack of physical evidence linking Lucas to the crimes to which he confessed. Lucas did not [sic] lead authorities to any bodies of victims."

> "We have found information that would lead us to believe that some officials 'cleared cases' just to get them off the books."

The grand jury completed its investigation in late June 1985 and issued a no bill on Lucas for the two homicides he had confessed to in McLennan County. It should be noted that the officers who took the confessions from Lucas never testified before the grand jury. Members of the Lucas Task Force did testify before the grand jury, only after strongly insisting that they be allowed to testify. No charges against the task force were issued by the grand jury.

Despite the findings of the *Lucas Report*, Henry Lee Lucas was indeed a serial killer, having been convicted of eleven homicides. He probably did not kill 360 people. However, it is very difficult to question the clearances of all 162 homicides attributed to Lucas in thirty states; authorities remain convinced of his involvement in at least one hundred homicides.

LUCAS'S LAST WORDS

The last time I interviewed Henry Lee Lucas was in May 1998. He was scheduled for execution the following day. It was visiting day on death row, and it was hard to conduct a conversation amid the din of the other inmates' discussions with their lawyers or loved ones.

Lucas admitted he was fighting for his life and was trying to get his death sentence commuted to life. He told me that he had not killed anyone and that the only reason he had confessed was to make law enforcement look bad. The following day, Lucas's sentence was commuted to life imprisonment by the then-governor of Texas, George W. Bush.

On March 12, 2001, Henry Lee Lucas died of natural causes.

6

KENNETH BIANCHI

"Hillside Strangler" **Kenneth Bianchi**
© Bettmann/CORBIS

Kenneth Bianchi and Angelo Buono were known as the "Hillside Stranglers." Together, they killed at least nine women in the Los Angeles area in 1977 and 1978; Bianchi killed two more women on his own before he was apprehended by authorities.

ADOPTED YOUTH

Kenneth Alessio Bianchi was born in 1951 to a young teenage girl in Rochester, New York. After Bianchi's mother became pregnant, she married a man who was not the father. She was allegedly an alcoholic and decided to put the baby up for adoption. The Monroe County, New York adoption report stated, "She [Bianchi's mother] appears to be a pathetic creature of limited intelligence."

When baby Kenneth was a few weeks old, a private adoption proceeding was initiated by his foster parents, Francis and Nicholas Bianchi. He was legally adopted by them in 1952 and given their last name.

Bianchi's adoptive parents were both born in 1919 and were of similar backgrounds: first-generation Americans raised in Italian Catholic families. They both left high school in their second year to take full-time jobs. As a child, Nicholas had a stuttering problem, which he never fully overcame. In December 1941, the two were married. Francis learned shortly thereafter that she could not bear children and had to undergo a radical hysterectomy.

OVERPROTECTIVE MOTHER

Francis Bianchi very quickly became an overprotective mother. Between December 1951 and May 1952, she took young Ken to the doctor eight times; nothing was found to be wrong with him other than a minor respiratory infection that was responding to treatment.

The family moved to Los Angeles in 1956 because of Ken's asthma. In January 1957, Ken fell from a jungle gym at the school playground and struck his nose and the back of his head. He also began to have petit mal seizures, and when he was upset he would roll his eyes. His mother thought he had epilepsy, but the doctors felt that his various problems were psychological. This angered her. Moreover, the doctors thought the eye rolling was simply a habit.

In 1958, the family moved back to Rochester, where Ken was admitted to Rochester General Hospital because he frequently urinated in his pants. His mother had done everything she could to stop Ken from doing this, going so far as to spank him before he went to the bathroom to ensure that he urinated enough not to dribble in his pants later.

Ken was diagnosed as having diverticulitis, a horseshoe kidney, and transient hypertension. Although these were physical findings, the doctor also stated that Ken had many emotional problems. In fact, the hospital report indicated that there was no problem with Ken until his mother came to visit him in the afternoon. Then he would complain about everything for his mother's benefit. Hospitalization was a trying experience for Ken, and the attending physician wondered whether his social or home environment was adequate. The hospital staff and investigating social workers suggested that Ken and his mother see a psychiatrist, but his mother refused.

Ken's parents were reported numerous times to the Rochester Society for the Prevention of Cruelty to Children because of concern over Ken's emotional state. On September 15, 1962, the society issued a report on its investigation of the Bianchis. The report focused primarily on Ken's mother. She was found to be "[d]eeply disturbed, socially ambitious, dissatisfied, unsure, opinionated and overly protective ... guilt ridden by her failure to have children...[and who had] smothered this adopted son in medical attention and maternal concern from the moment of adoption." The report also focused on Ken's mother's frequent attempts to have him tested because of his constant urination. Each test involved the probing of his genitals.

Ken's mother often kept him home from school for fear he would develop an illness and his urination problem would worsen. Ken was seen at DePaul Clinic in Rochester in 1962. Part of the clinic report stated:

> The boy drips urine in his pants, doesn't make friends very easily and has twitches. The other children make fun of him and his mother is extremely angry at the school because they do not stop the other children. The mother sounded as if she were very overprotective of this boy. When the boy fell on the playground in kindergarten early in the school year, she kept the boy home the total year. She indicated that she has become so upset because people keep telling her to take her child to a psychiatrist. She does not think he needs a psychiatrist and she went into great detail about how the doctors these days are just out for money and she does not trust any of them.
>
> The mother is obviously the dominant one in the family and impresses one as a quite disturbed woman. Mrs. Bianchi tends to displace her anger especially on doctors and hospitals and project the blame for the boy's problem onto other sources.

The DePaul Clinic report also more specifically addressed Ken's behavior:

Dr. Dowling reports that Kenneth is a deeply hostile boy who has extremely dependent needs which his mother fulfills. He depends on his mother for his very survival and expends a great deal of energy keeping his hostility under control and under cover. He is eager for other relationships and uses a great deal of denial in handling his own feelings. For example, he says that his mother and father are the best parents in the world.... To sum up, Dr. Dowling said that he is a severely repressed boy who is very anxious and very lonely. He felt that the only outlet whereby he could somehow get back at his mother was through psychosomatic complaints. Dr. Dowling felt that without this defense of the use of his somatic complaints he might very well be a severely disturbed boy.

Young Ken did not spend much time with his father, who worked a great deal of overtime during Ken's childhood. When Bianchi was fourteen years old, his father died suddenly at work. After this, Ken reportedly underwent a prolonged period of grief.

SEX AND MARRIAGE

In his teens, Bianchi frequently purchased hard-core sex material in adult bookstores in Rochester, New York. He sometimes borrowed the family movie projector and showed pornographic films to friends at their homes, telling his mother he was showing family movies. Bianchi smoked marijuana a few times but was never seriously habituated. His first sexual experience probably took place in his early teens.

Bianchi got married shortly after graduating from high school in 1971. He quarreled with his wife constantly, and after eight months she left him and filed for an annulment. Bianchi later referred to the marriage as being "dumped on."

After his marriage was annulled, Bianchi attended Monroe Community College in Rochester, where he took police science and political science courses. His grades were generally high Cs. Then Bianchi dropped out of college and took qualifying tests for the U.S. Air Force. He registered high on the electronics tests but did not enter the military. Instead, he worked as a bouncer at a bar for a while, then obtained a job with an ambulance service.

ADULT RELATIONSHIPS

Bianchi's mother remarried after his father's death, and Bianchi decided to travel to California. His mother had arranged for him to stay with Angelo Buono, his forty-seven-year-old half cousin who ran an auto upholstery business out of his home in Glendale, California, a suburb of Los Angeles.

After moving to L.A., Bianchi lived with a girlfriend for a short period. She broke up with him in late 1976; for more than a year after that, Bianchi harassed her by stealing items from her apartment, cutting up her sandals with a razor blade, ripping up her nightgown, and pounding on the outside walls of her apartment.

In early 1977, Bianchi moved in with another young woman who later bore him a son. Their finances were tight, but Bianchi bought a Cadillac even though he couldn't afford the payments. He simply ignored the bills until the car was repossessed.

In May 1977, Bianchi's girlfriend went to Las Vegas with a friend and was allegedly raped during her stay. She did not report the incident to the police or to Bianchi. It wasn't until later, when Bianchi had caught venereal disease from his girlfriend, that he learned of the rape. When she was examined by doctors, they discovered she was pregnant.

THE LOS ANGELES MURDERS

While Bianchi was living in L.A., the area was terrorized by a mass murderer dubbed the "Hillside Strangler." Over a four-month period in late 1977 and early 1978, eleven females between the ages of twelve and twenty-eight were found strangled in Los Angeles County. Seven of the victims had been raped. Eight were found within a six-mile radius of the city of Glendale. Two of the victims, ages twelve and fourteen, had been last seen together at a local shopping center in Glendale. Their bodies were found a week later near Dodger Stadium. Six of the victims were known to have been heavily involved in the nightlife of Hollywood Boulevard. One had been seen frequently in an area where prostitutes gather at Hollywood and Vine Streets. One was a local runaway who was well known on the streets of Hollywood. One had worked as a waitress in Hollywood. One had moved to Hollywood after being convicted of prostitution in the state of New York. One was a Hollywood resident and a chronic hitchhiker, and the last was frequently seen in the area trying to get into show business.

The nude body of the first victim was discovered alongside Forest Lawn Drive, near Forest Lawn Cemetery. She was a nineteen-year-old part-time prostitute. She had been manually strangled. Almost two weeks later, a second victim was found on a roadside in Glendale. The fifteen-year-old girl was nude and had ligature marks around the wrists, ankles, and neck. She had been raped and sodomized.

Between October 18 and November 29, 1977, eleven victims were found dumped by their assailants in a similar manner. The victims were all found nude, strangled, and left in remote areas of the county. The majority had been sexually assaulted. Most of them bore ligature marks similar to those on the second victim.

On December 14, 1977, a twelfth female victim was found strangled and nude in a residential area east of Silver Lake. An autopsy revealed she had not been sexually assaulted. The victim had been employed by an outcall "modeling" service and was known to have worked as a prostitute. She had been reported missing shortly after 10:00 P.M. on December 13 after she failed to make her customary check-in call at 10:00 P.M. The victim had been sent to what turned out to be a vacant apartment in Los Angeles. Her abandoned auto was found nearby. It was learned later that the original call for modeling services had been placed from a telephone booth in the Hollywood branch of the Los Angeles City Library.

Almost two months later, a thirteenth victim was found. The victim, a twenty-year-old female who lived in Glendale, was discovered nude and strangled in the trunk of her car, which was found in a ravine near a highway in the Angeles National Forest. She had been last seen near her home on the afternoon of February 16, 1978 and was discovered at 9:45 A.M. the following morning. This was the last known victim of the "Hillside Strangler."

THE WASHINGTON MURDERS

In March 1978, three and a half weeks after Bianchi's son was born, his girlfriend broke up with him and moved with her baby back to her hometown of Bellingham, Washington. In May of that year, the couple decided to give the relationship another try, and Bianchi also moved to Bellingham. As his girlfriend was breastfeeding their son, Bianchi limited his sexual relations with her. He stated later that he went out with other women during this time. He also apparently masturbated frequently.

When Bianchi arrived in Bellingham, he was hired by a uniformed private security firm. That summer, Bianchi left his security job and went to work for a department store for higher wages. Bianchi was reportedly popular with some of the security firm's clients, and the firm subsequently rehired him in a supervisory position.

Bianchi joined the Sheriff's Reserve program in Bellingham in March 1978; he was the first private security officer to be accepted by that organization. He was scheduled to attend a meeting of the Reserve on the night two girls disappeared in Bellingham; the Bellingham police subsequently learned that he did not attend the meeting.

The police became suspicious of Bianchi when they found out that he had been out in a security vehicle that night and that he had been made aware of missing keys from the home where the missing girls were supposedly going to housesit. They then learned that Bianchi had called a neighbor and told her not to go near the house that night because work was being done on the alarm system. Nothing appeared to be wrong in the house, although someone had evidently been there recently. When the strangled girls' bodies were found in their car on the following day, the police immediately arrested Bianchi. He surrendered willingly, stating he had killed no one.

MULTIPLE PERSONALITIES

Although Bianchi consistently and calmly maintained that he was innocent, the police found long blonde hairs believed to belong to one of the victims and pubic hairs matching those of Bianchi in the Bellingham house where the victims were supposedly housesitting. Bianchi's attorney requested the assistance of psychiatrist Donald Lunde, to whom Bianchi recounted a love-filled, joyous, and tranquil childhood. Bianchi's recollection did not match existing medical and psychiatric records, and Lunde was forced to conclude that Ken was repressing much of his past and might not remember committing the stranglings.

By now, his attorney was skeptical not only of Bianchi's alibis, but also of his sanity—although Bianchi resisted his attorney's argument to enter an insanity plea. Dr. John Watkins, an expert in hypnosis, was called in to try to restore Bianchi's memory.

During one of the hypnosis sessions, Dr. Watkins discovered the emergence of a second personality, called "Stevie Walker." Bianchi's second personality, who appeared sadistic and boastful, proudly talked about committing murders in Bellingham and Los Angeles. He stated that Angelo Buono, his cousin, had killed with him in Los Angeles.

RECOUNTING THE CRIMES

Through "Steve's" confession and countless hours of police work, officials came to the conclusion that ten of the thirteen victims attributed to the "Hillside Strangler" had been killed by Angelo Buono and Kenneth Bianchi. By one account, the killings began when Bianchi and Buono were sitting around Buono's house one day in L.A. They began talking about what it would feel like to kill someone—then decided to try it.

Except for the first victim, who was killed in Buono's automobile, the other nine victims were kidnapped and taken to Buono's home in Glendale, where they were tortured and killed. One was injected with a cleaning fluid and gassed with a hose from the oven. Another was tortured and burned with an electric cord before her death.

The killers first asked each of the victims to go to the bathroom in order to avoid involuntarily urinating right after death. The victims were each tied by their arms, legs, and neck to a special chair in Buono's spare bedroom. Each was then raped, sodomized with various instruments, and strangled to death. Nine of the bodies were then tossed on roadsides and hillsides in Los Angeles and Glendale. The last victim was put into the trunk of her car, which was pushed down a ravine.

Bianchi told police that he and Buono would flip a coin to see who would rape the victims first before they were murdered. He also stated that many of the victims had plastic bags placed over their heads before they were slowly strangled to death by tightening a rope around their necks. He stated that on one occasion he took Polaroid pictures of Buono raping one of the victims.

Buono had promoted Bianchi as a casting director and location scout for Universal Studios, so Bianchi played this role with a number of the victims. However, in most cases the victims were lured into going with Buono and Bianchi because the two were posing as police officers. Witnesses stated they had seen Buono with a badge and handcuffs, and police proved that he had owned a police-type badge by analyzing an impression left in a wallet found in his home. Bianchi was known by a number of people to have police badges. Also, the police learned that Bianchi had obtained an official Los Angeles County seal from an aide to a county supervisor. The blue and white Cadillac that Bianchi drove while in Los Angeles was impounded by the police with this seal still affixed to the windshield. Further, the daughter of the late actor Peter Lorre identified Buono and Bianchi as the men who posed as vice squad officers and tried to force her into their car on a Hollywood street during the fall of 1977.

The killings stopped when Bianchi moved to Washington state. Then, on January 11, 1979, Bianchi lured two Bellingham girls to an unoccupied house by offering them a housesitting job. He met them there and forced them into the house at gunpoint. He bound them with rope, sexually assaulted them, then strangled them. He then put them in their car and drove it to a deserted cul-de-sac, where he left the car. He was quickly linked to the girls' disappearance and arrested. When Bianchi's home was searched, a number of stolen items were found that had been taken from houses to which Bianchi had been assigned as a security guard.

Thus, almost a year after the last "Hillside Stranger" victim was found, the case was solved.

FAKING IT?

Based on the discovery of Bianchi's second personality, his attorney concluded that Bianchi was not legally sane at the time of the murders. He subsequently changed his plea to not guilty by reason of insanity.

Because of this change of plea, the judge in Bellingham called in Dr. Ralph Allison, an expert on multiple personalities and altered ego states, as an independent advisor to the court. Allison hypnotized Bianchi and was also confronted with Bianchi's second personality, "Steve," who again boasted of the murders. Through hypnosis, Dr. Allison took Bianchi back to his childhood and learned that the second personality, or alter ego, had been invented by Bianchi when he was nine years old. Allison concluded that Bianchi was a dual personality who was not aware of his crimes and who was incompetent to stand trial.

The prosecutor in the case, who disagreed with the conclusions regarding Bianchi's dual personality, requested that Dr. Martin Orne, a psychiatrist at the University of Pennsylvania Medical School, be called in to examine Bianchi. Rather than attempting to authenticate Bianchi's multiple personality, Orne devised tests to determine the authenticity of Bianchi's hypnotic trance.

For the first test, Orne told Bianchi before hypnotizing him that it was rare in cases of multiple personalities for there to be only two personalities. When Bianchi was hypnotized, another personality surfaced. This one was called "Billy." On another occasion, Orne asked Bianchi, while hypnotized, to talk to his attorney, who was not actually in the room. Bianchi complied with Orne's request, even shaking the hand of his attorney who was not there. When Bianchi's attorney was asked to enter the room, Bianchi asked, "How can I see him in two places?"

On the basis of (1) the third personality, which had been suggested by Orne prior to hypnosis, (2) the fact that a hypnotized person ordinarily does not question the existence of two of the same people, and (3) other tests, Orne concluded that Bianchi was faking hypnosis and thus faking his multiple personalities. Indeed, books on psychology had been found in Bianchi's home, including one on hypnotic techniques. This seemed to support Orne's conclusion; however, there was no real proof that Bianchi was faking a hypnotic trance and a multiple personality.

While checking his background in Los Angeles, investigators found a copy of Bianchi's academic transcript from Los Angeles Valley College. The transcript had an incorrect date of birth and listed courses that had been taken before Bianchi even moved to Los Angeles. It turned out that the original transcript belonged to a person named Thomas Steven Walker. Further investigation revealed that Bianchi had placed an advertisement in the *Los Angeles Times* requesting applications for a counseling position; applicants were to send in their résumés and college transcripts. When Walker sent in his transcript, Bianchi substituted his own name on the transcript and used the transcript to further his own career.

Even though an alter ego could presumably mimic a real identity, such as that of Steve Walker, Bianchi first saw Walker's name as an adult, whereas "Stevie Walker" had appeared under hypnosis when Bianchi regressed back to the age of nine. Although it is possible that two Steve Walkers appeared in Bianchi's life by coincidence, it is more likely that Bianchi was faking hypnosis.

PLEA BARGAIN

Because the multiple-personality theory was no longer believable, Bianchi's lawyer negotiated a plea with the prosecutors in Bellingham, Washington and Los Angeles County, California. His client would enter a plea of guilty to the murders in Bellingham and to five of the murders in California—if he would not be given the death penalty. In return, Bianchi would testify against his cousin Angelo Buono in California.

Shortly after Bianchi entered a plea of guilty in Washington, Angelo Buono was arrested in Los Angeles on October 18, 1979 for ten "strangler" murders. The only substantial evidence against Buono was Bianchi's testimony. Buono was also charged with a number of felonies and misdemeanors, including sodomy, pimping, pandering, and conspiracy to commit extortion and oral copulation. This last charge involved an outcall prostitution scheme that Buono and Bianchi were accused of operating in 1977.

Buono was arraigned on these nonmurder indictments on March 27, 1980. The first part of Buono's preliminary hearing dealt with the nonmurder charges; the second part dealt specifically with the ten counts of murder. It was almost a year later before Buono was bound over for trial after the longest preliminary hearing ever held in Los Angeles County (involving 120 days of testimony).

DENIAL—AND A FOILED PLAN

Shortly after his arrival in California for Buono's trial, Bianchi wrote a letter to Dr. Allison, one of the psychiatrists who had examined him in Bellingham. He stated that he had not personally killed any of the "strangler" victims—it was Buono who did the killing. When the Los Angeles district attorney's office confronted Bianchi with this change in his story, he said he had not told them initially that Buono was the killer because he was afraid they would not believe him if he did not also implicate himself.

In early October 1980, Bianchi's jailers seized some papers in his cell, including a forty-three-page document entitled "An Open Letter to the World" in which Bianchi denied participation in any murder. On October 2, just prior to the seizure of this letter, a woman who had been visiting Bianchi in jail was arrested in Los Angeles for attempting a "copycat" version of the two murders in Bellingham, Washington, to which Bianchi had confessed. She was charged by Bellingham authorities with the attempted strangling of a woman whom she had lured to a downtown hotel. The woman was also accused of sending a series of tape recordings to law enforcement authorities with a message that Bianchi was the wrong man and that more murders would be committed by the real killer.

The woman told law enforcement officers and the press that Bianchi could not have committed the "strangler" murders because he was in bed with her on the nights that the victims were abducted and killed. She claimed that she had met Bianchi in 1977. Police, however, learned that the woman's first contact with Bianchi was by mail in January 1980. Police believe that this woman's actions were coordinated by Bianchi during her visits to him in jail in an effort to clear himself of all charges. The woman was later convicted of attempted murder in Bellingham and was sentenced to life in prison.

THE TRIAL

When Buono's trial began in November 1981, jury selection took five months because of the highly publicized nature of the case. The trial lasted two years and two days, the longest trial at that time in the history of the United States. The prosecution's key witness was Kenneth Bianchi, who testified for a total of eighty days. He described how the abductions took place, how the victims were tortured and killed, and how the victims' bodies were discarded.

Bianchi's testimony, however, varied over the course of the trial. At one point he stated, "The strangulations I don't remember. I remember the women were alive and picked up and . . . dead and . . . dropped off." He said he didn't know what happened between these times. At other points in his testimony, however, Bianchi was graphic in his descriptions of the killings—even though the descriptions changed with his further testimony.

On March 14, 1982, the California Supreme Court ruled that witnesses whose memory had been enhanced through hypnosis could not testify in criminal trials. This ruling effectively barred the testimony of some witnesses for the prosecution who would have linked Buono to some of the victims. The ruling, however, did not bar Bianchi's testimony because the presiding judge ruled that Bianchi had "voluntarily and consciously faked hypnosis."

Late in the trial, in June 1983, the woman who had attempted the "copycat" killing in Bellingham testified for the defense. She had been found guilty of attempted murder in Washington. She stated that she and Bianchi had conspired to frame Buono for the "strangler" murders; they had planned to testify falsely that Buono confessed to the murders and told them he had an accomplice other than Bianchi. She further stated that Bianchi had directed her to go to Bellingham and commit a murder to show that the accomplice was still at large.

After 345 days and the testimony of over 400 witnesses, the case went to the jury on October 20, 1983. The jury found

Buono guilty of nine of the ten counts of murder. The not-guilty verdict was for the first victim. In this case, the body of the victim did not have the ligature marks of the other nine victims, and microscopic fibers from the chair in Buono's house were not found on her body, as they had been on the other victims. The verdicts of the jury included a finding of "special circumstances of multiple murder," which in California carries only two possible sentences: life imprisonment without parole or death.

AFTERWORD

On January 9, 1984, Angelo Buono was sentenced to life imprisonment without the possibility of parole. He is currently incarcerated in Folsom State Prison in California.

After Buono's trial, Kenneth Bianchi was returned to the state of Washington. He is currently incarcerated in Walla Walla State Prison until his first parole hearing some time in the year 2010. If he is ever freed by Washington, Bianchi will face five consecutive life sentences in California.

In late 1984, Bianchi legally changed his name—not once, but twice. He finally settled on the new name of Nicholas Fontana.

7

THEODORE
ROBERT BUNDY

Ted Bundy was convicted of three homicides in 1979 and 1980 and is believed to have killed at least twenty-eight women between 1974 and 1978. What makes Bundy's crimes so chilling is that, to all outward appearances, he was a charming, clean-cut, self-assured young man. His personable demeanor made it easy for him to control and manipulate women—then commit the most vicious of assaults.

YOUNG TED

The killer we know as Ted Bundy was born Theodore Robert Cowell on November 24, 1946. His mother was Eleanor Louise Cowell, and when Ted was born, she was living at the Elizabeth Lund Home for Unwed Mothers in Burlington, Vermont.

During the first few years of his life, young Ted lived with his grandparents, his mother, and her two sisters in the Roxborough section of northwest Philadelphia. In 1950, his mother had his last name changed to Nelson and moved with her son to Tacoma, Washington to live with relatives. In May 1951, his mother married John C. Bundy, who adopted Ted and changed his last name to Bundy.

John and Eleanor had two boys and two girls, half brothers and half sisters to Ted. The dominant force in the family was Ted's mother; Ted did not get along well with his stepfather and refused to use him as a role model. He had memories of his grandfather in Pennsylvania, who was closer to being a father figure for him.

Ted's mother worked as a secretary at the University of Puget Sound; his stepfather was a cook at an army hospital south of Tacoma. Bundy stated that his mother "paid all the bills and never used force or anger." He once said that he grew up thinking his mother was his sister and that he was a late baby born to his grandparents.

The Bundys were not financially well off, but neither were they poverty stricken; their socioeconomic level would best be described as "upper lower class." Following his mother's marriage, the family moved several times over a four-year period. While Bundy was adjusting to his new father, he was also dealing with the family's moves around the city. Bundy comments on this period in his life by saying, "Life was not as sweet, but not a nightmare." This was a difficult and sometimes lonely period of readjustment for the young boy.

Ted had a paper route, was a member of the Boy Scouts, and was active in the Methodist Church with his family. He liked school and did well in his studies, according to his parents. Bundy said, "We didn't talk a lot about real personal matters, certainly never about sex or any of those things. My mom has trouble talking on intimate, personal terms."

According to his fourth-grade teacher, "Ted was neither good nor bad, happy, well adjusted and always eager to learn." He reportedly displayed babyish tendencies up to the fifth grade in school. He was a loner who didn't want to get involved with too many people at a time. He could do superior work in school when he wanted to and liked to foster the impression that he always did superior work. He talked of being a policeman or a lawyer when he grew up.

It is not known when Bundy learned of his illegitimate birth. He was apparently never told by his parents. Bundy claimed he found out he was illegitimate at age thirteen when he discovered his birth certificate stating "father unknown." Others report that he learned this at age eighteen from his cousin, who taunted him about his birth. Still other reports have Bundy learning of his birth when he traveled to Burlington, Vermont in 1969 and checked his birth certificate there.

Although Bundy consistently maintained that his illegitimacy was not important to him, it did seem to upset him. It further strained relations with his stepfather, frequently to the point of outright defiance.

HIGH SCHOOL YEARS

On the surface, Bundy's teenage years appeared fairly typical for a young man growing up in Tacoma, Washington in the 1950s and early 1960s. Following junior high school, he participated in Little League baseball and high school football. He was a Boy Scout and ran unsuccessfully for the student council in high school. He was also a member of the high school cross-country team. However, he tried these activities only briefly before moving on to something else.

During high school, he felt at ease in only two environments—the ski slopes and the classroom. Bundy found a lot of enjoyment in skiing and is believed to have stolen expensive ski gear. Although he was considered a scholar by many of his fellow students, Bundy graduated from Wilson High School with only a B average.

During his high school years, Bundy was reportedly very naive about sex and never appeared interested in girls. He had one date in his three years of high school. Bundy later argued that he was "particularly dense, or insensitive, not knowing when a woman's interested in me. I've been described as handsome and all this shit or attractive. I don't believe it. It's a built-in insecurity. I don't believe I'm attractive." Bundy's best friend in high school describes him as a very sensitive person.

He was considered very private and introverted. His IQ was tested at 122. He earned above-average grades but was not considered an outstanding student. Bundy's neighbors remember him during this time as serious, nice, polite, not a troublemaker, and rather quiet.

COLLEGE HOPPING

Bundy had three goals in life: (1) to get married and have a family life, (2) to be a lawyer, and (3) to get involved in politics. His heroes were Senator J. William Fulbright, Nelson Rockefeller, and later, Governor Daniel Evans. After completing college, he dreamed of going to law school and remarked, "But money's a real problem." During the following three years, he attended two different law schools and for a brief period became very active in politics.

In the summer of 1965, after graduating from high school, Bundy worked at a warehouse in Tacoma and purchased his first car, a 1933 Plymouth coupe. That fall, he entered the University of Puget Sound in Tacoma. He purchased a 1958 Volkswagen during his first year of college. Bundy stated later, "I just love Volkswagens!"

During his first year of college, he "had a longing for a beautiful coed. But I didn't have the skill or social acumen to cope with it." Bundy's mother remembered, "He got good grades that first year [but] never got into the social life of the school at all. He'd come home, study, sleep, and go back to school."

In the fall of 1966, Bundy transferred to the University of Washington in Seattle to major in Asian studies. That year, he worked at the Seattle Yacht Club and became friends with the pastry cook there. She sometimes fixed snacks for him, and he often borrowed money from her. She once loaned him money to go to Philadelphia and gave him a ride to the airport. He was dressed in expensive clothes and had expensive ski equipment. He was going to stop off in Aspen, Colorado to do some skiing. When she called to complain to his mother, she learned that his mother did not know what he was doing, that he never called home, and that she did not know where he was living.

In the summer of 1967, Bundy attended the Stanford Chinese Institute in Stanford, California. He changed his major to urban planning and sociology in the fall of 1967 and withdrew from the University of Washington with several incompletes in the winter quarter of 1968. Then he traveled to Aspen, to California, and to Philadelphia to visit his grandparents. After returning to Seattle in the spring of 1968, Bundy committed numerous crimes of shoplifting and burglary, then became involved in politics as a volunteer in a campaign for the Republican nominee for lieutenant governor.

During his campaign activities, Bundy often got drunk. Meanwhile, he became the nominee's official driver and made a number of political contacts and acquaintances. According to Bundy, it was during this period—at age twenty-two—that he lost his virginity, being seduced by an older woman after he got intoxicated.

Bundy traveled to Philadelphia in early 1969 and attended Temple University, where he took classes in urban affairs and theatrical arts. He returned to Seattle in the summer of 1969 and rented a room near the University of Washington. He reentered the university in the summer of 1970, graduated in the spring of 1972 with a degree in psychology, and promptly applied to a number of law schools.

Although he was given high character references from his college professors, his academic record and his Law School Aptitude Test scores were not impressive, and he was rejected by the law schools. Bundy then became very active in Governor Dan Evans's reelection campaign. In February 1973, Bundy reapplied to the University of Utah College of Law with a glowing character reference from Governor Evans, and this time he was accepted. At the last minute, late in the summer, he decided not to attend law school that fall and lied to the school that he had suffered serious injuries in an auto accident.

Sex and Romance

Bundy's first extensive involvement with a woman occurred during his first year at the University of Washington in 1966. She was older, came from a wealthy family in San Francisco, and frequently paid for their dates together. It was at her urging that he attended Stanford in the summer of 1967.

For Bundy, the relationship was intense until she broke up with him later that summer. Ted's brother recalls that this "screwed him up for a while. He came home and seemed pretty upset and moody. I'd never seen him like that before. He's always in charge of his emotions." Bundy described this period as "absolutely the pits for me—the lowest time ever."

Bundy's second romance began in September 1969 when he met a divorcée with a young child. After three months of dating, they began to talk about marriage. Bundy changed his mind, but the relationship continued.

The two of them had a sexually active relationship, but after a while Bundy began sexually experimenting by tying her up with nylon stockings prior to having intercourse. On one occasion, he started strangling her during intercourse after tying her up. She stopped him, and the "experiments" ceased. Their relationship lasted for five years.

Meanwhile, Bundy kept in contact with his former girl-friend in San Francisco, and by 1973 the relationship was reestablished to the point where the woman thought they were engaged. Bundy then refused to write or call her, stating, "I just wanted to prove to myself that I could have married her." During this period, he had maintained his relationship with the woman in Seattle.

A Hard Worker

Bundy worked at a number of jobs to pay his way through college: at the Seattle Yacht Club as a busboy, at a Safeway store stocking shelves, at a surgical supply house as a stockboy, as a legal messenger, and as a shoe salesman. His summer jobs included working at a sawmill and a power company in Tacoma.

In 1968, Bundy was the office manager for the Draft Rockefeller headquarters in downtown Seattle. A co-worker described Bundy thus:

> Ted had control of what he was doing. He was really poised. He was friendly. He was always smiling. He was terribly charismatic. Obviously, he was someone who had a great deal of compassion in dealing with other people.

In 1971, Bundy was a work-study student at Seattle's Crisis Clinic; there he met Ann Rule, a volunteer, who later wrote a book about him (*The Stranger Beside Me*, New American Library, 1980). In 1972, he worked on Evans's political campaign. Posing as a political science graduate student doing research, he taped opponents' speeches and reported directly to the governor. He also worked as a counselor at a psychiatric outpatient clinic for four months that year.

In October 1972, he began working as the assistant director of the Seattle Crime Prevention Commission and conducted some research on rape and white-collar crime. He resigned from this position in January 1973 when he was not selected for the director's position. In the same month, Bundy obtained a consulting contract with King County to study recidivism among misdemeanor offenders in the county jail. In April 1973, Bundy was given a political job as an aide to the chairman of the Washington State Republican party.

THE KILLINGS BEGIN

On January 31, 1974, a twenty-one-year-old young woman was taken from her basement apartment in Seattle. Bloodstains were found on her nightclothes; the top sheet on her bed and her pillowcase were missing, as were some clothes. She had apparently been killed in her bed, dressed, and taken from her apartment. Twenty-seven days earlier, a young girl had been found viciously beaten and sexually assaulted nearby in a similar basement apartment.

On March 12, a nineteen-year-old girl disappeared without a trace on her way to a jazz concert at Evergreen State College in Olympia, Washington. On April 17, an eighteen-year-old girl left her residence hall on the Central Washington University campus in Olympia to attend a meeting across campus; she was not seen again. That same evening, two girls twice encountered a young man on campus, near the library. On each occasion, the man solicited their help in carrying his books, claiming an injury to his arm. He led them to his Volkswagen in a darkened area of campus before they fled.

On May 12, a nineteen-year-old female student at Oregon State University in Corvallis, Oregon took a walk across campus and was not seen again. On May 31, a young woman disappeared from outside a tavern in Seattle. On June 11, an eighteen-year-old girl disappeared from a well-lighted alley on the way to her sorority house in Seattle. Shortly before this girl disappeared, a young man on crutches with a cast on one leg had been seen nearby having difficulty in carrying his briefcase and was offered assistance by another young sorority girl. The man waited while the girl entered a house on an errand. When she returned, he had disappeared.

On July 14, two more young women disappeared from the Lake Sammamish Recreation Area near Issaquah and east of Seattle. One of the missing women, who was twenty-three years old, had last been seen around noon in the company of a young man with his arm in a sling who called himself Ted, according to witnesses. "Ted" told her his sailboat was in Issaquah, and he needed help putting it on his Volkswagen to transport it to the lake. She agreed to help him and left with her bicycle. This man was seen on five separate occasions that day, asking females for assistance with his sailboat. The other missing female, who was nineteen years old, was last seen around 4:30 that afternoon on her way to the restroom.

All these missing females were single, had long hair parted in the middle, and were of similar appearance. The first six disappearances occurred in the late evening; the last two occurred in broad daylight. All the disappearances happened within a 250-mile radius of Seattle.

Fifty-five days after their disappearance, skeletal remains of the girls missing from Lake Sammamish were found in the foothills of the Cascade Mountains, four miles east of the lake near Interstate 90. The remains of a third person were also found but could not be identified.

On October 12, 1974, the skeletal remains of two girls were found along a deer path 130 miles south of Issaquah near the Oregon border, seventeen miles from Vancouver. One girl was identified as a girl from Vancouver who had last been seen in August. The other girl was not identified.

SUSPICIONS

All the aforementioned disappearances occurred while Ted Bundy was living in Seattle. He was reportedly very familiar with the area east of Seattle, where six of the missing girls' bodies were found. Bundy was a man who understood police jurisdictions and boundaries, and who was familiar with their vulnerability—their imperfect exchange of information with one another.

During this period, Bundy was picked up at least twice by juvenile authorities in Tacoma for suspicion of auto theft and burglary. As Ann Rule noted, "There is no indication that he was ever confined, but his name was known to juvenile case-workers. The records outlining the details of the incidents have long been shredded—procedures when a juvenile reaches eighteen. Only a card remains with his name and offense listed."

Bundy's girlfriend in Seattle became suspicious of him during the disappearances of the girls in Washington and Oregon. He had a number of unexplained absences during the night, and he frequently slept during the day. Moreover, Bundy would periodically hide in the bushes near her home and jump out and frighten her. She found surgical gloves in his jacket pocket, and she observed a package of plaster of paris and crutches in his apartment. She stated that Bundy kept a lug wrench under the seat of her car and a knife in the glove compartment. His girlfriend also claimed that she once found a bag of women's clothing in his room.

THE KILLINGS CONTINUE—IN UTAH

In late 1974 and early 1975, Ted Bundy attended night classes at the University of Puget Sound Law School. However, he was not happy with the school and dropped out. In the spring of 1974, he applied again to the University of Utah and was accepted; he later stated that the two greatest goals in his life were to return to law school and to become active in the church.

In the fall of 1974, Bundy moved to Salt Lake City, Utah. He worked part time as a university security guard and was preparing to join the Mormon Church.

A month after Bundy moved to Salt Lake City, on the evening of October 18, 1974, a young girl disappeared while walking in the streets of Midvale, a suburban community near Salt Lake City. Her nude body was found a week later in Summit Park, in a canyon of the Wasatch Mountains east of Salt Lake City. She had been badly beaten, strangled with nylons, and raped. The autopsy determined that she had been killed elsewhere.

On October 31, 1974, another young girl disappeared from American Fork, Utah after leaving a Halloween party. (American Fork is approximately twenty-five miles south of Salt Lake City.) Eight days later in Murray, Utah (just south of Salt Lake City and north of American Fork), a young woman was lured to the parking lot of a local shopping mall by a man who proceeded to attack her with a tire iron. She escaped unharmed. The man was driving a light-colored Volkswagen.

In the early evening of November 11, 1974, a man posing as a police officer approached a young girl in a Salt Lake City shopping mall and told her that someone had been seen prowling near her car. He asked her to check the car to see whether anything was missing. After she checked the car and found nothing missing, the man then led her to what he said was a police substation. Finding the door locked, he asked her to accompany him downtown to sign a complaint against the prowler, who had allegedly been arrested by his partner. He showed her his police identification, then led her to a light-colored Volkswagen with scratches and dents and a tear in the back seat. He drove her for a short distance in his car, then abruptly stopped and tried to handcuff her. She struggled and fled the car, at which time he tried to strike her with a tire iron. She resisted and, with handcuffs on one wrist, escaped into the street, where a passing motorist stopped and picked her up.

Half an hour later in Bountiful, Utah, just north of Salt Lake City, a young man stopped a woman backstage at a high school musical and asked her to come outside to the parking lot and identify a car for him. She declined, stating she was too busy with the musical. Thirty minutes later, the man again asked the same woman for assistance in the parking lot, and she again declined. The man was seen a few minutes later pacing near the rear of the theater. Toward the end of the musical, this same man sat down in the audience near the woman he had asked for assistance earlier. His hair was mussed and he was breathing heavily. A young girl who was attending the musical with her parents left the theater during the third act to pick up her brother nearby, and she disappeared. During a search of the high school the following day, a handcuff key was found just outside the school's south door.

On November 27, the body of the girl missing from American Fork was found near a hiking trail on the north slope of Mount Timpanogos, in the Wasatch Mountains. Like the girl found in Summit Park, this girl had been sexually assaulted, bludgeoned on the head, strangled with nylons, and stripped naked. These girls were found within twenty miles of each other.

On January 12, 1975, a young woman disappeared from a ski lodge in Snowmass, Colorado. She was there with friends on a vacation from Michigan and was last seen on the second floor of the lodge. On February 17, 1975, her body was found lying in the snow between Aspen and Snowmass Village. The autopsy revealed that she had received severe head injuries and had been raped.

In March 1975, four of the girls missing from Seattle and Ellensburg, Washington, and Corvallis, Oregon were found on Taylor Mountain, southeast of Seattle and ten miles east of where the Lake Sammamish victims were found. The victims' skulls had been fractured.

That same month, a young woman disappeared from Vail, Colorado while on her way to visit a friend at a local bar. The next month, in April, a young girl disappeared while riding her bicycle in Grand Junction, Colorado. Her bicycle was found under a bridge, her sandals nearby. On April 25, a girl disappeared on her way home from high school in Nederland, Colorado; her body was found fifteen miles away off a county road. Her clothes were partially torn off, her skull was fractured, and her hands were bound.

BUSTED

That fall, in the early morning hours of August 16, 1975, a Utah Highway Patrol sergeant arrested Ted Bundy for evading a police officer in a southern subdivision of Salt Lake City. Bundy had briefly tried to outrun the officer in his Volkswagen and later stated that he had been smoking marijuana and was trying to air out the car before being stopped.

When he was stopped, Bundy was cooperative and, to the arresting officer, seemed almost too relaxed. He was also placed under suspicion for possession of burglary tools, based on the items found in his car: rope, two gloves, a mask made of panty hose, strips of torn sheet, a pair of handcuffs, a flashlight, and a box of black plastic garbage bags. He was released later that morning from the county jail on his own recognizance.

The handcuffs found in Bundy's car caused the Salt Lake county sheriff's office to connect him with an attempted kidnapping that had occurred the previous November. The assailant in that case had used handcuffs and had driven a Volkswagen. Two days after his first arrest, Bundy was charged with possession of burglary tools, and the police began to investigate him further. They searched his apartment and took pictures of his Volkswagen. He was placed under police surveillance and frequently tried to elude his watchers, sometimes successfully. Subsequently, he sold his Volkswagen and canceled his gas credit card.

As part of its investigation, the sheriff's office contacted King County, Washington, whose officers had notified them a year previously that Bundy was a suspect in an investigation of missing women in the Seattle area. Contact was also made with police in Colorado, because ski brochures from Colorado were found in the search of his apartment. A small ink mark was found on one brochure describing a motel in Snowmass, Colorado, where the unsolved murder of a woman had occurred.

On October 1, 1975, Bundy stood in a police lineup. His hair was clipped short and parted in a new way. But the kidnap victim and two witnesses identified him as the kidnap assailant. He was charged with aggravated kidnapping and attempted criminal homicide. Bundy spent eight weeks in the Salt Lake City County jail and posted bond on November 11, 1975. On November 26, 1975, he was bound over for trial at a preliminary hearing and charged with aggravated kidnapping. Bundy was again placed under police surveillance while awaiting trial. Again he tried to elude the police and frequently seemed to be toying with them.

PSYCHOLOGICAL EVALUATIONS

Prior to the trial, Bundy's attorney requested a psychological evaluation of his client. The psychologist found the following:

Good social presence, ego strength and good self-concept, positive self-identity. Bundy was highly intellectual, independent, tolerant, responsible and with normal psychosexual development. He had a healthy curiosity about his father. The worst thing was that he showed some hostility on tests. He is an extremely intelligent young man who is *intact psychologically* [emphasis added].

In late February 1976, Bundy was tried in a bench trial. During the trial, he frequently changed his appearance. For three days in a row, he wore different clothing, changed his hairstyle, and wore different glasses. The prosecution's case rested primarily on the victim's identification of Bundy and her memory since the attempted kidnapping.

Bundy was found guilty, and a presentence investigative report was ordered by the judge. Not satisfied with the results of the presentence report, on March 22, 1976, the judge delayed sentencing and ordered Bundy to Utah State Prison for a ninety-day diagnostic evaluation.

The diagnostic report issued on Bundy on June 22, 1976 contained a series of negatives and positives:

Plus Side
High intelligence, no severely traumatizing influences in childhood or adolescence, few distortions in relationship with mother and stepfather, no serious defects in physical development, habits, school adjustment or sexual development and emotional maturation, adequate interest in hobbies and recreational pursuits, average environmental pressures and responsibilities, and no previous attacks of mental illness.

Minus Side
When one tries to understand him, he becomes evasive, somewhat threatened by people unless he feels he can structure the outcome of the relationship, passive-aggressive features were evident, hostility toward diagnosis personnel.

Bundy's test results on the Minnesota Multiphasic Personality Inventory reflected a somewhat different view of the man:

A fairly strong conflict was evidenced in the testing profile, that being the subject's fairly strong dependence on women, yet his need to be independent. Mr. Bundy would like a close relationship with females, but is fearful of being hurt by them. In addition, there were indications of general anger, and more particularly, well-masked anger toward women.

The final diagnostic report was written by a Dr. Van Austin. Bundy was not found to be psychotic or suffering from schizophrenia. However, he was found to exhibit some characteristics of a personality disorder. Among the features of an antisocial personality disorder that were cited were lack of guilt, callousness, and a tendency to compartmentalize and rationalize his behavior. Van Austin concluded, "I feel that Mr. Bundy is either a man who has no problems or is smart enough and clever enough to appear to be on the edge of normal." The doctor further stated that he could not predict Bundy's future behavior because there was much more to his personality structure that was not known.

SENTENCING, PRISON, AND ESCAPE

On June 30, 1976, Bundy was sentenced to one to fifteen years in prison, with eligibility for parole in approximately fifteen months. He began serving his sentence in the Utah State Penitentiary in July.

Bundy was placed in medium security and given a work assignment in the print shop. Prison officials and guards considered him to be a respectful, pleasant, and cooperative prisoner. He had no problems with the inmates because he provided legal advice to them.

Later that year, a search of Bundy's cell revealed escape contraband: a forged Social Security card, an Illinois driver's license, an airline schedule, and a road map. He was disciplined by serving fifteen days in isolation, then was transferred to maximum security as an escape risk.

In January 1977, Bundy was extradited to Colorado to stand trial for murder. He was incarcerated in the Pitkin County jail in Aspen. The judge in Aspen allowed Bundy to act as his own attorney and to appear in street clothes without any restraining devices.

During this time, Bundy continually asked to have his jail security reduced on the grounds that it hampered his defense preparation. A deputy at the jail stated, "He's smart and very observant. He's making himself just as personable as can be to everyone around here. He's fine until he wants something." In April, Bundy was moved to the Glenwood Springs jail forty miles from Aspen. In April and May of that year, police and other prisoners warned jail officials that Bundy might try to escape; he had been practicing jumping off his bunk in his cell.

On June 7, 1977, Bundy successfully escaped from a window of the courthouse in Aspen by jumping through a second-story window. He was caught in a stolen car after spending six days in the mountains nearby.

After being captured, Bundy resumed preparation for his defense. He worked actively as his own lawyer with legal advisors appointed by the court, he interviewed forensic experts, and his briefs on various motions to the court were considered superior. At a pretrial evidentiary hearing, he cross-examined his previous kidnap victim so that his kidnap conviction would not be introduced against him at the trial. Late in the year, he was granted a change of venue, and his trial was assigned to Colorado Springs; he was housed in the Glenwood Springs jail.

On December 30, 1977, Bundy sawed through a light fixture in the ceiling of his cell and escaped. He was free for forty-three days—enough time to resume his murderous ways.

MOST WANTED

After his escape, Ted Bundy was a man on the move. It was later revealed that he had traveled to Chicago, Illinois; to Ann Arbor, Michigan; and on to Tallahassee, Florida.

In early January, when Bundy arrived in Tallahassee by bus, he was traveling under a false identity. Each day, he changed his appearance by parting his hair differently, by wearing different glasses, and by cutting off his mustache and growing it again. He committed a number of property crimes:

shoplifting of food; theft of a bicycle; theft of numerous credit cards from women's purses in libraries and restaurants; breaking into an automobile; and stealing a television, radio, and typewriter.

In the early morning hours of January 15, 1978, Ted Bundy killed again. He entered the Chi Omega sorority house in Tallahassee shortly after 3:00 A.M. and within approximately fifteen minutes had beaten five different girls as they slept in their rooms on the second floor of the house. He killed two of these girls by strangling them with panty hose. They had been beaten viciously about the head and body. One of the deceased had bite marks on her left buttock, and one of her nipples had been bitten off. A mask made of panty hose was found next to one of the victims.

One and a half hours later, Bundy struck again four blocks away from the sorority house. He attacked and beat a girl as she was sleeping in her apartment. The attack was heard in the adjacent apartment, and police were summoned. Bundy escaped, and the victim survived. At 5:00 A.M. that same day, Bundy was seen in front of his apartment house, four blocks from the Chi Omega house.

The next few weeks found Bundy busy with a variety of crimes. On January 21, he stole a student's wallet and used the student's credit cards for the next ten days. By February 1, he had obtained a birth certificate of the owner of the stolen wallet. On February 6, he stole a Florida State University van and the license plates from another car. On February 7, he bought gas with a stolen credit card in Jacksonville. On February 8, he bought gas in Lake City and tried to pick up a fourteen-year-old girl by posing as a fireman; the girl got the license number of the van. That night, he stayed at a motel in Lake City and left the following morning without paying the bill. That morning, he abducted a twelve-year-old girl from outside her school in Lake City. Her partially decomposed body was found on April 7, thirty-five miles from Lake City.

On February 10, Ted Bundy was placed on the FBI's "Ten Most Wanted" list. The text of the FBI wanted poster described him as an escapee from Colorado wanted for questioning in thirty-six sexual slayings, beginning in California in 1969 and extending through the Pacific Northwest into Utah and Colorado. Below three different-looking photos of Bundy, the text of the poster read:

> Age 31, born November 24, 1946. Height: 5'11" to 6'. Weight: 145 to 175 lbs. Build: Slender, athletic. Caution: Bundy, a college-educated physical fitness enthusiast with a prior history of escape, is being sought as a prison escapee after being convicted of kidnapping and while awaiting trial involving brutal sex slaying of woman at ski resort. He should be considered armed, dangerous, and an escape risk.

On February 11, Bundy locked the door to his apartment, wiped it clean of fingerprints, and left by the fire escape.

The following day, he was stopped by a Leon County deputy near his apartment. The deputy observed a license plate in the car next to which Bundy was standing. Bundy fled before he could be questioned any further. That day, he stole three different cars; the third one he drove west, leaving Tallahassee. On February 13, Bundy was caught using a stolen credit card at a restaurant in Crestview but escaped.

CAPTURE

The next day, on February 14, Bundy was stopped while driving a stolen car in Pensacola. When he resisted arrest, shots were fired by the police officer. He was subdued and placed in the Pensacola jail.

At a minimum, Bundy faced sixty-seven felony counts in Florida for stolen credit cards, forgery, and auto theft. An inventory of his stolen Volkswagen included a bicycle frame, a portable television, stereo equipment, clothing, a sleeping bag, a notebook with student identification, over twenty stolen credit cards, and a number of photos of girls and women.

At the time of his arrest, Bundy was using a false identification, and the police did not know his real identity. When his identity was learned, he immediately came under suspicion for the January 15, 1978 murders of two women and the assault of others in a sorority house in Tallahassee. Police learned that on February 11, he had been confronted by a Leon County deputy in Tallahassee about stolen license plates in his car. Bundy had fled on foot and escaped the officer.

Shortly after his arrest, Bundy was interviewed extensively by Pensacola investigators. He readily confessed that he had stolen the television and credit cards. He also admitted to stealing three cars in Tallahassee. He told three Pensacola detectives that his "problem" had first surfaced in Seattle while walking on a street one night: A girl on the street ahead aroused a feeling he'd never had before. He wanted to possess her by any means necessary, so he followed her home until she entered the house, and he never saw her again. Bundy stated he had become a voyeur during law school in Seattle while walking the streets at night.

Bundy's girlfriend from Seattle claims that he called her on February 18 and confessed to the murders he had committed. In her book, written under a pseudonym, she quotes him as saying:

> There is something the matter with me. It wasn't you. It was me. I just couldn't contain it. I've fought it for a long, long time ... it got too strong. We just happened to be going together when it got under way. I tried to suppress it. It was taking more and more of my time. That's why I didn't do well in school. My time was being used trying to make my life look normal. But it wasn't normal. All the time I could feel that force building in me.
>
> I don't have a split personality. I don't have blackouts. I remember everything I've done. Like Lake Sammamish.

A few days after his arrest, Bundy was transferred to the Leon County jail in Tallahassee. On July 27, 1978, he was indicted on two counts of murder, three of attempted murder, and two of burglary in the crimes committed at the Chi Omega sorority house on January 15. Four days later, Bundy was indicted for murder in the death of a twelve-year-old girl in Lake City, Florida. He pled not guilty to each indictment.

TRIALS—AND CONVICTIONS

The court determined that Bundy could not receive a fair trial in Tallahassee and changed the venue of the Chi Omega trial to Miami. During the trial in Miami, Bundy was involved in the cross-examination of witnesses and eventually fired his defense team, proceeding as his own counsel with the defense team as standby counsel. He continually objected to the presence of television cameras in the courtroom but was overruled by the judge.

On July 24, 1979, Bundy was found guilty. He was given two death sentences and three ninety-year sentences, which would run consecutively.

In January 1980, Bundy was tried for the murder of a twelve-year-old girl in Lake City, Florida. On February 7, 1980, he was found guilty as charged. He received the death penalty and was returned to death row in a Florida prison, one of eight places he had been incarcerated since his arrest in Salt Lake City in 1975.

It must be remembered that Bundy was convicted only for the murders that occurred in Tallahassee and Lake City, Florida in early 1978. He was never convicted for the murders he was suspected of having committed in Washington, Utah, Oregon, and Colorado.

WHO WAS TED BUNDY?

By all accounts, there were two Ted Bundys—the charming, public Ted and the dark, murderous, private Ted.

The public Ted Bundy was considered a sharp dresser and a compulsively neat and orderly person. He was regarded as a young man with charming ways, good looks, and a steady social life when he wanted it.

A former girlfriend stated, "If you know him, you can't help but have a great deal of affection for him as a human being." However, she also noted that he was constantly on guard against anyone getting close to him. This girl's father said Bundy was "extremely moody on occasion. He can be very nice, pleasant, helpful, and then all of a sudden he'll sour on you. It'll look like he's really thinking hard about something."

According to police research, Bundy outwardly made a good impression and was energetic, skillful, bright, moving from job to job, gaining his education and upwardly mobile. But he committed petty thievery, used his boyish good looks and charm to exploit and manipulate, and lacked the inner discipline to finish any major task. Robert Keppel's profile of Bundy describes him as a "self-serving manipulator who lied at will, pinched goods from his employers, and stole his girl-friends' cars."

After conducting a background check on Bundy and watching him in the courtroom, the prosecutor in Aspen said:

> As long as he's functioning as a lawyer everything's real cool with Ted. Then when something reminds him that he's the prisoner, you sense those flashes of anger, hostility. He's always got to be the superstar. But he's only good in the first quarter of whatever game he's in. Then something happens.

To the police in Utah, Bundy was a "loner, always short of money, a leech, and very moody." While in Utah, Bundy was to some extent leading a double life. He was becoming heavily involved in the Mormon Church but he never mentioned this involvement to his friends in the neighborhood where he lived. He sometimes had relationships with two women at the same time, as he did in 1973 when he was engaged to two different women. Later, when he was in prison in Utah, he kept two intense relationships going through visitations and correspondence.

Over the years, Bundy's charm became well known and was a decisive factor in both of his escapes from prison. His charm affected the jailers, guards, secretaries, and officials at the Aspen courthouse and the Glenwood Springs jail in Colorado. For example, after a month of being incarcerated, Bundy was on agreeable terms with almost everyone around the jail in Glenwood Springs. He got along just as well with those who didn't trust him as with those who did.

Despite his charm, however, Bundy was still a loner in some social circles. At the Crisis Clinic in Seattle, most of the students had strong liberal views. Bundy, however, was a strongly conservative Republican. In Utah, the students and neighbors with whom he drank and smoked marijuana were also of a different political philosophy.

Because he could control and manipulate women, they were important to him, and he was frequently in their company. Yet at the same time, he was apart from them and never let them get too close.

Author Ann Rule described two Ted Bundys emerging in 1973:

> One, the perfect son, the University of Washington student who had graduated "with distinction," the fledgling lawyer and politician, and a charming schemer, a man who could manipulate women with ease, whether it be sex or money he desired, and it made no difference if the women were eighteen or sixty-five.

ATTITUDES

At first impression, Ted Bundy projected the image of an individual who was in control and cared little what others thought of him. However, his attitudes reflected a somewhat different person.

It is difficult to determine accurately what value Bundy placed on human life, because he never confessed to his murderous crimes. Only a few of his comments reflect his attitudes toward his victims, and they are anachronistic. For example, following his arrest in Florida, he reportedly told his girlfriend in Seattle, "I want to make it right with all the people I've hurt." However, he would state a short time later that the girl he tried to kidnap in Utah was "lucky she got away." Regarding the location of his twelve-year-old victim in Florida, he said, "I'm the most cold-hearted son of a bitch you'll ever want to meet."

While he was in a Florida prison, Bundy told interviewers, "I feel less guilty now than I've felt in any time in my life." For Bundy, "guilt doesn't solve anything, it only hurts you." Other than the alleged statement to his girlfriend in Seattle, Bundy reportedly never showed remorse for his actions or his victims, which he claimed numbered over one hundred.

Bundy's attitude toward authority is self-evident in many of his recorded statements, as well as from occurrences in his early life. In grade school, he was characterized as being beyond any discipline from his teachers. When things went wrong for Bundy, he would blame an authority figure or the system, as he did when he failed to achieve success in law school or made sporadic attempts at various areas of study while in college.

He took a great deal of pride in outsmarting law enforcement officers. In fact, he bragged about losing the officers who had him under surveillance in Utah. He wrote to Ann Rule, "I have a standing policy from this point forward never to talk to a law enforcement officer about anything except the time of day and the location of the toilet." He frequently castigated his pursuers: "I never underestimate the inventiveness and dangerousness of such men [law enforcement officers]. Like wild animals, when cornered can become very unstable." He reportedly told a neighbor in Tallahassee that he was a lot smarter than the police and could get away with anything he wanted.

Bundy seemed to like to taunt the police. To the investigators of the Chi Omega house killings, he said, "The evidence is there. Keep digging." He urged the investigators in Utah to search for straws to make the broom. Regarding the investigators in Washington, he stated, "They're not going to find any evidence there, because there is no evidence there to find." In continuing to proclaim his innocence, he accused the police of wasting taxpayers' money with all their conferences and task forces. The police, for Bundy, had their heads in the sand. He claimed that the police and the prosecutor's charges against

THE NEED TO KILL

him were "grossly exaggerated, their accusations purely ficti-
tious and totally without merit."

Throughout his incarceration and criminal trials, Bundy
continued to maintain his innocence of any murders. He constantly tried to reach the media to convey this message. Even
though he seemed to enjoy being a celebrity, he sometimes
contradicted himself regarding his own self-perception. He
stated to a detective that it was important how people perceived him; he was not just a fiend, there was more to him
than that. But he wrote to a magazine editor in Seattle, "I am
still too young to look upon my life as history. I am at a stage
in life, an egocentric stage, where it matters only that I understand what I am and not what others may think of me."

He told one interviewer, "I just liked to kill, I wanted to
kill." In an interview with James Dobson, Bundy claimed that
pornography had led him to kill:

> I'm telling you from personal experience, the most graphic
> violence on screen, particularly as it gets into the home; to
> children who may be unattended or unaware that they may
> be a Ted Bundy who has vulnerability to that, that predispo-
> sition to be influenced by that kind of behavior, by that kind
> of movie and that kind of violence.

BUNDY'S LAST CON

After being found guilty on two counts of murder in February of 1980, Ted Bundy was married to Carole Boone in a
Miami courtroom during the penalty phase of his criminal
trial. They later conceived in a Florida prison, and his wife
gave birth to a baby girl.

A few days before his execution, Bundy began confessing
his crimes. Although a number of these confessions were
taken seriously by law enforcement officials, Bundy was most
likely trying one more con—a con to save his life. By confessing to these additional crimes, he was trying to avoid the
death penalty.

It didn't work.

The State of Florida executed Ted Bundy on January 24, 1989. For many, he still remains a very troubling enigma. Although he did, in fact, kill a large number of people, many of his victims may never be identified.

8

JERRY MARCUS

Jerry Marcus
From the author's files

Jerry Marcus murdered seven women between 1970 and 1986, yet didn't attract a lot of media attention. Perhaps it was because the murders occurred in small communities; perhaps it was because Marcus and his victims were all black. Whatever the reasons, Marcus is that type of killer who is the most frightening—the nice guy next door who is never suspected of having a murderous dark side.

CHILDHOOD YEARS

Jerry Marcus was born on June 14, 1951, in Tuskegee, Alabama. He had three brothers, Edwin, Anthony, and Ronald, and one sister, Beverly. As a young boy, Jerry played Little League baseball, then became involved in sports in high school, playing baseball and football and running track.

Jerry's mother and maternal aunt were very loving and supportive, and remain so today. However, this was not true of his father. Ruth and Eddie Marcus never had a sound marriage, and Eddie used to mentally, physically, socially, and spiritually abuse his wife and children beyond physical and emotional recognition.

Marcus indicated that although he loved his father, he was whipped a lot and struck with his father's fists as well:

> There were numerous occasions when I wanted to end my dad's life, but my plans never went through because my mom truly loved him no matter now bad he beat her up or mistreated her, she always went back to him knowing how he is when he's drinking a lot.

Between the ages of eight and ten, Jerry felt a "badness" deep inside his heart and mind toward others, except for his best friends and family members. These feelings of anger confused the young boy, because his family had always been religiously inclined. However, he admitted that he often skipped out on attending services and church school. Persuading neighborhood kids to give him a copy of the church bulletin, he would show this to his aunt and mother to prove that he had attended the services.

During this time, Marcus began to abuse animals:

> I tortured cats a lot, especially when they were pregnant, I would toss the cat around and around until it became drunk, then I would set its tail on fire. I got a kick out of that. When I played with fire, I felt amusement, what it would feel like to stick my finger in it, how it would feel to be caught in a fire with no way out. I poured hot water on stray dogs that came for a free meal around the house. When I tortured these animals, I felt pride, joy, happiness, and being in total control of my naughtiness.

By age twelve, Marcus began to feel shame concerning his family and the abuse that he felt sure everyone knew about. Perhaps because he thought that everyone knew intimate details about him and his family's life, Marcus began to window peep. "I began window peeping at the age of 13. I admired looking at girls and women in their bras and panties."

During the period 1964–1967, when Marcus was between thirteen and fifteen years of age, his mother separated from his father and took a job in New York State. At this point, Marcus moved in next door with his aunt to avoid his abusive father.

Prior to this time, because of family problems, Marcus's mother had left the family home on several occasions to stay next door with her sister. Her husband, Eddie, told her that if she didn't come back he would kill all his children. When she returned to the family home, Eddie kept her locked up in the house for days. Marcus and his older brother Ronald each took two rifles and went to their father's house to get their mother back, but she shouted for them to go away or their father would kill them all.

Marcus later recalled his feelings toward his father: "I just wanted to take a brick and bust his brains out of his head. I hid one evening outside with a brick ready to kill my dad, but he never came outside."

HIGH SCHOOL AND COLLEGE

Marcus attended Tuskegee Institute High School, where he was considered to be a sharp student, quick to answer questions and excelling in mathematics. He was also a good singer and an artist for the yearbook: "I was a creative child and I valued everything that I'd worked hard for without a handout from family members or others. I took my education more serious than playtime."

Marcus did very well in school, was regarded favorably by his teachers, excelled in mathematics, and to this day is very literate. He participated in extramural sports in grade school and high school, and earned a football scholarship that enabled him to attend Knoxville College. He had many friends throughout his school years, most of them female.

"He had quite a few girlfriends in high school. He was a leader and always showed me the utmost respect," said Thomas Calhoun, a former coach and teacher of Marcus. "He was like a son to me. He came to me with his problems, we talked about them, and once I gave him some money when he needed it. I was very surprised when I heard about everything that had happened. Marcus was never violent, even when he played football."

After high school there was no money for him to attend a "big" college. When he asked his father for financial support, he was told that he wouldn't get "one red cent" because he had run away from home to live with his aunt during high school. So his aunt came up with the money for his fees, and Marcus enrolled in Alexander City State Junior College to study health and physical education.

Marcus commuted to school with John Bentley, a classmate from high school who had a car, and his cousin, Earnest Brown, who also attended class there. They commuted in this fashion until Marcus and his cousin met the Wise family and moved in with them, paying $50 a month for room and board.

Early in 1969, Marcus dropped out of City State Junior College and returned to Tuskegee to care for his aunt, who was recovering from a stroke. He cared for her until she became mobile again in 1971.

That same year, Marcus began working at John Andrew Hospital on the Tuskegee Institute campus as a custodian in the surgical area. This is when the killings began.

A CRIME OF OPPORTUNITY

It was the fall of 1970. Marcus was off duty and driving through the campus of Tuskegee Institute when he spotted Constance Collins walking by Tatum Hall. She was a student nurse whom he recognized from the hospital. Marcus stopped and asked whether she wanted a ride to work. Recognizing Marcus from the hospital, she accepted the ride.

Marcus drove her to the Emergency Room area but as he stopped the car, the situation took a deadly turn. When Collins attempted to get out of the car, Marcus grabbed her arm, pulling her back into the car. He asked her where she lived and whether he could call her. Collins panicked and started fighting back, screaming for help. Marcus then restrained her from behind while covering her mouth with his hands. He told her to stop screaming, that he would let her go, but she continued to fight back and scream. Marcus panicked and slid his hands down from her mouth to her neck, choking her to death right outside the Emergency Room entrance.

He then drove away from the hospital, traveling aimlessly on Montgomery Highway until he eventually pulled off onto Peterson Street. When he spotted an abandoned, hutlike building at the end of the street, he dumped her body, fully clothed in her gray nursing uniform, onto the ground and drove away.

A month later, Marcus returned to the site and found everything gone, including the body. At that point, he threw away her books, which he had been carrying around with him. Although in his later written confession Marcus indicated that he killed Collins on a "sex urge," the victim was not sexually assaulted. Apparently, he reached such a state of panic when she would not cooperate that he redirected his passion, drawing from the murder itself all the sexual pleasure that he craved.

Marcus was never considered a suspect in Collins's murder.

ANOTHER VICTIM

Marcus' next attack was a year later. Margaret Sturdivant, another nursing student, was walking home from work, carrying her books and dressed in her gray student nursing uniform. Marcus offered her a ride. She accepted because she had seen him working on campus.

With little warning, Marcus felt his heart start to race; he says he could almost taste the adrenaline as it started pumping into his bloodstream. He detoured from her route home and drove to the local park, where he persuaded her to leave the car. Marcus began discussing problems he was having at work and with other women, but Sturdivant was tired and simply wanted to go home to her family. Marcus then became physically aggressive. Sturdivant resisted, kicking him in the groin while attempting to flee. She tripped and fell with Marcus on top of her, attacking and raping her. She again attempted to attract attention and to cry out for help, but Marcus forcefully pushed her face into the loose dirt and suffocated her. He held her face down in the dirt until he was sure she was dead, then he hid her body in the nearby woods and discarded her clothing.

This attack demonstrated more aggressiveness and better planning on Marcus's part. He later recalled the crime:

> I can still see her face buried in the ground as I tried to calm her down. When I turned her over, she wasn't breathing, so I disrobed her and left her body in the woods. I always remembered when my dad got mad at mom, and he tore her clothes off her to disgrace her publically [sic] in front of me and my brother.

Sturdivant's body was recovered on November 22, 1971. Again, Marcus was not regarded as a suspect.

ASSAULT AND CAPTURE

In 1971, Marcus was accused of assault with intent to ravish by two student nurses from Tuskegee University. When later questioned about this incident, Marcus said that he had been falsely accused. He indicated that he was procuring needles and phenobarbital from John Hopkins Hospital for the students who accused him. Marcus said that when he grew afraid that he would lose his job and that his aunt would find out about the thefts, he refused to steal anything else for the students; they supposedly retaliated by accusing him of assault.

Prior to his trial, Marcus was admitted to Brice Mental Hospital in Tuscaloosa, Alabama, where he remained for approximately two months. The hospital staff found that Marcus demonstrated a personality trait disorder manifested by ambivalence, poorly controlled hostility, guilt, and frustration with irritability. He was considered legally sane and competent to face trial.

A jury found Marcus guilty of the crimes, but the Alabama Court of Criminal Appeals reversed the ruling on the grounds that the confession was improperly allowed as evidence. On March 12, 1972, the original charge of assault with intent to ravish was reduced to one of assault and battery. Five days later, on March 17, Marcus was convicted and sentenced to six months in jail; the sentence was lenient because he had no prior criminal record.

Marcus spent his six months in jail but felt that his life and reputation had been destroyed forever:

> So, I began to hate girls because two other girls had falsely accused me of doing something that I didn't do. I had too many girls to take or make them do anything on the sex side.

After his release, Marcus quietly slipped back into society—marrying his high school sweetheart, working to support his new family, going to school, and caring for his aunt, who had become ill. He appeared to be attempting to neutralize his criminal behavior, disregarding his previous actions as though they had never occurred and blaming others for the behavior that eventually led to his incarceration.

LOVE AND MARRIAGE

When Marcus was fourteen years old and in tenth grade, he met Gwen Synegal, whom he considered the love of his life. She was one of the smartest and most intelligent girls he ever met:

> I always felt intimidated by her smartness. She's the jealous type, dazzle, charm, a great sense of humor, easy to impress, wouldn't let me be me totally, a total mysterious woman towards "voodoo," shows a lack of passion, stubborn to the core when angry, a very attractive lady. She never wanted me to attend Knoxville College but to work at a gas station for the rest of my life. I could never please or satisfy her desires.

Even though Marcus and Gwen's relationship was not approved of by either family, they were married in 1972, soon after Marcus was released from the assault and battery conviction. Throughout the marriage, Marcus was unfaithful. He separated from Gwen and their family between 1975 and 1979 and during this time left Tuskegee to attend school in Knoxville, Tennessee. Also during this time, he became intimately involved with two other women and had children with both of them.

In subsequent police reports, Marcus talked about Gwen and how she practiced voodoo and was a witch. He made no reference to himself as participating in her activities. He feared her and noticed that she saved nail clippings and hair that she trimmed from his head; she also kept large Clorox bottles filled with water in all the closets. Gwen supposedly "deprived" Marcus of sexual activity for weeks at a time; this was when he started "dating other ladies behind her back."

There is no written evidence that Gwen was aware of the incidents that occurred in Tuskegee. After her initial interview with the authorities in 1986, she has refused to comment further.

BACK TO COLLEGE

In September 1975, after Jerry and Gwen had separated, coach Marian Quinn of Knoxville College in Tennessee sought out Marcus to play football on his team. Quinn and Marcus had attended the same high school in Tuskegee and played ball together there. As a result, Marcus became a student at Knoxville College and remained there until 1979.

After Marcus first moved to Knoxville, he became involved with Lynn Bishop, who was also a student at the college. She graduated in 1978 and moved back to Starkville, Mississippi, pregnant with Marcus's son.

In 1979, Marcus met Lennise Gillette, who was also a student at Knoxville College, and they also conceived a son. Marcus then dropped out of college to work full time on campus as a custodial supervisor. He lived alone at the Wesley House, which was considered a living area for "indigents." It was during this period that Marcus and Gwen formally divorced, following a brief reconciliation in 1977. Marcus continued working at Knoxville College, and Lennise became pregnant again with a second son.

During 1983, Marcus was fired from his job at Knoxville College after he gave out the master key for the basketball locker room and items were stolen. He was formally charged with aiding and abetting, but the charges were subsequently dismissed. As far as the college administration knew, Marcus had never been in any type of trouble before.

THE KILLINGS RESUME

Marcus's urge to kill had apparently been satiated for more than a dozen years, but the loss of this job apparently helped to revive his murderous impulses.

In October 1984, Marcus met Francine Davis. Because he had lost his job on campus, he had been living on food stamps and unemployment compensation; she worked at the local food stamp office. Davis and Marcus soon became sexually intimate.

Early one weekend morning, Marcus went over to Davis's house so they could go to the park and play tennis. Afterward, they stopped at the home of a friend of Marcus's, where he showered while Davis waited for him. Then they returned to Davis's apartment so she could shower. While she bathed, Marcus "cased" her apartment. He found an envelope with his name on it and, looking inside, discovered what appeared to be some of his food stamps and some cash. Marcus realized that while he had been showering, Davis must have taken the items.

Initially, he was hurt rather than angry at her for taking his stamps and cash, but then he redirected this hurt back at her. The longer she stayed in the shower, the angrier he allowed himself to become. When Davis came into the room wrapped in a bathrobe, Marcus turned on her, seizing her by the arm and spraying Mace directly into her face. Davis attempted to pull away from him, crying, "What do you want, what do you need? Don't kill me," but he threw her onto the floor.

As his hands fumbled at his waist, he realized he was not wearing a belt. His eyes flitted around the room. Suddenly he saw what he was looking for. Jerking a narrow black cord away from the back of the television set, he wrapped it around her neck and choked her. Then he pulled the cord away from her neck, her body limp in his hands, and carried her into the bathroom. Marcus's head was spinning, but he remembered the effort of strangling Constance Collins and wondered whether he had really killed his victim. He held Davis's head under water, still furious with her but determined to make sure she would never reappear to accuse him of attempted murder: "I put her head under the water and held it until the bubbles quit coming up. It took a long time."

Marcus then pulled her body from the tub, dried her off somewhat, and put her in her bed to make it appear that she had died while sleeping. He also wrote a suicide note implicating her former husband, Arthur; took a few pieces of gold jewelry and a boom box; and left the apartment. After that, he went to his girlfriend's house for the night. The next day, he sold the stolen items at a local pawnshop—and left town.

ANOTHER MURDER—AND A CONFESSION

When Marcus left Tennessee, he traveled to Los Angeles with an unidentified male companion. From Los Angeles, the two took a bus to Houston, Texas, then split up, with Marcus staying at the Salvation Army while searching for work in that area. By June 1984, Marcus had hitched a ride to Waugh, Alabama and found a factory job as a steel worker, which he held until July 1985. During this time, he became heavily involved with alcohol and drugs, and he lost his job after not showing up for work. Early in 1986, Marcus moved back to Tuskegee and started doing construction work on the Tuskegee campus.

Marcus's next brush with the law occurred in late spring of 1986. On May 8 of that year, a missing persons report was filed by the Tuskegee Job Corps Center concerning Yvette Chambers, who had last been seen with her boyfriend, Carl Washington. When Washington was questioned by local police, he indicated that he had last seen Chambers on the afternoon of May 4, as she was getting into a vehicle with other male subjects—one of whom was Jerry Marcus.

When Marcus was questioned on May 14, he told several different stories. The initial story indicated that he had picked up both Chambers and her girlfriend, Janice, on May 5 at around 4:00 P.M. They drove around to get some beer and marijuana, hung around a local lake until about 7:00 P.M., then drove back to the Job Corps, where they dropped Janice off. Marcus and Chambers then returned to the store to get more beer and food, and they picked up some more marijuana. This interaction occurred in the same local park where the Sturdivant killing had occurred in 1971, approximately fifteen years previously, as well as where Marcus had played tennis with Davis before killing her in 1984.

By the afternoon of the same day of this initial questioning, Marcus had changed his mind. In his second sworn statement, he indicated that he had dropped Chambers off at a hair salon and had gone to pick up his girlfriend, Lynn Bishop. The story remained the same until after the beer and marijuana, when Chambers and Marcus supposedly drove to a club in Hardway, Alabama. Marcus said he went inside, leaving Chambers in the car for approximately thirty minutes. When he came back outside, both Chambers and his car (Lynn's car) were gone. After about fifteen minutes, Chambers returned with another male in the vehicle, whom Marcus told to get out. This man was not identified.

Marcus said he got into the car and started driving Chambers back to Tuskegee on Highway 80; then without warning, he pulled off of the road and started slapping her. She attempted to get away but Marcus started tearing off her clothes, forcing her back into the car. She spit in his face and bloodied his nose during the struggle. Marcus then reached into the backseat of the car and retrieved a belt, which he tightened around her neck. As he started getting out of the car, dragging Chambers by the neck, he heard something pop. After that, she didn't move anymore. He panicked, pulling her body upright and shaking her to provoke some response. Getting none, he dumped her body in the trunk of the car and started driving across the bridge.

Marcus then began having second thoughts. He pulled the car over to the side of the road and removed the body from the trunk, throwing it over the Highway 80 bridge. He heard a dull thump and the splash of water as the body made contact. He then jumped into the car and drove back to Tuskegee. As he drove into the campus of the Tuskegee Institute, he began to calm down and headed to a service station, where he threw the clothes he had torn off Chambers's body into a Dumpster. Then he drove home.

On May 27, Chambers's body was recovered from under the bridge on Highway 80. The cause of death was undetermined, partially owing to advanced postmortem decomposition.

Despite his confession, Marcus had not yet been arrested. This gave him the opportunity on June 17 to modify his statement. This time, Marcus said Chambers had revealed to him that Washington planned to kill her and that she feared for her life. Marcus then dropped Chambers off at the Chicken Coop restaurant, telling her he had to pick up his girlfriend, Lynn Bishop, from work. After he took Bishop home, he went out again, supposedly in concern for Chambers's safety. Spotting Chambers and Washington together, he followed them to the bridge on Highway 80. Marcus then indicated that as he drove by their car, he noticed the passenger's door was open and Chambers and Washington were arguing. He said that he didn't think Chambers was wearing any clothes; he also thought that Washington's shirt was halfway off. When he turned the car around and returned to the scene, he told officials, the two of them were gone.

ANOTHER VICTIM

On May 30, 1986, while Marcus was attempting to cover up his previous contact with Chambers, he had the urge to kill again. The victim this time was named Lenore Wright.

That evening, Marcus and Wright had eaten dinner at a Kentucky Fried Chicken, then drove out to a local lake to smoke marijuana and drink some beer. When Marcus told Wright that his girlfriend was coming to town and that they planned to get married, Wright put her feet on the dashboard and, kicking, broke the windshield. Realizing it was going to cost $400 to have the windshield repaired, Marcus lost his temper, wrapped his hands around her neck, and choked her until he thought she was dead. He started to drive away, but then Wright began to regain consciousness. Marcus stopped to strangle her again.

At this point, his story takes a more sinister turn, revealing Marcus's capability for planning and his attention to detail. Marcus drove his car to the rear of Wright's house, a concealed area surrounded by trees, and deposited the body on the back porch. He then drove his car about a block away to the parking lot of an apartment complex, left it there, and returned to Wright's house on foot. When he was unable to open the back door, he went to the front and let himself in. Heading to the rear of the house, he opened the back door and pulled her body through the doorway to the front of the house. Marcus then placed her body on the bed and turned on the gas stove, hoping that the house would blow up and cover up his crime.

Marcus was considered a suspect in Wright's murder and was questioned again, but there was not sufficient evidence to charge him. A year went by, and police continued to question Marcus about the deaths of both Yvette Chambers and Lenore Wright. No arrest was made; no charges were filed.

Jerry Marcus was laid off from his construction job early in 1987, due to bad weather conditions. He then moved to Starkville, Mississippi to live with Lynn Bishop (now his fiancée) and her mother.

ALCOHOL, SEX, AND MURDER

On April 10, 1987, at about 11:00 A.M., Marcus picked up a woman named Dot Davis at her mother's home in Starkville. He was driving his fiancée's car, a 1984 blue Ford Tempo. Marcus and Davis drove to the welfare office in Starkville, then headed out to Highway 389, buying some beer and parking near a fishing spot to drink it. Around 2:30 P.M., they returned to Davis's sister's house to check on her kids, and Davis received a phone call from her boyfriend. This call prompted her to urge Marcus to drive her to Columbus, Mississippi so they could "party" at a club called Goldie's Disco in Catfish Alley. They spent some time at the club, then left to buy a pint of whiskey from the ABC package store. Afterward, they drove back to Highway 45, drinking, smoking, and killing time until dark.

When they returned to the liquor store to get more beer, Marcus searched for $60 that he had put in the console of Bishop's car. It was gone. When he asked Davis about the money, she at first denied any knowledge of the cash; then she said she needed the money and would pay Marcus back later. They drove off the highway onto a gravel road a mile or so from the crossroads, went under an underpass, and pulled onto a dirt road where they parked and had sexual intercourse. But all the time Marcus kept remembering the money Davis had taken.

Marcus' anger began building in that familiar way, leaving him breathless—better than sex, better than almost anything. He asked her about the money again. This time Davis made the mistake that cost her her life, saying, "You got your money's worth." Marcus gave her one more chance to stop his escalating passion to kill, saying, "Dot, let's not play games, I need my money." Davis must not have seen the rage in his eyes as she replied, "You'll get your money back, but not right now."

Marcus felt she expected him to beg for his money back. He reached down for his belt on the floorboard and looped it around her neck from behind, taking her by surprise. Even though it was springtime, it was hot inside the car, and the driver's side door was already open; Marcus dragged her body out of the car by the belt around her neck. He held her down on the ground, pulling the belt tighter until blood started coming out of her nose and a foamy substance out of her mouth.

As quickly as Marcus's anger had escalated out of control, suddenly it was gone, replaced with panic. He picked up Davis's nude body, threw it into the trunk of the car, and drove away, skidding on the gravel road and throwing her clothing out the window. They were already in an isolated area, and after driving a quarter of a mile or so, he stopped the car and dumped the body near the side of the road. As he drove away, he discarded the belt that he had used in at least three previous murders.

Marcus then returned to Starkville and fell asleep in a service station lot. When he awakened the next morning, he attempted to file a false police report indicating that he had been robbed; this would furnish a cover for having Lynn Bishop's car out all night.

THE FINAL VICTIM

When Marcus went to the police on April 11 to file the false robbery report, they wanted to talk to him about something else—the murder of Dot Davis, whose nude body had been found the previous evening. Investigators questioned Marcus for several hours but then released him for lack of evidence.

Things were unraveling for Jerry Marcus. On April 16, police officials brought him in for further questioning. This time he modified his confession concerning the Chambers killing the year before, indicating that although he had attempted to blame Carl Washington for the murder, he himself was really responsible. He also confessed to the murder of Dot Davis.

The next day, April 17, police discovered the body of Wydeane Ellerbee near Marcus's former house in Tuskegee. Back on September 16, 1986, Ellerbee had asked Marcus to accompany her to pick up some cocaine. He agreed and gave her $25 to purchase the drug while he waited in the car. When

Ellerbee came back outside, she said there was just a little of the coke so she had done it herself. Did he know where they could find some more?

Marcus took Ellerbee back to the house where he was currently living with his mother. From there, he made some phone calls, trying to find more coke. When he was unable to locate more drugs, Ellerbee became impatient, which prompted Marcus to ask her about the $200 she owed him. She pulled away from Marcus and turned, walking down the back steps of his mother's house; he looped his belt around her neck from behind and pulled her toward him, choking her and dragging her into the back yard.

Ellerbee was too heavy for Marcus to lift, so he returned to the house and got a long black cord from the television set, remembering that he had used this type of cord successfully with Francine Davis. He tied it around Ellerbee's hands and dragged her down the wooden steps into a wooded area beyond the back yard of his mother's house. Marcus then drove Ellerbee's car back into town and retrieved his own car, returning home that same night.

The next day, Marcus returned to Ellerbee's body lying on the ground in the wooded area behind his mother's house. He attempted to dig a grave, but the ground was too hard. Lacking a better idea, he concealed the body with a cover that he took from the couch in his mother's house. Over the next few days, Marcus kept pouring dirt over the body to attempt to cover up the smell of decay that his mother had started to notice.

Her body wasn't discovered until the following spring, the day after Marcus confessed to the Davis killing.

On May 16, 1987, Jerry Marcus was formally indicted for the murder of Dot Davis. He subsequently confessed to the other murders, writing lengthy confessions in almost perfect handwriting, drawing maps to the locations of his kills, and leading officers to the kill sites.

THE KILLER ON SERIAL KILLERS

After his arrest, Marcus demonstrated the same humble, gentle behavior that everyone had known of him, graciously assisting the officers investing his crimes. This time, however, the gentleness was frightening; authorities now knew that it was this behavior that victims trusted, leading them to their deaths.

During this period, Marcus wrote a long description of serial killers and what law enforcement officers should look for in these individuals. In this document, he described the sick mind and how such an individual will look good in the public eye, then become a schemer and a mastermind when he is alone.

Marcus went on to describe himself as an athlete, "as cool as ever," in the fast lane, choosing the finest women. He indicated that the girls in high school were okay but that he preferred college girls because they had more to offer. He wrote that when he was in high school he was very shy but that at night he became someone else, as a "peeping tom."

Marcus described himself (in the third person) as a shy type, hanging around bars or clubs, looking for prostitutes for sex. He warned the reader to beware of the shy type, because "these individuals could become a brutal person if rejection permits itself." He discussed anxieties and how they build up to be "dealt with prostitutes." When the shy type finds someone who will trust him and go off with him, her life is in danger; especially if drugs and drinking are involved, the woman could easily be hurt or killed.

Marcus then talked about college and how he became involved with women, drugs, and drinking, indicating that this was the start of his sick mind. He wrote that once the mind is poisoned by these things, it will automatically change into a "schemer or mastermind," influenced by money, women, and drugs; and when those people are "mastered," they become his victims.

ATTITUDES

Throughout his life, Marcus was regarded by others as a giving and conscientious individual. "He was the type who would try to do anything asked of him," said Thomas Lee Calhoun, Marcus's former football coach and teacher. Lynn Bishop's grandmother, Katie Jones, indicated that she was surprised because Marcus had seemed like such a nice fellow who hadn't said all that much and kept to himself most of the time. Maxey Peterson of Peterson Building and Construction of Louisville, Kentucky indicated that Marcus was smart and a good worker. "He was an easygoing, quiet kind of fellow and I was always pleased with his work," said Peterson. The Lowndes County sheriff, Lewis Harper, said that Marcus had cooperated with detectives and described him as a "big man who is just as humble as he can be."

When Marcus began killing his victims, perhaps he was reliving his resentment toward his mother's tolerance of abuse from his father and her inability to protect him as a child. "My uncaring dad, my role model, didn't provide me with a safe place from poverty, neglect, drugs, and violence," Marcus once wrote.

It is interesting that even though Marcus loved his mother and his aunt very much, he became a repeat killer of women. Perhaps he was subconsciously modeling after his father in his rage toward both parents—his father for the repeated physical and mental abuse that affected the entire family and his mother for being unable to control the abuse and for her willingness to be punished repeatedly. During his youth, Marcus was unable to help his mother or himself; the more hatred he developed toward his father for abusing his mother, the more of this hatred he transferred to girls:

> The more I killed and got away with, the more I wanted to see them suffer the way my mom did by the hands of my dad. I saw all the bad things that my dad did to my mom, so by him teaching me how bad he treated mom, I knew it was wrong, but I had to find out by experimentation how it would feel to actually hurt a female physically the way my dad did.

Although Marcus belongs to the category of male serial killers who kill women, his known killings would not be considered heinous because he did not abuse or torture his victims before or after the act. He apparently did not collect trophies, such as clothing or body parts, and there is no evidence that he bragged about his kills to other individuals. Even though Marcus indicated that he robbed several of his victims of jewelry, small amounts of money, and some stereo equipment, the value of the stolen goods was minimal. And he did not mutilate the victims' bodies; evidence indicates that he was capable of killing with or without sexually compromising his victims.

When questioned about his feelings toward his victims and women in general, Marcus seemed to differ from the norm of serial killers. During the times when he interacted with his victims, rather than being stimulated and excited, he considered his respect for women and himself to be at its lowest point because of his lack of moral values and self-respect. In fact, Marcus claims that he kept teaching himself to become dangerous when alone with a girl as they smoked marijuana and drank alcohol. According to Marcus, his unsatisfactory lifestyle drove him to do more bad than good toward those girls.

> As a youngster, I started living out my fantasies toward putting pain on something that had life. I used to hurt a lot, and I would try to shoot or kill anything that got in my eyesight. The anger from those college girls began to make me feel uncomfortable about girls, so I was riding around in my car hating every girl that I saw on the street. Something in the back of my mind said that it was O.K. to hate girls, so I began hating girls, and I got my first edge to pick one up, take her off somewhere, and punish her. I always felt insecure about myself, I had low self-esteem, and hated all the girls smarter than me.

THE LAST WORD

Jerry Marcus murdered seven women: Constance Collins, Margaret Sturdivant, Francine Davis, Yvette Chambers,

Lenore Wright, Wydeane Ellerbee, and Dot Davis. Although this killer was convicted many years ago, his case has not attracted widespread public attention. This could be for many reasons: (1) The murders occurred in small communities, (2) Marcus is black and his victims were also black, and (3) Marcus was not a horrific killer.

Research has demonstrated that Jerry Marcus is a serial killer of a different type, perhaps a type that hasn't yet been fully defined. He impressed everyone with his gentle personality and his willingness to help. Teachers, employers, and coworkers all noted his ability to listen and follow instructions. He dated and entertained women continuously without any of them ever suspecting that each date might be her last.

Yet Jerry Marcus is the type of killer that should be feared the most: the type that is never suspected; the nice guy next door; a fellow student at college; the guy who worked maintenance in surgery; the one who respected his elders and his teachers and never rejected authority or discipline.

Jerry Marcus is currently an inmate at Parchman Penitentiary. He is a good writer, and he works with other inmates, teaching them to read and write. In his most recent communications, Marcus indicates that he has rededicated his life to God, having recently joined a religious group within the prison:

> The living spiritual world has put my life back on the right track. I am whatever people want me to be as long as its part of "God's Will." God has put me on a positive level mentally, spiritually, socially, and physically. I've asked God for His forgiveness, and to please give me His wisdom and understanding.

9

JOSEPH MILLER

Joseph Miller
Peoria County, Illinois, Sheriff's Office
From the author's files

Joseph Miller is a Chicago-area serial murderer who had two separate killing sprees. After being convicted for two murders in the mid-1970s, he served fifteen years in prison; six months after his parole, he was killing again.

CHILDHOOD

According to a Cook County, Illinois birth certificate, Joseph Frank Miller was born at Cook County Hospital in Chicago on January 15, 1955. Although the middle name Robert and its corresponding initial are cited in his later life, it is apparent that this is not Miller's given middle name. Miller's father is recorded as James Miller, a twenty-three-year-old newspaper-company salesman. Shirley Lorraine Watkins is listed as the mother; the document indicates that she was a native of Iowa and was eighteen years old when Joseph was born. According to the certificate, the boy was Shirley Watkins's first child.

Joseph Miller never knew the whereabouts of his natural father. His mother married several times during his childhood, but it is uncertain whether Shirley Watkins ever married

James Miller. One of young Joseph's stepfathers was apparently named Donald Frank Tarczon, a name that Joseph Miller would use at various times during later stages of his life. The future killer may have experienced problems with one or more of his stepfathers; one, he claimed, had a severe temper and exercised strict discipline within the household. Although Miller said he was afraid of this paternal figure, there is no specific record of abuse.

Curiously, when Miller was a child, his mother repeatedly told him he had a twin brother. At some point in his later childhood, he located a copy of his birth certificate and learned this was not the case. ("I wonder why she told me that," Miller later mused.)

It is apparent that Joseph Miller's early home life was fraught with neglect or, at the very least, a lack of attention the boy felt he deserved. He frequently ran away from home, usually to return within a short time. On one occasion, when he was in ninth grade, Miller left home for a relatively long period. Although the actual length of time is not known, basements of abandoned buildings, hallways in office and apartment complexes, and outdoor park benches served as Miller's living quarters during this absence from home. Nonetheless, regardless of the duration of these ventures, Miller always returned home. He thought his family would appreciate him more following his time away.

ENTERING ADULTHOOD

In 1971, when he was seventeen years old, Miller entered the U.S. Army. He registered under the name of his stepfather, Donald Frank Tarczon; military officials discovered this misrepresentation in August 1972 and dishonorably discharged Miller for having fraudulently enlisted.

In January 1972, Miller married. He and his wife, Marcia, spent their short time together living near Chicago. This initial marriage ended in divorce under unusual circumstances two years later. Miller later told an Illinois Department of Corrections interviewer that his dishonorable discharge formed the basis for his divorce, "since the Army told me that Donald Frank Tarczon didn't exist, and that was the name I was using, I wanted to be married under my own name." The couple remarried shortly thereafter, with Miller using his given name.

Life with Marcia was apparently less than nurturing; she attempted to make up for shortcomings at home by having extramarital affairs. Miller seems to feel that he did not provide her with a productive relationship, and he expressed guilt at his self-reported inability to satisfy her sexually. He later told an interviewer, "My wife was running around with other guys because I could not give her enough love and care and our sex life was terrible because of me."

Miller spent his entire life in the lower working class. Aside from the time he spent in the armed forces, his employment history was erratic. Over the years, Miller held a variety of jobs, usually semiskilled, including work as a truck driver, factory work, and odd jobs in restaurants. Nothing suggests that Miller ever obtained any postsecondary or vocational education that might have helped him find a more lucrative or stable means of employment. As a result, money was always in short supply.

FIRST CRIMES

Miller lived and worked most of his life in and around the Chicago area. His sole record outside of Illinois is an arrest by the Petersburg, Virginia police in May 1972 for grand larceny of an automobile. Miller was given a two-year suspended sentence for this act.

On January 15, 1973, Miller was arrested for auto theft by officers of the Skokie, Illinois police department. He used the name Joseph R. Tarczon on this occasion and was given one year of court supervision as a penalty.

Several months later, he was charged with two counts of theft by the Chicago police. He was sentenced to one year of probation for this crime; Miller told authorities he was Joseph R. Tarczon on this occasion, as well.

The Chicago city police arrested Miller once again in February 1974 for criminal trespass to land. This record also indicates he referred to himself as Joseph R. Tarczon.

ROAD TO MURDER

Then in 1975, Miller's illegal actions became more personal—and more violent. On January 29 of that year, he was arrested again by Chicago police and charged with sexual assault. In May, the charge was reduced from rape to simple kidnapping, and Miller was yet again given probation, this time for five years. This time, Miller used his true name.

A battery charge in Chicago followed in September 1976, and this led to an additional charge of probation violation. The Bloomingdale, Illinois police department arrested Miller on April 10, 1977 for driving with a suspended driver's license and contributing to the delinquency of a child. This event landed Miller in jail and led to his subsequent confession to the murders of two women near Chicago.

The women were Ann Maxham and Martha Kowalski; both died of strangulation, and their bodies were dumped in remote, wooded areas. Miller readily admitted the murders of the two women, whom he described as prostitutes. He later told an interviewer he would watch the young women for several days before approaching them, then engage them in conversation and attempt to "date" them. During their rendezvous, he said, "[s]omething would snap and I began beating them." Miller did not detail the nature of these beatings but said that following the attacks he would attempt to break the young women's necks. Once the victim was dead, he would wash her in a tub of hot water to "clean them up as best I could." Miller said he then wrapped the bodies and took them to remote roadside areas, where he dumped them. He claimed that the last body he disposed of in this manner was dumped near his home in an attempt to "try and get some people to stop me."

Miller's then-wife, Marcia, played a pivotal role in the events surrounding her husband's arrest in these murders. When Miller confessed to the murders of the two women, he must have indicated in some way that Marcia had assisted him with the disposal of the body of one of the victims. The officers investigating this homicide as well as the murder of the second woman may have explained to Miller that Marcia could face charges for her alleged assistance. This apparently led to his confession—in order to save his wife the possibility of a related trial and conviction.

Miller was convicted of the Maxham and Kowalski killings and was sentenced to thirty years in prison to be served at the Illinois River Correctional Center in Canton, Illinois. After the sentencing, he and Marcia divorced for a second time. He later told a prison official, "She is out of my life. Although she told me she would wait for me, I don't believe her."

BODIES IN THE DITCH

After spending only fifteen years behind bars, Joseph Miller was released on parole in April 1993. He was paroled to the Chicago area but moved very soon thereafter to Peoria. It was there that he resumed his killing spree.

At about 4:30 P.M. on Saturday, September 18, 1993, children walking along rural Cameron Lane in Peoria noticed a dead body in the culvert adjacent to the roadway. Just as detectives were beginning to examine the immediate area, a crime scene technician called out and announced that he had found another body, approximately twenty-five feet from the first. Detectives at first thought the technician was joking; he wasn't.

The first body was identified as that of Marcia L. Logue, a thirty-four-year-old white woman who had on occasion worked the Morton Square Park area as a prostitute. Logue's nude body was only slightly decomposed at the time of discovery. Two indications of foul play were immediately apparent: A cloth pillowcase had been stuffed in her mouth, and there were deep red creases encircling the skin of her ankles and wrists, indicating she had probably been bound.

The second victim was Helen E. Dorrence, another prostitute who frequented the same area in Peoria. Like Logue's, Dorrence's body was unclothed; but owing to more advanced bodily decay, detectives were unable to determine whether she had ligature marks similar to those noted on Logue.

At approximately 8:30 A.M. on Sunday, September 26, a Peoria County sheriff's deputy patrolling the area of Christ Church Road was flagged down by two pedestrians. A foul odor had captured the attention of the couple; when they peered into a ravine next to the roadway, they saw what appeared to be a human foot protruding from vegetation layered at the bottom of the ditch. For the second time in just over a week and within about two and one-half miles of the Cameron Lane scene, investigators found another nude female body dumped in a relatively remote locale.

An autopsy was performed on the third body, and despite extreme decomposition, she was identified as Sandra L. McMahill-Cseszcegi. Cseszcegi, who was forty-two years old when she died, had also been known to engage in prostitution activity in the Morton Square Park vicinity.

Coroner's juries ultimately ruled all three deaths to be homicidal. Marcia Logue had been beaten and stabbed several times; her body also showed signs of having been strangled, in addition to probable asphyxiation caused by the pillowcase stuffed in her mouth. Photographs taken during her autopsy depicted severe reddish-purple bruising on her buttocks, and incisions revealed that the trauma extended approximately one inch beneath the skin. Along the sides and backs of her thighs, there appeared to be numerous weltlike bruises of various lengths and severity. One in particular was very distinct; it seemed to show a lengthwise geometric pattern and an uneven end. Asphyxiation due to possible strangulation was thought to have caused the deaths of Helen Dorrence and Sandra McMahill-Cseszcegi. Logue and Dorrence had also been subjected to sexual abuse and assault; McMahill-Cseszcegi's body had been too decomposed to permit such a determination.

MISSING PERSON

While the county authorities were attempting to piece together this growing series of unusual murders, their counterparts in the City of Peoria's police department learned of the disappearance of eighty-eight-year-old Bernice Fagotte. On September 4, a close friend of the elderly woman called the police and explained that mail and newspapers were accumulating at Fagotte's home in the city's West Bluff neighborhood. Fagotte had also reportedly missed several doctors' appointments. The responding patrol officers found no signs of natural death at her residence; however, they learned that Fagotte's 1991 maroon Oldsmobile four-door Cutlass was also missing.

Suspicions about the widow's fate intensified after crime scene technicians were summoned to examine her house. They discovered what were later determined to be droplets of blood on a pillowcase found on her bed. Almost three weeks after the missing persons report was made, the maroon Oldsmobile was found parked unoccupied, with its doors locked, in the city's East Bluff area. The car was processed for evidence and inventories; technicians located a green tapestry rug in the vehicle and a large bloodstain on one of the interior seats. The amount of blood was such that the underlying foam cushion was also soaked.

A BREAK IN THE CASE

Following the discovery of Sandra McMahill-Csesznegi's body, a task force of city, county, and state law enforcement personnel had been formed to investigate the killings. The break in the case came on September 28, when a caller to a dedicated tip line advised that Joseph Miller might be a suspect.

Having seen the news coverage of the bodies found near Peoria, a correctional officer at Illinois River approached a parole agent and pointed out that these murders appeared to be similar in circumstance to the killings for which Miller had served time in his institution. The agent soon learned that

Miller had been paroled back to Chicago but that he had requested and been granted permission to move to Peoria.

Over the course of the next twenty-four hours, investigators explored the Miller angle. Progress was also being made in the Bernice Fagotte case—progress that would ultimately involve Miller as a suspect in her disappearance.

A neighbor of Fagotte's was interviewed and told police that he had introduced Mrs. Fagotte to Joseph Miller; Miller had then been hired by the widow to perform odd jobs and yard work at her home. The neighbor described Miller as having become somewhat of a "pest" to Fagotte. When asked whether he had ever been to Miller's apartment, the neighbor said that he had visited the apartment approximately two or three weeks before, only to have Miller dissolve their friendship when the neighbor accused him of having stolen a tape recorder. A photograph of the green tapestry rug found in Fagotte's car was shown to the neighbor, who immediately professed to having seen this rug, or one just like it, in Miller's apartment during previous visits there. He then added that he had not seen the rug during his last visit, just weeks before.

CRIME SCENE INVESTIGATION

Having connected Miller to the disappearance of the elderly woman, investigators obtained a search warrant and went to Miller's apartment. Detectives were met at the door by a heavy man with brown hair and a mustache: Joseph Miller. Curious about the nature of the detectives' visit, Miller signed a consent form granting permission for a search of his residence; the detectives had chosen to attempt to get Miller's consent instead of immediately handing him the warrant. While lab technicians from the city and county police surveyed the apartment's interior, Miller voluntarily accompanied Hawkins to the sheriff's office for questioning.

The clues needed to tie Miller to the deaths of Dorrence, Logue, and McMahill-Csesznegi, and to implicate him further in the disappearance of Bernice Fagotte were located within the walls of apartment 208 at the Pennsylvania Terrace tower. Crime scene investigators recovered a single women's white tennis shoe; several strands of white nylon rope were found in the bedroom. When detectives and laboratory technicians turned over the mattress of Miller's bed, they found a sizable amount of blood staining the material. Other bloodstains and spatters were located in the bedroom, on the bed's headboard, on an electrical outlet and surrounding wall adjacent to the bed, and on a pillowcase.

Through DNA analysis and comparison, the remnant blood found in Miller's apartment that night was ultimately determined to have come from all of the three murdered women. The largest sample of blood—that found on the underside of Miller's mattress—was connected to Marcia Logue.

INTERVIEW—AND INDICTMENT

During the hours of interviews that followed his trip to the Peoria County sheriff's office, Miller never completely confessed to involvement in the murders of the three women or the disappearance of Fagotte. But when detectives showed him a Polaroid photograph of a knife recovered from the elderly woman's Oldsmobile, the suspect identified it as his property. Miller told detectives that he used the knife to open paint cans, but he spontaneously added, "I know you won't find any blood on there, because there isn't any." Miller was asked why he thought police might expect to find blood on the knife; he simply responded that he did not know. But Miller did say, "I knew you would be coming to talk to me because of those missing women," citing his past convictions as the reason for this belief.

The fact that his knife had been found in Fagotte's car led to Miller's arrest on suspicion of having at least burglarized the woman's home. The DNA test results that would eventually connect him to the murders were yet to come, but shortly after his arrest, a Peoria County grand jury indicted Miller on a charge of having burglarized Bernice Fagotte's home sometime between August 26 and September 30, 1993. When the blood test results were returned from the state police crime lab, he was also charged in the deaths of Helen Dorrence, Marcia Logue, and Sandra McMahill-Csesznegi. The fate of Bernice Fagotte remained a mystery for nearly a year.

TRIAL AND CONVICTION

In 1994, a change of venue moved Joseph Miller's triple murder trial from Peoria County south to Sangamon County, Illinois. The trial lasted about one week, and Miller did not take the witness stand in his own defense. The forensic evidence was overwhelming, and Miller was subsequently found guilty of the deaths of the three Peoria women. A sentence of death was imposed in all three cases, as was a lesser sentence for the residential burglary charge.

For the second time in his life, Miller was transferred to the custody of the Illinois Department of Corrections. This time, he was taken to a solitary cell on death row at the Menard Correctional Center to await lethal injection.

Despite the efforts of scores of police and volunteer searchers, Bernice Fagotte's whereabouts were still unknown—even after Miller's trial and sentencing. After Miller's placement on death row, investigators learned that Fagotte's body was hidden in Springdale Cemetery, one of the largest cemeteries in the state, located near the Illinois River within the city limits of Peoria. The woman's skeletal remains were found there, well hidden under a blanket of leaves and grass; she had been strangled to death.

No trial was held for the murder of Bernice Fagotte. Miller pled guilty to the charge of killing her and, as a result, was given a sentence of natural life in prison.

ATTITUDES

During interviews with detectives following his arrest in Peoria, Miller was evasive when answering questions, and he never confessed to his crimes. Although he was willing to talk for hours on end to some interviewers, he would attempt to change the subject or otherwise avoid talking about the crimes he was suspected of having committed.

Why did Joseph Miller kill? His life seems to have been plagued by an array of debilitating relationships and situations. Although not much is known of relationships or scholastic performance during childhood, it is clear that his early adult life was arduous.

It's possible that Miller may have harbored ill feelings toward women he considered to be prostitutes. He labeled as "prostitutes" the two women he was convicted of killing in the Chicago area. With the exception of Bernice Fagotte, all of Miller's known victims have been engaged in sex-trade activities.

THE POSSIBILITIES FOR CLOSURE

Law enforcement officials do not know with certainty how many people Joseph Miller killed. Former Cook County prosecutor Kenneth Gillis recalled, "There were a number of women—hitchhikers and prostitutes—who turned up dead or missing [around northern Chicago and nearby suburbs] at that time [the mid-1970s]. After we put Miller away, all of that ended." Detectives in Peoria have similar suspicions.

Joseph Miller is the only person who knows how many victims he has claimed. Given his past demeanor, it is unlikely that he will ever reveal the true extent of his actions.

10

JEFFREY DAHMER

There are few serial killers as horrifying as Jeffrey Dahmer, who murdered seventeen young men in and around Milwaukee, Wisconsin. He lured them to his apartment, had sex with them, killed them, then dismembered and disposed of their bodies. He kept trophies from most of his crimes—photographs, skulls, even complete skeletons. Dahmer's grisly crimes were the work of a seriously disturbed mind; experts agree that his behavior was sick, bizarre, and (fortunately) unique.

FASCINATION WITH DEATH

Growing up in Ohio, young Jeffrey Dahmer had trouble making friends; he seemed to trust no one. In grade school, the other youngsters noticed that Dahmer never had any sympathy for others. When other students got hurt on the school playground, he would laugh or watch the scene without compassion.

Dahmer's morbid curiosity about death, bodies, bones, and flesh began at an early age. He started with a collection of insects preserved in jars full of chemicals; then he began to collect dead animals that had been run over on the roads near his home. Once while fishing with some other boys, he chopped up the fish he had caught into little pieces so he could see their insides. Another time, a group of boys walking in the woods behind the Dahmer home found the head of a dog impaled on a stick. They were so shocked at the sight that they took photographs, but they didn't tell the police until years later, after Dahmer had been arrested in his apartment in Milwaukee. Neighbors of the Dahmers also found frogs and cats impaled or staked to trees. A boy who grew up across the street from the Dahmer home said that young Jeffrey kept chipmunk and squirrel skeletons in a backyard shed and maintained a pet cemetery nearby, with small crosses to mark each grave.

When on occasion a neighborhood dog would disappear, no one suspected that Jeffrey was killing dogs for his autopsies. In 1975, when Jeffrey was fifteen years old, a neighbor boy walking in the woods behind the Dahmer home discovered a mutilated dog carcass. The head was mounted on a stick next to a wooden cross. The body, skinned and gutted, was nailed to a nearby tree. Dahmer's father had given him a chemistry set; according to Jeffrey's stepmother, "He liked to use acid to scrape the meat off dead animals." No one, including his parents, seemed to think this behavior warranted much attention or concern.

Most psychiatrists agree that cruelty to animals is one common childhood characteristic of the sadistic criminal. Many experts on serial killers believe that these killers often start out by torturing and killing animals as youngsters. Jeffrey Dahmer's behavior should have been a warning. Had this warning been heeded, a number of lives might have been saved.

ODD BEHAVIOR

By high school, Dahmer was considered so weird that no one wanted to associate with him. He played on the tennis team but was not a popular student. He was very shy toward girls but was aggressive toward authority figures.

A neighbor remembers Dahmer's ritual as he walked to the school bus stop: four steps forward, two steps back, four steps forward, one step back—day after day, week after week. Little kids thought it was funny and stared at him. He seemed to be seeking attention everywhere he went. He reportedly faked epileptic fits in the classroom and at the nearby mall. He frequently drew outlines of nonexistent bodies on the floors at school.

One of Dahmer's former classmates, now a sociology professor, considered him a friend for a short time. However, "at sixteen years of age, he was lost," she said. "He seemed to cry out for help, but nobody paid attention to him at all.... He would come in with a cup of Scotch—not coffee, with something in it, Scotch whiskey: If a sixteen-year-old drinking in an 8:00 A.M. class isn't calling out for help, I don't know what is."

THE FIRST VICTIM

Jeffrey's parents were headed for divorce when he killed his first human victim. It became a bitter battle as Lionel and Joyce Dahmer fought over custody of Jeffrey's younger brother, David, who was then twelve years old. Because Jeffrey was already eighteen, he was not an issue in the custody battle.

Jeffrey's father was the first to sue for divorce, charging his mother with "gross neglect of duty and extreme cruelty." Dahmer's mother countersued, filing the same charges against his father. In the court documents of the divorce, Jeffrey's father accused his mother of having an "extreme mental illness."

During the time Jeffrey's parents were arguing over custody of his brother, they divided the house, each living on one side. His father set up a warning system with a string of keys to alert him if his wife was trying to enter his half. Both parents pressured Jeffrey to side with them in the divorce. He later said that his parents were "constantly at each other's throats" before they divorced.

Joyce Dahmer ultimately won custody of David. She took the boy and moved to Wisconsin, leaving Jeffrey with no money and instructing him not to tell his father where they had gone. Shortly thereafter, Jeffrey's father moved out of the house to a motel.

On June 18, 1978, Stephen Mark Hicks, an eighteen-year-old white male from Coventry, Ohio, was hitchhiking to a rock concert. Jeffrey Dahmer met him and brought him back to his empty home, where they had sex. When Hicks tried to leave, Dahmer struck him in the head with a barbell, killing him. Dahmer then smashed Hicks's body to bits with a sledgehammer, put the remains in plastic bags, and buried them in the woods behind his house.

Dahmer may have been abandoned by his parents, but now he was someone very different. He now had a self-image: He was a killer.

A BRIEF RESPITE

After graduating from high school, Dahmer entered Ohio State University in Columbus. He spent most of his first semester drinking; he never made it through the second semester. A classmate remembers the last time she saw him. "He was passed out on a street in Columbus," she said.

After his failure with college, Dahmer joined the army and served in a medical unit in Germany. According to his roommate, "Jeff would drink his gin. He had an eight-track stereo with headphones, and he'd sit there and get plastered. He'd be on a two- or three-day drink. He wouldn't even leave his room to go eat." Dahmer was discharged from the army in 1981 because of his drinking.

Returning home from the army, Dahmer was arrested in a hotel lobby where he was drinking vodka and threatening people. On his way to jail, he kept insisting that the police stop the car and beat him up.

In 1982, he moved in with his grandmother in West Allis, a suburb of Milwaukee. He began hanging out in gay bars and sometimes brought men home through a private entrance to his grandmother's basement.

THE KILLINGS RESUME

Nine years passed between Dahmer's first and second murders. However, this time he did not stop with only one victim—he killed and killed again.

In Milwaukee, Wisconsin in November 1987, Steven W. Toumi, a twenty-five-year-old white male, was reported missing by his parents. He was already a victim of Jeffrey Dahmer, who had picked him up at Club 219 in Milwaukee and taken him to a room at the Ambassador Hotel. There the two got drunk and passed out. Dahmer subsequently claimed that when he awoke, Toumi was dead, with blood dripping from his mouth. So Dahmer bought a large suitcase at a nearby mall and put the corpse inside. Then he took the suitcase by taxi to his grandmother's house, where he had sex with the corpse in the basement. Dahmer then dismembered the corpse, placed the body parts in plastic bags, and threw them in the trash. Toumi's remains were never found.

From that point, Dahmer's crimes—and victims—started to mount:

- **January 16, 1988** Dahmer met James Doxtator, a fourteen-year-old Native American boy, outside Club 219 and offered him some money to pose nude. Dahmer took the boy to his grandmother's, where they had sex. Dahmer then gave him a drink with sleeping pills in it, and when the boy fell asleep, Dahmer strangled him. Dahmer dismembered the body with a knife and a sledgehammer, placed the remains in plastic bags, and put them in the trash.
- **March 24, 1988** Richard Guerrero, a twenty-five-year old Mexican American, met Dahmer near Club 219 and agreed to go home with him. After they had sex in his grandmother's basement, Dahmer drugged his victim with sleeping pills and strangled him. Dahmer had sex with the corpse, dismembered it, and threw the remains away.
- **September 26, 1988** On September 25, Dahmer moved from his grandmother's house to 808 North 24th Street,

Apartment 213, in Milwaukee. The next day, he offered a thirteen-year-old Laotian boy money to come to his apartment, where he attempted to seduce the boy and laced his drink with sleeping pills. Somehow the boy managed to leave. When he passed out at home, his parents took him to the hospital, and the police were notified. Dahmer was arrested the next day for sexual assault. He pled guilty to the charge and was sentenced to five years' probation and one year at a correctional center in a work-release program.

■ **March 25, 1989** Dahmer met Anthony Sears, a twenty-four-year-old African American, at the La Cage Aux Folles bar and offered him money to be photographed. The two drove to Dahmer's grandmother's, where they had sex, after which Dahmer drugged Sears and strangled him. Dahmer disposed of his victim as before; however, he kept the head, which he boiled so that only the skull remained. Dahmer painted his trophy with gray paint.

■ **June 1990** Raymond L. Smith, a twenty-eight-year-old African American, met Dahmer at Club 219 and agreed to go to his apartment to be photographed. Dahmer drugged him, strangled him to death, and had sex with his corpse. Dahmer dismembered and disposed of the remains as he had before. He kept Smith's skull as another trophy.

■ **Late June 1990** Dahmer offered money for sex and the chance to pose for pictures to Edward W. Smith, a twenty-eight-year-old African American he met in the Phoenix Bar. They returned to Apartment 213, where they had sex. Afterward, Dahmer drugged and strangled Smith. Dahmer disposed of Smith's dismembered body in trash bags. His only trophies were pictures of the dead man.

■ **September 24, 1990** Ernest Miller, a twenty-four-year-old African American, was lured by Dahmer from in front of an adult bookstore. After taking a number of pictures of Miller, Dahmer drugged him and, when he passed out, cut his throat with a hunting knife. Dahmer placed the corpse in his bathtub, removed the flesh from the body, and photographed the skeleton. This time, his trophy was the entire skeleton. Dahmer put some of the flesh from the corpse in his freezer and later claimed he had eaten the flesh.

- **Late September 1990** The girlfriend of David Thomas reported him missing on September 24, 1990. This twenty-two-year-old African American died at the hands of Jeffrey Dahmer. His trophies this time were photographs taken by Dahmer as he dismembered Thomas's corpse.

- **February 1991** Curtis Straughter, an eighteen-year-old African American, met his death after Dahmer lured him from a bus stop to his nearby apartment. Sex, followed by strangulation, more sex, then dismemberment—it was becoming a ritual for Dahmer. He photographed the corpse and kept the skull.

- **April 7, 1991** Errol Lindsey's mother last saw her son when he left home to have a key made. This nineteen-year-old African American made a fatal mistake. He accepted Jeffrey Dahmer's offer of money to go to Apartment 213. All that remains of Lindsey is his skull and some horrific photos of his corpse.

- **May 24, 1991** The next victim Dahmer lured to his death was a deaf-mute, Tony A. Hughes. They met in front of the 219 Bar. Dahmer communicated with this thirty-one-year-old African American in writing, convincing him to go to Apartment 213. Another skull trophy was added to Dahmer's collection.

- **May 27, 1991** Like Dahmer's other victims, fourteen-year-old Konerak Sinthasomphone was lured with money; once in Dahmer's apartment, he was drugged with sleeping pills. However, in this case Dahmer left to get some beer before killing the young Laotian boy. Sinthasomphone awoke, and Milwaukee police officers found him staggering in the street near Dahmer's apartment. Dahmer told police that the boy was drunk and had done this before. He stated that he would "take care of his friend." The police escorted Dahmer and the boy back into Apartment 213, where the remains of Tony

Hughes lay decomposing in the back bedroom; the officers didn't notice. After the police left, Dahmer strangled the boy, photographed the corpse, and after having sex with it, dismembered the remains and kept the skull.

■ **June 30, 1991** Dahmer traveled to Chicago for his next victim. There he met Matt Turner, a twenty-year-old African American, at a bus station after they had both attended the Gay Pride Parade in Chicago. Turner agreed to pose nude for money, and they returned together to Dahmer's apartment in Milwaukee. When Turner passed out from a drink laced with sleeping pills, his horrific fate was sealed. After dismembering the corpse, Dahmer placed Turner's head in the freezer and his torso in a fifty-seven-gallon barrel.

■ **July 5, 1991** Returning to Chicago, Dahmer lured his next victim from Carol's Speakeasy by promising money in return for posing in the nude. Jeremiah Weinberger, a twenty-three-year-old Puerto Rican man, stayed in Apartment 213 with Dahmer for two days before deciding to leave. This triggered the deadly ritual again. Another head was added to Dahmer's freezer and a second torso to the fifty-seven-gallon barrel.

■ **July 15, 1991** Jeffrey Dahmer found his sixteenth victim just around the corner from his Milwaukee apartment building. Oliver Lacy's remains would be found in Dahmer's apartment. Seven days later, police found this twenty-three-year-old African American's head in the refrigerator and his disemboweled body in the freezer. His heart was also in the freezer.

■ **July 19, 1991** Joseph Bradehoft, a twenty-five-year-old white man, fell prey to Dahmer's lure of money for posing in the nude while they were riding a bus in Milwaukee. In Apartment 213, Bradehoft's head was added to Dahmer's gruesome refrigerator collection, and his torso was stuffed into the fifty-seven-gallon barrel, which was getting full. Bradehoft was Jeffrey Dahmer's seventeenth and last homicide victim.

BEATING THE SYSTEM

Since June 1978, Jeffrey Dahmer had beaten the system. Immediately after his first murder, he had been stopped by police in Bath, Ohio; there was a dismembered body in garbage bags on the back seat of his car but Dahmer told the officers he was taking the bags to the dump, and they let him drive on. In April 1988, a man reported that he had been drugged and robbed by Dahmer; Milwaukee police spoke to Dahmer but lacked evidence to pursue the charges. In March 1989, a friend of Anthony Sears reported him missing; the friend even took police to the street corner where he had left Sears with another man. The other man was Jeffrey Dahmer, whose grandmother's house was nearby. But the police turned up nothing.

In February 1989, when Dahmer was released from the Milwaukee County jail, where he had been sentenced under work release, he was on probation. Procedures required that his probation officer meet with him twice a month and make regular home visits. However, Dahmer's probation officer, who was supervising 121 clients at the time, requested that she be excused from making home visits with Dahmer. She argued that she had a heavy caseload and that Dahmer lived in a bad neighborhood. Her supervisors agreed to waive the home visit requirement with Dahmer. Jeffrey Dahmer was then free to pursue the creation of his "inferno" in Apartment 213.

The most notorious incident, mentioned earlier, was on May 27, 1991, when Dahmer's intended victim escaped, and the police unwittingly helped the murderer return the victim to the apartment—and to his death. The following Milwaukee police transcript details the conversation afterward between the police officer and his dispatcher:

> *Police Officer:* Intoxicated Asian naked male. (Laughter) Was returned to his sober boyfriend. (More laughter)
>
> *Dispatcher:* 10-4 64 and 65.
>
> *Police Officer:* 10-4. It will be a minute. My partner is going to get deloused at the station. (Laughter)

The "intoxicated Asian naked male" became Jeffrey's Dahmer's twelfth victim and his youngest. The officers considered the incident to be a routine domestic dispute between homosexuals—but it became routine only for Dahmer, who, after the police left, strangled the young boy as he had his other victims.

THE KILLER, DISCOVERED

Just before midnight on Monday evening, July 22, 1991, two Milwaukee police officers sitting in their squad car were approached by a short African American man with handcuffs dangling from his left wrist. The man, thirty-one-year-old Tracy Edwards, told the officers about a "weird dude" who had handcuffed him in a nearby apartment. The officers were reluctant to respond but eventually agreed to go with Edwards to the apartment to investigate.

Once inside the Oxford Apartment Complex, the officers noticed a heavy rancid odor. Jeffrey Dahmer opened the door for the three men. Dahmer was asked for the key to the handcuffs, and he told the officers the key was in the bedroom. One of the officers walked into the bedroom and looked into an open dresser drawer. He was horrified: There were Polaroid pictures of dismembered bodies, skulls, and a skeleton hanging from a showerhead.

Dahmer later recounted the details of that evening to the *Inside Edition* television program:

> It was the night of the arrest.... I heard a knock on the door and the police were there with the last victim. They asked me where the key was to the handcuffs. My mind was in a haze. I sort of pointed to the bedroom and that's where they found the pictures and they yelled, "Cuff him" and I was handcuffed. And it was the realization that there was no point in trying to hide my actions anymore, the best route was to help the police identify all the victims and just make a complete confession.

Dahmer was immediately arrested. As the officers began to search the apartment, one of them opened the refrigerator door. He found a severed human head staring out at him. And the search of Apartment 213 had only just begun.

PIECING TOGETHER THE HORROR

People who knew Jeffrey Dahmer in Milwaukee described him as a quiet, rather shy young man who didn't have much to say. Little did they know that he methodically assaulted and dismembered the corpses of his victims, placing their skulls on his death shrine in his apartment and their entrails and body parts in his refrigerator and freezer.

Like other psychopaths who became infamous serial killers, Dahmer appeared to be a very quiet person. But he was filled with a rage or force that controlled him. This rage was driven by a particularly dangerous chemistry: an antisocial trait, so that he flouted the law with impunity; a "borderline" personality that made him vulnerable to explosive rage when he felt he was being abandoned; and a bizarre sexual deviation that culminated in necrophilia.

Dahmer appears to have been both a sadist and a necrophiliac. Sadists find sexual pleasure in the suffering of their victims; the sexual thrill stops when the victims die. But for necrophiliacs, the thrill starts with the death. For Dahmer, the pleasure was in both the suffering of his victims and what he could do with them after their deaths.

Dahmer's victims were lured into his lair, where he could control the situation and the assault of his prey. He didn't stalk them on the streets, then quickly slay them for the police to find. He needed time with his dead victims. Indeed, time was important to Dahmer—time to have sex with the corpses, time to dismember and fillet the bodies at his leisure, and time to select a trophy before disposing of the victim's remains.

Whether his urge to kill was driven by a longing for simple companionship or for sex, Dahmer killed for it. He wanted to be with the victims. He wanted to keep them with him. As his obsession grew, he began saving body parts. Wanting to remember their appearance, he took pictures of the corpses. They belonged to him.

Soon the offer of money for posing in the nude or for sex, the killing, having sex with the corpse, the dismemberment and examination of the body, the trophy selection, and the disposal became habit-forming for Dahmer. He was performing a ritual each time he convinced his prey to come with him to the slaughter. His reverse sculpturing of their bodies became the driving force of his existence: the search for his next work of art.

DEFINING THE VICTIMS

Most serial killers select easy prey, victims with little prestige or power in society. If they are reported missing, the authorities spend little time looking for them. Often, victims are not missed for weeks or months. Some are never missed, because no one cares enough to note their absence. They are almost always strangers to their killer and are generally easy to dominate, lure, or manipulate.

The victims of serial killers are selected because of their vulnerability, but this does not mean the serial killer is a coward. In fact, it means he is smart; choosing vulnerable victims reduces the time and effort of the selection, the lure, or the "con." For Dahmer, it provided more time for the control and the kill.

Dahmer was a gay man, and he selected his own kind. He understood their sexual frustration and their problems in meeting sexual partners. He knew how the rest of society felt about them. He knew that their parents had not sat down with them when they started dating men and warned them about certain kinds of men to avoid. Persuading his victims to go with him was seldom a problem, because he knew what they wanted. Except he wanted something more. Unfortunately for his victims, their deaths were required to fulfill his wants.

A victim's lifestyle is frequently the critical factor in falling prey to a serial killer. Prostitutes and gay men very often become the victims of serial killers. Dahmer chose gay boys and men from age fourteen to thirty-one; most of them were African American.

THE AFTERMATH

When Jeffrey Dahmer picked up a young man in one of the gay bars he frequented in Milwaukee, the result was almost always death. Few young men escaped after entering number 213 of the Oxford Apartment Complex.

Neighbors said Dahmer always brought his guests in through the back door of the complex. Unbeknownst to the neighbors, all his guests would eventually leave through this door as well—their torsos floating in a chemical bath in a large blue barrel, their arms and legs in plastic bags, some of their skulls in cardboard boxes labeled "Skull Parts," and some of their frozen heads in Dahmer's refrigerator. They would be carried out by police officers, hazardous waste removal specialists, and staff from the County Medical Examiner's Office. When Dahmer's guests left Apartment 213, their remains passed by a bright yellow tape that read, "POLICE LINE. DO NOT CROSS." For these victims, the warning came much too late.

As Dahmer's refrigerator was removed on a dolly down the back steps of the Oxford Apartment Complex, Doug Jackson, a short black man, stood watching from the neatly kept lawn of the complex. "My head could've been in that refrigerator," he said in a low, cracking voice. A few days earlier, Dahmer had invited Jackson to his apartment for a beer. His girlfriend had talked him out of going. He was very thankful.

For months after the grisly discovery in Apartment 213, many people in Milwaukee would double-check the locks on their doors and windows before going to bed. Some would keep a log of phone numbers and addresses of where their children were supposed to be. Many would pay more attention to "things that go bump in the night." And if they had them, many would load their guns and put them within easy reach.

Milwaukee police received numerous calls to check out suspicious strangers, day and night. A mind-numbing fear and paranoia seemed to envelop the city. Milwaukee had become a city of victims—victims of fear, horror, and disbelief over what had gone on behind the door of Apartment 213.

The breweries, beer halls, German restaurants, and various ethnic neighborhoods that had long been linked to this midwestern city in eastern Wisconsin on the shores of Lake Michigan were forgotten. When people heard "Milwaukee," they immediately thought of Jeffrey Dahmer. Of course, for some who had been mesmerized by Anthony Hopkins's portrayal of Dr. Hannibal Lecter in the movie *Silence of the Lambs,* Milwaukee would become the "City of the Lambs," whose silence had been shattered by the screaming of innocent, slaughtered lambs in July 1991.

THE TRIAL

Dahmer chose to plead guilty but insane, which changed the nature of his criminal trial. The question was no longer one of guilt but rather of responsibility.

It was not for the court to determine the strange or perverted behavior of Dahmer or, for that matter, his bizarre motivations. The question was whether he had understood what he was doing and whether he knew the difference between right and wrong. Further, Wisconsin criminal statutes required that the court determine whether Dahmer could have stopped himself. The burden was no longer on the state to prove him guilty. It was now the burden of the defense to demonstrate his insanity.

Trial Judge Laurence C. Gram, Jr. had warned the jurors that they were going to hear testimony unlike anything they had heard before. That was exactly what happened. During the first two days of testimony, the jury heard the reading of Dahmer's confession, in which he related how he skinned the victims, boiled and cleaned their skulls, and even ate the biceps of one man after seasoning it with salt, pepper, and A-1 sauce.

Dahmer's defense attorneys would have to prove that he was suffering from some form of mental illness at the time of his crimes and that he lacked the capacity to understand the wrongfulness of his actions or to conform his conduct to the law. This made the trial a battle of psychiatrists; those hired for the defense testified about Dahmer's mental illness, and those hired by the prosecution testified about his sanity.

Dr. Fred Berlin of Johns Hopkins University, testifying for the defense, told jurors that Dahmer's intense sexual craving was a "cancer of the mind." Berlin viewed Dahmer as "out of control.... The power of what was driving him basically took over." Berlin further stated, "I don't think the normal man could even force himself to walk around thinking about having sexual contact with dead bodies."

Dr. Park Dietz, testifying for the prosecution, stated that Dahmer suffered from a variety of sexual disorders but that none would have made him unable to know right from wrong or unable to stop himself from killing. Dietz described Dahmer's sexual urges as "less than many teenagers experience in back seats with their girlfriends." (Dahmer wore condoms when having sex with his dead victims.)

Dr. George Palermo, a court-appointed psychiatrist, said Dahmer was "sick" but "not psychotic" and was "legally sane at the time of the offenses."

Dr. Frederick Fosdal, testifying for the prosecution, said Dahmer suffered from necrophilia "before, during, and after" killing seventeen young males but that the disorder did not prevent him from stopping. Fosdal stated, "He was able to refrain and had some control as to when he followed through on his sexual desires." Fosdal also noted that Dahmer appreciated the wrongfulness of his acts, was prepared to and did have the capacity to conform to the law, and could have controlled his behavior at the time of the acts.

Four of the testifying psychiatrists referred to Dahmer as a necrophiliac. Two of them classified him as having an antisocial personality disorder. One described Dahmer's behavior as clinically rare, unusual, and bizarre—behavior for which there was no current diagnostic category.

The jury heard from a total of twenty-eight witnesses before the attorneys provided their summation of the case. "He couldn't stop killing because of a sickness he discovered, not chose," Dahmer's defense attorney, Gerald Boyle, told the jurors. "He had to do what he did because he couldn't stop. This isn't a matter of choice," Boyle said.

Prosecutor E. Michael McCann described Dahmer as a sane, cowardly killer who sacrificed others for his own sexual pleasure and who was now "seeking to escape responsibility. Please, please, don't let this murderous killer fool you with this special defense," McCann told the jurors.

After twelve days of testimony, the jurors deliberated for a little more than five hours to find Jeffrey Dahmer sane on all sixteen counts of murder. Fortunately for Dahmer, the State of Wisconsin did not allow the death penalty; instead, he was sentenced to fifteen consecutive life sentences plus an additional ten years for habitual criminality on each of the fifteen counts. The judge structured Dahmer's sentences in such a way that he would never again see freedom. He would have the rest of his life to contemplate his murders, away from society, behind bars.

WHAT MADE HIM A MONSTER?

It is difficult to understand what made Jeffrey Dahmer commit such horrendous acts against his fellow human beings. The crimes he committed were just not normal. After all, what normal person would systematically murder and mutilate seventeen victims? Our morbid fascination with him and his terrible acts may be a way of attempting to define him as separate and different from the rest of society. We seem to need the comfort of knowing that this serial killer is an aberration, that he is not one of us. To consider him normal would mean that anyone could be capable of these savage acts of terror and death.

Perhaps some understanding can be gained from reading the 179-page confession Dahmer made to Milwaukee police. Excerpts follow:

> My consuming lust was to experience their bodies. I viewed them as objects, as strangers. If I knew them, I could not have done it. It's hard for me to believe that a human being could have done what I've done, but I know I did it. It would be me who has to stand before God and admit my wrongdoing.

> I realize what I have done is my fault, but I have to question if there is an evil force in the world and if I am influenced by it. If I am to be honest with myself, I would have to admit that if I was set up in another apartment and had the opportunity, I probably would not be able to stop.

> A power higher than myself had been fed up with my deeds and decided it was time for me to be stopped.

DAHMER'S DEMISE

For the remainder of his life, Jeffrey Dahmer's home was to be a prison cell at the Columbia Correctional Facility in Portage, Wisconsin. Columbia, with its five guard towers rising as tall as the silos of nearby dairy farms, is the newest and most secure of the state's maximum-security prisons.

"He's very glad that he's in there," his mother, Joyce Flint, told reporters in 1994. "He still has those thoughts."

Those thoughts would soon end. Jeffrey Dahmer was killed in prison by another inmate on November 28, 1994.

Stopping the Horror

11

COMPARING SERIAL KILLERS

There are a number of similarities, as well as differences, between the seven murderers—Gacy, Lucas, Bianchi, Bundy, Marcus, Miller, and Dahmer—discussed in the previous section of this book. Examining these similarities may give us a better understanding of the violent criminals who kill a number of victims in different locations over a period of time.

SOCIAL ENVIRONMENT

All the murderers we examined were born into working-class families or families of lower socioeconomic status. Two of the killers, Bundy and Gacy, moved into a middle-class stratum; the others remained within their original social class. In educational achievement, the subjects ranged from Bundy, who made an attempt at law school, to Lucas, who barely finished the fourth grade.

Bundy, Lucas, Marcus, and Dahmer all abused alcohol, and Lucas may very well have been an alcoholic. Lucas's parents were reportedly alcoholics, but there was no history of alcoholism in Bundy's family. Both Gacy and Marcus had fathers who abused alcohol. There is evidence that all seven of these killers had used marijuana, but none had formed a habit or addiction to the substance.

Bundy, Gacy, Dahmer, and Buono all maintained a neat, orderly lifestyle. Bundy's apartment was always spotless, and Gacy and Buono kept their houses very clean. Buono also was known as a meticulous worker. Gacy ordered his life to the extent that he kept a log of his activities during the day. Dahmer's apartment, though horrific, was kept orderly and neat.

All of the murderers first experienced sexual intercourse sometime in their teens. The sexual relationships of Bundy, Gacy, and Buono all involved some form of violence. They used bondage on their sexual partners, and Buono and Gacy were both sadistic and dominant in their sexual relations with others. Gacy, Bianchi, and Buono all read and showed a strong interest in pornography. Bundy claims to have been exposed to pornography.

All of the killers had experienced some form of childhood health trauma. Gacy was frequently beaten by his father and also experienced blackouts, which were never accurately diagnosed. Bianchi experienced urination problems and reportedly had severe respiratory infections. Lucas suffered the loss of his eye in an accident. Marcus was severely beaten by his father. Miller reportedly was subjected to severe discipline by two of his stepfathers, and Dahmer had to deal with his parents' acrimony during their divorce.

Bundy, Gacy, and Bianchi all had a strong interest in law enforcement, going back to early childhood. Lucas claims to have "studied" law enforcement.

Bundy was considered a loner in high school, but Bianchi and Gacy reportedly had relatively normal social relationships in high school. Neither Buono nor Lucas ever attended high school. Marcus was seen as a loner during his high school years, even though he participated in athletic activities.

FAMILY BACKGROUND

Bundy, Bianchi, and Lucas were all born to unwed mothers. Bundy was adopted when he was five years old, after his mother's marriage. Bianchi's mother relinquished him to a foster home, and he was adopted before his first birthday. Miller knew very little about his natural father. Lucas's real father is unknown. Bundy was apparently the only one of these four who was troubled by the circumstances of his birth.

Bundy, Bianchi, and Lucas all had dominant mothers. Bundy's mother paid the bills and spoke for the family. Bianchi's mother smothered him with her protectiveness and administered his punishment, sometimes harsh. Lucas was beaten and neglected by his mother, who gave the orders in his family. Gacy was heavily influenced by his mother, whom he tried to protect when she was beaten by his father.

Gacy, Bianchi, Lucas, Miller, and Marcus all had parents with emotional problems. Gacy's father never showed his emotions except when he was intoxicated, as he was almost every night. When his father came home from work, he would start drinking until his anger surfaced, then would physically abuse Gacy's mother. Bianchi's mother was described as a disturbed woman who apparently experienced a great deal of guilt over her failure to bear children. She was extremely overprotective of Bianchi and became paranoid over his illnesses. Lucas's mother reportedly forced him to watch her engage in sexual intercourse with a number of men. Until he was six or seven years old, she dressed him as a girl. Miller's early childhood showed evidence of child neglect, because he frequently ran away from home. Marcus had to deal with an abusive father who beat him and his mother.

All of the killers had been married, then divorced. Both Gacy and Miller were married twice, and Buono was married three times. Marcus fathered three children out of wedlock.

Gacy, Lucas, and Dahmer appear to have experienced some confusion regarding their sexual identity. Also, these murderers came from families with a history of alcoholism. Gacy, Marcus, and Bundy all experienced problems with their fathers.

PERSONAL RELATIONSHIPS

All of the murderers except Lucas were apparently very manipulative of situations and people. Lucas could also be considered manipulative but in a much less sophisticated manner, as a result of his limited education and the severe economic deprivation of his childhood.

On the surface, all of these men appeared harmless to most people. In five of these men, however—Gacy, Bianchi's "Stevie Walker," Marcus, Miller, and Lucas—it is apparent that a strong emotion of hatred lay just beneath the surface. All of these seven murderers had been unable or unwilling to establish lasting relationships with others.

CONTACT WITH AUTHORITIES

All of these murderers appeared to be well informed about police procedures and practices. Bundy, Marcus, and Lucas appear to have understood problems of interjurisdictional communication among police and killed in more than one jurisdiction as a way of eluding detection. Bianchi and Buono were very conscious of the danger of leaving any physical evidence of their killings. When Bianchi killed on his own, however, it was a different story. Gacy seemed to understand that missing teenagers, especially young homosexuals, might not be actively sought and were apt to be investigated only in a routine fashion.

All of the men except Bianchi had known criminal records prior to their final arrests. Some had more extensive records than others.

Three of the men—Bundy, Marcus, and Lucas—had juvenile delinquency records; Lucas's early criminal activities were the most serious and consistent. Gacy, Dahmer, Miller, and Bianchi had no known juvenile records.

Gacy was on parole from Iowa for sodomy during his killing spree. Miller was on parole for two killings in Chicago, for which he served fifteen years. Marcus committed a number of criminal acts before and during his murder spree, including kidnapping and attempted rape (reduced to an assault and battery charge). Bundy had been convicted of attempted kidnapping and committed his three murders in Florida after his second escape from authorities in Colorado. Lucas committed his first killing at age fourteen and committed a range of other felony crimes. Dahmer killed while on probation for sexual assault and enticing a child for immoral purposes.

All of the men except Buono, for whom psychiatric reports may never have been written, were referred to by psychiatrists or psychologists as having antisocial personalities. All have been labeled as sociopaths or psychopaths. Mental health professionals did not always offer consistent diagnoses of these men but in some cases disagreed strongly about an individual murderer. A common theme in the psychological and psychiatric evaluations of these seven men was that they were strongly resistant toward authority, were obsessed with controlling and manipulating others to their own advantage, and almost never shared their true feelings with others.

When arrested for the last time, only Bundy physically resisted the police. All the other men offered no resistance and submitted to authorities calmly.

HOW THEY KILLED

All of these men killed over a period of at least a year except Buono and Bianchi, who, when acting together, killed their victims over a four-month period. Lucas first killed as a fourteen-year-old boy. The others reportedly first killed in their twenties or thirties, except for Buono, who was in his forties.

Bundy, Gacy, and Dahmer used lures to attract their victims. Bundy used a faked injury, and Gacy used offers of homosexual relations for money. Dahmer offered his victims money to pose in the nude. Bundy, Gacy, Buono, and Bianchi all posed as police officers, using the force of official authority to persuade their victims to accompany them. All of the murderers carried some sort of deadly weapon most of the time. In all cases, automobiles were used to abduct victims and to transport their corpses.

All seven of the murderers used strangulation as their primary means of killing. Lucas strangled a number of his victims but also used a variety of other means, primarily a knife. Bundy and Lucas used "overkill" on their victims. Long after his victims were dead, Bundy continued to beat them, and many of Lucas's victims were mutilated after death.

Although all the murderers were very mobile, Gacy and Buono-Bianchi killed in only one location. Bundy and Lucas, however, killed in numerous police jurisdictions in many different states. Marcus killed in three different states. Taking Buono and Bianchi as one example, each of these men killed at least nine people. All of them also committed both property crimes and other violent crimes.

VICTIMS

Gacy's victims were all young Caucasian males. Bundy, Miller, and Bianchi and Buono killed only females, in most cases under twenty-five years of age and Caucasian. Lucas and his accomplices killed a number of males, but 75 percent of Lucas's victims were females, and over 90 percent were Caucasian, with a mean age of almost thirty-one but with an age range of eighty years. Marcus, the only African American serial killer under discussion, killed only black women, most of them under twenty-five years of age.

Many of the serial murderers' victims were particularly vulnerable to assault or abduction because of their lifestyle or perceived powerlessness. Bundy's victims were young women who moved about by themselves or were alone in the late evening hours. Most of Gacy's victims were young homosexuals "cruising" for sexual contacts in areas known to be frequented by gay men. Dahmer found his victims in gay bars near his apartment. Bianchi and Buono approached many young women who had a history of prostitution and, therefore, were used to being accosted on the street. Lucas reportedly killed forty-two victims who were hitchhiking when abducted. He also abducted many of his victims while they were traveling alone, at a distance from their homes. Miller's victims were prostitutes. Marcus placed his victims in positions of powerlessness prior to killing them.

SELF-CONCEPT

All of these murderers seemed to see themselves as controlling others either through manipulation or by physical force. In many cases, they failed to recognize their own faults and tended to rationalize their behavior by blaming others.

With the possible exception of Buono, who projected a macho image, all appeared to have concerns about their masculinity. Lucas and Gacy had problems with their sexual identities going back to childhood experiences. Dahmer seemed to fight against acknowledging his homosexuality. Lucas, emphasizing that his primary accomplice in murder was a homosexual, made a point of differentiating himself from this accomplice, although Lucas did admit to being the passive partner in homosexual relations with his accomplice. Gacy, when arrested, stressed to police that he was bisexual, not homosexual.

Marcus described himself as "shy" and implied that he was very cunning in his murders. Miller, though never confessing to his murders, seemed to enjoy the attention he received from law enforcement after his arrest. All of these men seem to have been unwilling or unable to delay their own gratification.

ATTITUDES

Once they were arrested and in custody, Bundy, Bianchi, and Lucas tended to reveal their attitudes toward authority, symbolized for them by their captors. Bundy bragged to the police of his escapes and mocked his previous jailers. He taunted police into digging deeper to find evidence in his killings. Bianchi, faking hypnosis, patronized his examiners and showed pure defiance. Lucas acted on many occasions as all-powerful, controlling whether or not he would see people and choosing to whom he would confess; in his view, he, and not the police, was clearing the cases. Lucas bragged about turning law enforcement "upside down." Buono defiantly ignored almost everyone during his trial.

All except Buono seemed to enjoy their celebrity status and thrived on the attention they received. Bianchi's response to celebrity was sometimes difficult to determine, but he did not shun the limelight and usually seemed to enjoy the fact that he was known worldwide. Although Bundy complained constantly about the presence of television cameras in the courtroom, he constantly sought contacts with the media during his incarceration. When Gacy confessed to police and lawyers, he found himself the center of attention and seemed to want to retain this attention through his clinical, almost professional method of discussing his victims and how he had killed them. After his arrest, Gacy kept a scrapbook of newspaper clippings about his case.

Only Bianchi and Lucas ever showed any remorse for their killings. When Bianchi cried while speaking in open court in Washington, some felt he was truly sorry and a very sick man, but others saw his tears as merely expressing frustration over his circumstances. Lucas, after being "saved by the Lord," now claims to understand all the grief he has caused the relatives of his victims. However, few who have interviewed him, including this author, believe he is sincere; many doubt that Lucas is capable of feeling remorse for the murders of his victims, which include his mother and his common-law wife, whose deaths he rationalizes as accidents.

None of the murderers strongly professed a religious belief except for Lucas, whose claims are widely discounted, and Marcus, who joined a religious group in prison. Bundy, who regularly attended a Methodist church as a boy, was baptized into the Mormon faith in his twenties. Yet when arrested for the last time in Florida, he asked for a Catholic priest. Gacy's religious activities appear to have been undertaken only for social gain. Bianchi and Buono, both of Catholic heritage, reportedly professed no strong commitments to the Catholic faith.

RECALL OF EVENTS

Buono has never discussed his killings and still maintains his innocence. Bundy only theorized about the person who committed the murders he is believed to have done. Bianchi remembered his victims under hypnosis, apparently faked, but was reticent to discuss the details of how they were killed. Gacy allegedly remembered some of his victims but may have repressed the memory of his killings or perhaps simply was incapable of remembering as a result of blackouts caused by alcohol use. He is recalled by his wife and relatives as having had a very good memory.

Lucas's memory is a mystery. He has described his victims in graphic detail that has been verified by the police. He may have had what is known as an "eidetic" memory—an exceptionally detailed, vivid recall of visual images—or he may have had hypernesia, defined as the unusually vivid and complete recall of information, similar to a photographic memory.

WHAT DOES IT ALL MEAN?

None of these serial murderers had what could be described as a "normal" childhood. It appears that their later antisocial behavior was at least partly caused by unfavorable family or social conditions during their formative years. Some had abusive parents; all came from families with a history of alcoholism; all experienced some sort of childhood health trauma.

Economic conditions may also enter into the equation. These men were all born into lower-class families. Many, as adults, had trouble holding onto jobs.

Whatever the causes, one early sign of problems appears to be a difficulty in establishing long-lasting interpersonal relationships. All of these serial murderers were divorced; many experienced confusion regarding their sexual identities. All were described by experts as having antisocial personalities.

Still, it remains difficult to describe accurately those attributes possessed by potential serial murderers, at least on a predictive basis. Although some of the killers discussed here exhibited noticeably odd or disturbing behavior, others were outwardly personable and in some instances extremely charming. Once again, the old axiom proves true—appearances definitely can be deceiving.

12

INVESTIGATING
SERIAL MURDER

Technically, the unsolved murder is never closed. But as other murders occur, "old" cases receive a lower priority; scarce resources must be allocated on the basis of cost-effectiveness and probability of closure. The result is that investigative manpower is constantly reallocated from older to newer cases. The older cases, then, go uninvestigated—and unsolved.

When an unsolved murder is part of an identified series, however, law enforcement agencies are under a great deal of pressure to continue the investigation—regardless of the current likelihood of solving the crime or the cost-effectiveness of pursuing the case. When a killing is labeled a "serial murder," everything changes; pressure from politicians, the media, and the general public creates heightened expectations, and agencies involved in the investigation of a serial murder will use a variety of methods to catch the serial killer.

There are several ways for the relevant law enforcement agencies to respond to a string of serial murders. The most common responses include forming a task force for the coordination of multiple-jurisdiction investigations; holding conferences with all agencies that are involved in the investigation; acting as a clearinghouse of information about the serial crimes; or using psychological profiling. Other responses to serial murder are employed less frequently. These include using specially developed computer software programs, conducting geoforensic pattern analysis, using the services of a psychic, and paying an identified serial killer for criminal evidence necessary to locate all of his murder victims.

This chapter discusses each of these response types, as well as the various problems that investigative agencies frequently encounter when pursuing serial murder cases.

TASK FORCES

The formation of a task force is one of the most traditional methods of responding to a multijurisdiction criminal investigation. As Michigan State Police Captain and author Daniel C. Myre (*Death Investigation*, International Association of Chiefs of Police, 1974) states:

> The investigation of a major crime sometimes requires various police departments to unite and form a single investigative unit with a central headquarters. Such major crime investigative centers are only as good as their organization and information retrieval systems. To eliminate duplication of effort and insure that evidence is handled properly by all investigators, a major crime center must have a definite command structure and well-defined rules of procedure.

An example of a successful serial murder task force was the one formed in July 1980 to look into the problem of missing and murdered children in the Atlanta, Georgia area. This task force effort, although coming under some criticism at the time, eventually resulted in the arrest and conviction of Wayne Williams for murdering two of the twenty-eight identified homicide victims. Williams was suspected as being responsible for the deaths of many of the other victims.

CONFERENCES AND CLEARINGHOUSES

Law enforcement conferences are a tradition in police work, held on an annual basis by various professional associations. Only very recently, however, have such conferences attempted to deal with serial murder. These conferences tend to be of two types: those dealing with numerous unsolved murders and those responding to the ramifications of the identification and confessions of a serial murderer.

A response similar to the conference approach is the creation of an information clearinghouse. Again, such a response may occur because a serial murderer has been apprehended or because of a number of unsolved murders involving multiple law enforcement jurisdictions.

An example of a successful information clearinghouse on a national scale was the Lucas Homicide Task Force in Texas. This organization, though called a task force, performed the function of an information clearinghouse by communicating with law enforcement agencies that requested information on Lucas, coordinating interviews with Lucas, compiling and distributing information to requesting agencies, and providing for Lucas's security. In addition, the Texas Rangers directly investigated sixteen homicides committed in Texas in which Lucas was a suspect and assisted in numerous other investigations within the state. By the end of February 1985, the task force had cleared a total of 210 homicide cases, 189 of which were directly attributed to Lucas.

PSYCHOLOGICAL PROFILING

Psychological profiling is an attempt to provide investigators with more information on a serial murderer who is yet to be identified; a more current and perhaps more descriptive term for this strategy is *investigative profiling*. The purpose of this profiling is to develop a behavioral composite combining sociological and psychological assessments of the offender.

Profiling is generally based on the premise that an accurate analysis and interpretation of the crime scene and other locations related to the crime can provide clues to the type of individual who committed the crime. Because certain personality types exhibit similar behavioral patterns (in other words, behavior that becomes habitual or routine), an understanding of these patterns can lead investigators to potential suspects.

The origins of criminal profiling are obscure. It is known that during World War II, the Office of Strategic Services (OSS) employed psychiatrist William Langer to profile Adolf Hitler. The material assembled by Langer included a psychological description of Hitler's personality, a diagnosis of his condition, and a prediction of how Hitler would react to defeat. Furthermore, such cases as the Boston Strangler and New York City's Mad Bomber in the 1960s were profiled in a similar manner by Dr. James A. Brussels.

Over the past twenty years, three types of investigative profiling have emerged—the FBI model, developed primarily by the Federal Bureau of Investigation; the Cantner model, developed in 1985 by Dr. David Canter, a psychologist at the University of Surrey, England; and the Geoforensic model, developed by Dr. Milton Newton and based on the use of geographic topical analysis. Each of these methods will be discussed next.

FBI Model

The FBI became involved in psychological profiling in 1970. Agent Howard Teten was teaching an applied criminology course at the FBI Academy, and students from various police departments would bring their criminal cases to him for analysis. The FBI began formally developing psychological profiles shortly thereafter.

The profiling process used by the FBI typically involves five steps:

1. A comprehensive study of the nature of the criminal act and the types of persons who have committed this offense.

2. A thorough inspection of the specific crime scene involved in the case.

3. An in-depth examination of the background and activities of the victim(s) and any known suspects.

4. A formulation of the probable motivating factors of all parties involved.

5. The development of a description of the perpetrator based on the overt characteristics associated with his/her probable psychological makeup.

FBI Agent Robert K. Ressler, a former member of the profiling team in the Behavioral Science Unit, noted:

> All people have personality traits that can be more or less identified. But an abnormal person becomes ritualized even more so and there's a pattern in his behavior. Oftentimes, the behavior and the personality are reflected in the crime scene of that individual. By studying the crime scene from the psychological standpoint, rather than from the technical, evidence-gathering standpoint, you could recreate the personality of the individual who committed the crime.
>
> If the crime scene is abnormal, it would indicate their personality is abnormal.

Most homicide investigators appear to be convinced of the potential value of the psychological profile. The process is not without its limitations, however. The FBI surveyed 192 users of its profiles and found that less than half the crimes for which the profiles had been solicited were eventually solved. Further, in only 17 percent of these 88 solved cases did the profile help directly to identify the subject. Although a "success" rate of 17 percent of those 88 cases may appear low (and even lower if one includes the unsolved cases), the profiles are not expected, at least in most instances, to solve a case but simply to provide an additional set of clues in cases found by local police to be unsolvable. In over three fourths of the solved cases, the profile did at least help focus the investigation.

CANTER MODEL

A primary difference between the profiling developed by David Canter and that done by the FBI is that Canter is continually building an empirical base from which to operate, whereas the FBI model is based almost totally on intuition of the profiler and his or her experience in profiling previous crimes. Whereas the FBI model spends little effort on the victim of the crime, Canter's model considers victim information as crucial to the development of the investigative profile. Canter relies on statistical analysis and the use of probabilities derived from his continually updated empirical base. He also bases his findings on the accepted theoretical concepts of psychology, whereas FBI profilers rely almost solely on their own experience.

For Canter, research into the development of more accurate investigative profiles means interpreting the "criminal's shadow." This shadow, or story, of the criminal, which Canter refers to as the "inner narrative," evolves from a series of cryptic signals provided by the actions of the offender. These cryptic signals include:

- The personal world the individual inhabits
- The degree of care the offender takes in avoiding capture
- The degree of experience the offender shows in his crime
- Unusual aspects of the criminal act that may reflect the type of individual involved
- Habits of the offender that may carry over into his daily life

In effect, Canter is saying that even though the serial murderer may be characterized as killing in a random manner, the killer will in fact act in a very coherent manner. Unless a person is totally out of control, random behavior does not occur.

GEOFORENSIC PROFILING

Geoforensic profiling—also called "geographic profiling"—provides an analysis of spatial behavioral patterns of the offender and is based to some extent on the interrogation technique called "map tracking," developed by U.S. Army

Intelligence. Map tracking was used to debrief a captured combat soldier from his point of capture backward in time and space to his origination point or to the point at which he has no more information of intelligence value. Use of geographic targeting in crime analysis includes distance to crime research, demographic analysis, centrographic analysis, criminal geographic targeting, point-pattern analysis, point-spread analysis, crime site residual analysis, spatial-temporal ordering, and directional analysis.

These various analytical techniques are particularly useful in responding to serial rape and serial murder. By an examination of the spatial data connected with a series of crime sites, a criminal geographic targeting model generates a three-dimensional probability map that indicates those areas most likely to be associated with the offender, such as home, work site, social venue, and travel routes. At the very least, this profiling strategy can assist investigators in focusing their resources on specific geographic areas and can narrow the alternative scenarios to explore.

FORENSIC CONSULTANTS

Forensics means the use of scientific knowledge to answer legal questions. Because investigators are in effect attempting to answer legal questions so that the killer can be charged by the state with his crimes, it follows that forensic scientists will, from time to time, be asked to assist in serial murder investigations.

Forensic scientists from a variety of disciplines have provided assistance in such cases. Experts on DNA, which is generally referred to as "genetic fingerprints," are frequently used in serial murder investigations when semen is found at the crime scene on the body of the victim. Hypnosis experts may be used to enhance the memories of crucial witnesses. Police forensic artists may be used in instances where witnesses are available. The forensic pathologist is a frequent contributor to a serial murder investigation regarding specific information surrounding the actions of the killer, the victim, cause of death, time of death, manner of death, and other physiological evidence found from the autopsy of the victim.

Aside from the normal forensic assistance in a serial murder investigation, forensic anthropologists have been used to reconstruct the head of an unidentified victim from the skull; forensic entomologists have been useful in determining time of death from the examination of maggot larvae on the victim's body; and forensic odontologists have assisted in the examination of teeth of the victims for identification purposes. This group of investigative response strategies is always used in some fashion in a murder investigation, frequently as a complement to the other response strategies described.

CENTRALIZED INVESTIGATIVE NETWORKS

It is important when investigating a series of murders to verify that similar patterns or modi operandi are present, suggesting a serial murder. This usually requires the gathering of information from different jurisdictions. Once this information is collated and a strong probability of serial events is identified, the information can be shared with the group of relevant investigative agencies. An investigative network is then in a position, through state-of-the-art investigative techniques, to attempt to locate and apprehend the serial murderer.

Such centralized investigative networks are currently operational at the national and state levels in the United States, on a national level in Great Britain, and to some extent in Canada.

FBI's VIOLENT CRIMINAL APPREHENSION PROGRAM

The U.S. investigative network, referred to as the Violent Criminal Apprehension Program (VICAP), is located at the FBI National Academy in Quantico, Virginia as a component of the National Center for the Analysis of Violent Crime. The Behavioral Science Unit at the Academy is the central site for the network; this unit also provides a psychological profile of the perpetrator of an unsolved violent crime when requested by a local agency.

VICAP is a centralized data information center and crime analysis system that collects, collates, and analyzes all aspects of the investigation of similar-pattern, multiple murders on a nationwide basis, regardless of the location or number of police agencies involved. VICAP is described as a "nationwide clearinghouse ... to provide all law enforcement agencies reporting similar pattern violent crimes with the information necessary to initiate a coordinated multiagency investigation." VICAP attempts to identify any similar characteristics that may exist in a series of unsolved murders and to provide all police agencies reporting similar patterns with information necessary to initiate a coordinated multiagency investigation.

Cases that currently meet the criteria for VICAP include:

- Solved or unsolved homicides or attempts, especially those that involve an abduction; are apparently random, motiveless, or sexually oriented; or are known or suspected to be part of a series
- Missing persons where the circumstances indicate a strong possibility of foul play and the victim is still missing
- Unidentified dead bodies where the manner of death is known or suspected to be homicide

NEW YORK STATE'S HOMICIDE ASSESSMENT AND LEAD TRACKING SYSTEM

By the mid-1980s, a number of states had initiated efforts to develop statewide analysis capabilities similar to the system evolving with VICAP. In 1986, fourteen states were involved in such an effort. The first statewide system to become fully operational, in 1987, was New York State's Homicide Assessment and Lead Tracking (HALT) System. Although HALT is far from realizing its full potential, it has become a model for other states to follow in terms of its design, computer software, functions, and established cooperative relationship with VICAP.

The HALT program was designed to provide a systematic and timely criminal investigative tool to law enforcement agencies across the state. Through computer analysis of case incident information supplied by police agencies, HALT is able to determine when similar crime patterns exist in two or more jurisdictions. When patterns are identified, the appropriate local agencies are notified.

INTERPOL

INTERPOL is primarily a criminal information exchange service that provides its members with studies and reports on individuals and groups involved in crime internationally. According to the Interpol General Secretariat, "The purpose of INTERPOL is to facilitate, coordinate, and encourage international police cooperation as a means for embattling crime."

INTERPOL has become an increasingly important tool for criminal investigation in the United States to satisfy investigative leads that go beyond U.S. borders. To address the need for an international channel of communication for state and local law enforcement officials, each of the fifty states is setting up a point of contact within its own police system to serve as a focal point for all requests involving international matters.

Although INTERPOL was not specifically designed to respond to serial murder, the in-place system of this organization is uniquely qualified to provide assistance to investigators of a serial murder with potentially transnational characteristics. As each of the fifty states develops its liaison program, INTERPOL will become better known to the law enforcement community as a tool for international information and assistance.

OTHER CENTRALIZED SYSTEMS

Another statewide system, similar to HALT, is the Homicide Investigation and Tracking System (HITS). This system collects murder and sexual assault information and identifies similar characteristics across cases.

North of the border, the Royal Canadian Mounted Police has implemented the Violent Crime Linkage Analysis System (VICLAS). This system uses a modified version of the FBI's VICAP form to conduct computer analysis.

SPECIALIZED RESPONSE TEAMS

The FBI has recently developed a strategy to assist local law enforcement agencies in conducting major criminal investigations. The Critical Incident Response Group (CIRC)—originally known as the Rapid Start Team—is a team of FBI agents and computer specialists numbering from eight to twenty that can be on the site of an investigation within four hours. The team provides laptop and desktop computers, telephone modems, customized software, a portable generator, and a tent for the team to use. The team then assists the task force in transferring data into a specialized database; team members also recommend an organizational structure for the task force.

The CIRC is assigned to the task force on an indefinite basis; however, the overall goal of the team is to train the local departments involved and to provide the appropriate software for the investigation. The team provides five basic services:

1. Helping to organize and delegate jobs within the task force
2. Compiling and analyzing clues on the computer
3. Establishing an electronic message system for the task force
4. Providing links to national databases
5. Establishing communication links to national or international police forces

SOLICITATION FROM THE PUBLIC

When and if an agency chooses to make public the fact that it is investigating a series of homicides believed to have been committed by the same killer, it logically follows that the agency's leaders would ask the public for assistance in providing information to the investigation. Frequently, when the police announce that they are searching for a serial killer, they will set up a bank of telephones connected to a central number so that the public can call in information or leads to the police.

Making an investigation public is a strategic decision with a number of ramifications. A centralized telephone number made available to the public will require an additional allocation of investigative personnel to operate these telephones. Because of the large volume of information generated from these telephone banks, a number of potential suspects will be identified, necessitating investigative follow-ups. In addition, a great deal of information will be received from the public, necessitating the computerization of this data so that it can be managed effectively.

For example, in the Green River Murder investigation, 18,000 suspect names were collected, many from tips called in by the public to an advertised telephone hotline number. On December 7, 1988, a two-hour television special seeking assistance from the public was aired; it was entitled "Manhunt Live: A Chance to End the Nightmare." As a result of this program, the telephone company in Washington reported that more than 100,000 people had attempted to call the toll-free number. (Fewer than 10,000 actually got through to the detectives operating the telephones for the broadcast.) Unfortunately, this massive and unique effort to solicit information from a national television audience was to no avail: The Green River Killer has not yet been identified.

OFFENDER REWARDS

On January 14, 1982, Clifford Robert Olson pleaded guilty in a Vancouver, British Columbia courtroom to the rape and murder of eleven young boys and girls. Olson's plea was entered in exchange for a promise by Canadian authorities to establish a $90,000 trust fund for his wife and son. In addition to the plea, Olson agreed to identify the locations of some of the buried victims.

Although the intensely negative reaction of the public to this negotiated plea may preclude the probability of such an unusual event recurring, it is certainly noteworthy. One can only imagine the frustration of the criminal justice officials in Canada that led to such a negotiation. It is not unrealistic to contemplate that such a negotiation in the United States in such well-known cases as those of Ted Bundy and Henry Lee Lucas might have resulted, at the very least, in a resolution of cases and an end to the "not-knowing" of the relatives of their victims.

In other cases, serial murderers have agreed to confess to their murders in return for prosecutors not seeking the death penalty against them or in return for incarceration at a specific location. One notable example of this type of plea bargaining is the case of Robert Hansen, who bargained with the legal system to ensure his incarceration away from the state in which he was convicted. In 1984, Hansen agreed to plead guilty to the murders of seventeen women and the rape of thirty additional women in Anchorage, Alaska. In return for this plea and confession, which enabled Alaska state troopers to locate and unearth his buried victims, Hansen was assured of incarceration at a federal prison outside of Alaska, and state officials agreed to assist in the relocation of his family to another state.

PSYCHICS

Psychics invariably become involved in highly publicized serial murder investigations, either by making predictions about the killer to the media or by secretly providing advice to agencies or individual investigators. In many instances, police agencies have been reluctant to admit to the use of psychics, given the risks of criticism from the public and from other members of the law enforcement community.

Despite this reluctance, there are several documented instances of psychics providing crucial guidance in serial murder investigations. One good example concerns the John Wayne Gacy case. During the early stages of searching for a missing teenage boy in December 1978, Des Plaines, Illinois police began to suspect strongly that Gacy was responsible for the boy's disappearance. A local psychic was used to uncover information about the missing youth. Information given to the police by this psychic was subsequently interpreted as very accurate in describing Gacy, his method of killing his victims, and his disposal of their bodies. (The young boy missing in Des Plaines had been one of Gacy's victims.)

Another less successful example is that of Peter Hurkos, a famous Dutch mystic who claimed to have helped solve a number of murders in the United States and Europe during the early 1960s. In January 1964, Hurkos was asked to assist the Massachusetts Attorney General's Office in its investigation of a series of homicides that had occurred in and around Boston since 1962; the homicides were already being referred to as the "Boston Strangler" case. After spending a week in Boston, Hurkos identified a fifty-six-year-old shoe salesman with a history of mental illness as the killer. Hurkos assured the police they had to look no further. Boston police then coordinated an exhaustive investigation of this suspect, eventually ruling him out as a suspect in the killings. Not long after this, Albert DeSalvo—the *real* Boston Strangler—confessed to the killings.

Although some investigators claim that psychics are useful, the majority remain skeptical. However, the involvement of a psychic in a serial murder investigation may provide an unintentional benefit to the investigation. Psychics approach the investigation from a very different perspective, and it is this perspective that may, through the questions asked by a psychic, cause investigators to begin to ask new questions. This in turn may result in new information that inadvertently provides further progress in the investigation.

PROBLEMS WITH INVESTIGATING SERIAL MURDER

The investigation of a serial murder poses numerous issues for the investigating agency or agencies. These issues involve questions of investigative tactics and strategies, the allocation of personnel to the investigation, the necessary expenditure of funds to meet the increased expenses of such an investigation, news media relations, the management of large amounts of information, inter- and intra-agency communication, and the organization of the investigative effort to include control and coordination. In other words, a serial murder investigation is a major undertaking. It is frequently complicated by the involvement of multiple jurisdictions, the scope of the investigation, and the resources necessary to carry it out.

A review of serial murder investigations conducted over the last decade reveals seven major problems common to such investigations:

1. Contending with and attempting to reduce linkage blindness
2. Making a commitment to a serial murder investigation
3. Coordinating investigative functions and actions
4. Managing large amounts of investigative information
5. Dealing with public pressure and limiting the adversarial nature of relations with the news media
6. Acknowledging and assessing the value of victim information
7. Becoming aware of strategies employed in previous serial murder investigations

LINKAGE BLINDNESS

A review of serial murders occurring over the last few years reveals that most serial murderers are caught by chance or coincidence and not by ratiocination or scientific investigation. Law enforcement agencies today are simply not adept at identifying or apprehending the murderer who kills strangers, moves from jurisdiction to jurisdiction, and crosses state lines.

Why, in this age of information and rapidly advancing computer technology, are multijurisdictional crimes of murder so difficult for law enforcement to solve?

The answer is *linkage blindness*.

I coined the term *linkage blindness* in 1984 to denote a major problem in the law enforcement criminal investigation function applicable to serial crime in general. The term describes the nearly total lack of sharing or coordinating of investigative information prevalent among today's law enforcement agencies. Linkage blindness occurs because:

- Police do not exchange investigative information on unsolved murders with police agencies in different jurisdictions.
- Police do not exchange investigative information on unsolved murders in different command areas within the same jurisdiction.
- Police do not share or coordinate investigative information on unsolved murders very well between individual officers.
- Very little networking of information and sources relating to unsolved murders occurs between the police.

Simply stated, the exchange of investigative information within and between police departments in this country is very poor. As a result of this poor communication, linkages between similar crime patterns or modi operandi are rarely established across different geographic areas. The serial killer can take advantage of this linkage blindness and continue to kill until competing agencies agree to cooperate and share vital information.

Intergovernmental conflict between law enforcement agencies is unfortunately a somewhat common occurrence. The reasons for these conflicts are as varied and as numerous as there are agencies; however, there seems to be a common basis for most of this conflict. The basis is a real or perceived violation of an agency's boundaries or geographical jurisdiction, or of the specific responsibilities of an agency to enforce specific laws over a wide geographical area. Agencies large and small continually practice boundary maintenance in order to protect their jurisdictions from intruders—other police agencies moving onto their turf.

In discussing the mobility of serial killers and the difficulty of a multiple law enforcement agency investigation, Author D. Keyes (*Unveiling Claudia: A True Story of Serial Murder,* Bantam, 1986) describes what Bill Steckman, a homicide sergeant in Columbus, Ohio, was up against when he was investigating that area's ".22 Caliber Murders":

> [M]ost serial murderers moved from city to city, stalking their victims across city, county or state lines, over weeks, months and even years. Because different law enforcement agencies were involved—county sheriff's deputies, city police and the FBI, each concerned primarily with their own cases—detectives often didn't notice the patterns. Conflicting investigative methods, interdepartmental jealousies, and prosecutors overreacting to the political pressures of a fearful and outraged public, often gave serial killers the advantage. Among the most difficult criminals to apprehend; most often, when they were arrested, it was by accident.

Because of these conditions, it is difficult to provide an optimistic prognosis for controlling serial murder in this country. It is equally disheartening when one realizes that law enforcement's response to the phenomenon of serial murder is only symptomatic of the greater problem of serial criminality. The traveling criminal who repeats criminal acts in different law enforcement jurisdictions is indeed exploiting a systemic weakness, which frequently contributes to his or her continued immunity from detection or apprehension.

LACK OF COMMITMENT

Most law enforcement administrators are unwilling to make a public commitment to initiating a serial murder investigation. Because the public has been sold the concept that the police are responsible for the crime in their jurisdictions, chiefs and sheriffs are loath to admit that there is a serial killer running loose throughout their jurisdictions killing strangers at will.

Given that employment stability for police chiefs can be tenuous, it is no wonder that they strive to put their best appearance before the public. Serial killers make the police look bad. To commit to trying to catch one can make the police look inept in the public's eye.

COORDINATING INVESTIGATIVE FUNCTIONS AND ACTIONS

The reallocation of personnel to the serial murder investigation also requires that very skilled and experienced homicide investigators of supervisory and command level ranks must be reassigned. This means that ongoing cases and newly reported crimes will be responded to by less skilled investigators, supervisors, and commanders. Depending on the length of the serial murder investigation, this could eventually have a negative effect on the agency's clearance rate.

It must be remembered that a serial murder investigation is a major and complicated effort that requires a tremendous amount of coordination. Commanders must know the status of assigned personnel and be able to monitor their activities at all times. In other words, the left hand needs to know what the right hand is doing so that no mistakes are made and important pieces of information are acted on and not lost in the confusion of multiple tasks and different assignments.

MANAGING LARGE AMOUNTS OF INVESTIGATIVE INFORMATION

In a serial murder investigation, the amount of information and data generated is almost always unmanageable without the aid of the computer. However, even in today's high-tech age, many police agencies operate with little computer literacy. In fact, most police departments use their computing machines simply as fast-retrieval file cabinets.

To exploit the computer's ability to process information, the team of investigators must be able to cross-reference and retrieve aggregate data very rapidly. Command-level personnel who understand the need for such a capability may not be available to the agencies involved. Outside consultants may be required, but this has not always worked very smoothly in these sensitive and stress-filled investigations.

PUBLIC AND MASS MEDIA PRESSURE FOR INFORMATION

Most law enforcement agencies, though adequately prepared to withstand a great deal of public pressure to capture criminals and prevent crimes, are ill prepared to deal effectively with the mass media. The fact that serial murder investigations frequently involve more than one police jurisdiction only complicates the task of media relations. In some recent serial murder investigations, reporters have gone from one public source to another, seeking information about the investigation. Coordination with their counterparts in the other agencies involved is a topic that is almost always neglected in training courses in police-media relations.

If not handled correctly, the mass media can cause a great deal of chaos for personnel assigned to the investigation. In some cases, the media become almost frenzied in their search for information. This was certainly the case in Gainesville, Florida in late 1990, when five people were slain within seventy-two hours in that city. This serial killing soon turned into a media carnival, with some journalists using parabolic microphones to eavesdrop on members of the police task force. Michael Reynolds, a Reuters reporter, characterized his peers in Gainesville as exhibiting "brainstem behavior" and "[like] rats on methedrine, jabbering about semen and blood and missing nipples."

Often, the result of intense mass media pressure added to already existing public pressure is that the press comes to be viewed as an adversarial and intolerant critic of the investigatory effort. A great deal of antagonism is therefore generated between investigators and journalists, resulting in poor and sometimes slanted reporting of the progress and effectiveness of the investigatory efforts. However, it must be remembered that, whereas at times the media seem to get in the way of an investigation, in the final analysis they are much more likely to have a positive effect than a negative one. The publicity generated by the media is likely to bring witnesses forward who are useful to the investigation.

Low-Priority Victims

When a victim of a homicide comes from a powerless and marginalized sector of our population, there is little pressure to solve the case and apprehend the killer. As homicide investigators are assigned additional homicides to investigate, the "less-dead" victims receive less and less priority. Without public or mass media pressure, these less-dead victims become less and less important.

Because the less dead are likely to constitute most of the serial killer's victims, law enforcement agencies inadvertently place a low priority on solving a homicide that has a fairly high probability of being part of a serial killer's pattern. Thus, because law enforcement differentiates the value of homicide victims, the serial killer remains free to kill and kill again. When this occurs, society's throwaways are indeed thrown away.

Lack of Knowledge of Prior Experiences

Different law enforcement responses to serial murder have been employed over the last ten to twenty years. Unfortunately, most law enforcement agencies are not familiar with the experiences of their counterparts or the problems they have faced. Consequently, when an agency is confronted with a serial murder investigation, investigators are not aware of the various options, responses, or combinations of responses available to them.

THE FUTURE OF SERIAL MURDER INVESTIGATION

Going forward, a number of questions remain to be answered in order to increase the effectiveness of law enforcement's response to serial murder:

- Is there a correlation between the demographic or geographic patterns of serial murder? (For instance, there appears to be a disproportionate number of serial murderers who have killed in the Pacific Northwest.)
- How effective is VICAP in assisting local law enforcement agencies in responding to serial murder?
- What investigative strategies or techniques are the most successful for law enforcement's response to an unsolved and potentially serial murder?
- Is collecting information on unsolved murders and communicating this information the most effective method of reducing the linkage blindness?
- What are the necessary components of a training program for criminal investigators that would increase their effectiveness and efficiency in the investigation of serial murder?

The unfortunate fact is that serial murderers defy deterrence; we simply don't know who the next victim will be. Until more research is conducted on serial murder, only the most general deterrence strategies can be suggested—and these are of little use to the average citizen.

Researcher G. Nettler, after evaluating the phenomenon of serial lust murder, had just one recommendation to make:

"Lock your doors."

13

SERIAL MURDER IN THE TWENTY-FIRST CENTURY

What kind of serial killers will haunt our world in the twenty-first century? Given the selectivity of our mass media, our newspapers and television news programs will find them somehow more horrific than even Jeffrey Dahmer. Possibly they will be mass serial killers, using letter bombs, mailing anthrax, putting poison in our water supply, or spreading poison gas in the subways of our urban centers.

The only thing we can be relatively sure of is that the phenomenon of serial murder will continue—and possibly grow. As Ted Bundy told authors S.G. Michand and H. Aynesworth (*The Only Living Witness*, Linden Press/Simon & Schuster, 1983): "It has always been my theory that for every person arrested and charged with multiple homicide, there are probably a good five more out there."

Finding the "five more" before they kill has to be our goal.

GETTING SMARTER ABOUT THE PHENOMENON

As you will have no doubt noticed by now, there are more questions about serial murder than there are definitive answers about the phenomenon. That is perhaps appropriate, because we still have a lot to learn about serial murder. In particular, we need to learn more about the victims of serial murder, about the murderers themselves, and about how we go about identifying and apprehending these killers.

Victims

Here are just a few of the questions that need answers regarding the victims of serial murder:

- Are groups of people who lack prestige or power the most common victims of serial murderers, or is their vulnerability a precipitating factor, creating "attractive" targets of opportunity for the serial murderer?
- Does the sexual preference or chosen vocation of serial murder victims reduce the priority that law enforcement gives to their murders?
- How does the serial murderer select a victim, and how have selected victims escaped death?
- Can at-risk populations reduce the probability of their victimization by a serial murderer?

Serial Murderers

As a society, we have many questions about those warped individuals who commit serial murder. The most pressing of these questions include:

- What are the characteristics of serial killers that can help us distinguish them from normal individuals? How can the identification of such characteristics—presumably at an early age—be used to prevent these individuals from becoming serial murderers?
- Is the apparent fact that most serial murderers are males a significant characteristic of the phenomenon?
- Why are a large number of serial murders committed by a team of killers? Do the theories regarding solo serial killers also apply to these teams of killers?
- What techniques or methodologies will better develop our understanding of the causes of serial murder?

IDENTIFICATION AND APPREHENSION

To reduce the incidence of serial murders, it is necessary to understand the phenomenon better. Here are some of the key questions we need to answer:

- Is the incidence of serial murder increasing in the United States? If so, why?
- Why does the United States appear to have so many serial murderers, compared with other countries?
- What more do we need to know about the phenomenon of serial murder in order to develop strategies and policies for intervention, prevention, and deterrence?

A VIOLENT CULTURE

Some of the answers to these questions may be found in the very fabric of our society. American culture has cultivated a taste for violence that seems to be insatiable. We are a people obsessed with violence, and consequently our entertainment industry is driven by such violence. The violence of our contemporary popular culture, reflected in movies, television programs, magazines, and books of fact or fiction, has made the shocking reality of this violence seem a routine risk that we all face. Our own sense of humanity is anesthetized, almost to the point of unconsciousness. We sit in front of the television set and obliterate our sensitivity to the humanity of the serial killer's victims. Instead, we desire to learn more about the killer. The killer becomes our total focus.

In the same way, we want to hear or read about the torture and mutilation deaths of female victims almost as though such acts were an art form. The serial killer becomes an artist, in some cases performing a reverse type of sculpture by taking the lives of his victims with a sharp knife. Pick up a paperback mystery or a police procedural. Many that sell are about the hunt for a serial killer. We as a society enjoy serial killing, albeit vicariously.

Elliott Leyton, a wise observer of cultures, stated:

If we were charged with the responsibility for designing a society in which all structural and cultural mechanisms leaned toward the creation of the killers of strangers, we could do no better than to present the purchaser with the shape of modern America.

THE KILLERS OF THE NEW MILLENNIUM

Our violent culture seemingly breeds violent offenders—yet we still don't know near enough about who is likely to become a serial murderer. The research we have is inconclusive, if not confusing. Some serial killers are abused as children; some grow up as normal as the kid next door. Some serial killers are introverted and socially inept; others are outgoing and quite skilled at interpersonal relations. Some are obsessed with death and killing; others exhibit no outward characteristics of their secret impulses.

In other words, we can't predict who the next serial killers will be; we don't know what they will look like, where they will live, or how they will act. We only know that they will exist, as they have always existed, and that their victims will continue to mount.

In this already terror-tinged twenty-first century, the next generation of serial killers is indeed among us—and, until they are stopped, they will continue to kill and kill again.

REFERENCES AND
SOURCE MATERIAL

REFERENCES

Abrahamsen, D. (1973). *The murdering mind.* New York: Harper & Row.

———. (1985). *Confessions of Son of Sam.* New York: Columbia University Press.

American Psychiatric Association. (1968). *Diagnostic and statistical manual of mental disorders.* Washington, DC: American Psychiatric Association.

———. (1980). *Diagnostic and statistical manual of mental disorders,* 2nd ed. Washington, DC: American Psychiatric Association.

———. (1987). *Diagnostic and statistical manual of mental disorders,* 3rd ed., revised. Washington, DC: American Psychiatric Association.

———. (1994). *Electronic DSM-IV,* HDT Software. Jackson, WY: Teton Data Systems.

Apsche, J. A. (1993). *Probing the mind of a serial killer.* Morrisville, PA: International Information Associates.

Atkinson, R. (1984, February 20). Killing puzzle. *Washington Post,* pp. 1, 14–15.

Ault, R. L., & Reese, J. T. (1980, March). A psychological assessment of crime profiling. *FBI Law Enforcement Bulletin,* pp. 1–4.

Baden, M. M. (1989). *Unnatural death: Confessions of a medical examiner.* New York: Random House.

Banay, R. S. (1952). Study in murder. *Annals, 284,* 26–34.

———. (1956). Psychology of a mass murderer. *Journal of Forensic Science, 1*(1), 1–7.

Bardach, E. (1996). Turf barriers to interagency collaboration. In D. Kettl & H. B. Milward (Eds.), *The state of public management.* Baltimore, MD: Johns Hopkins University Press.

Barnes, M. (Producer and Director). (1984). *The mind of a murderer* [Videotape]. Washington, DC: Public Broadcasting Service.

Barrington, R. C., & Pease, D. M. S. (1985). HOLMES: The development of a computerised major crime investigation system. *The Police Journal, 63*(3), 207–223.

Bayley, D. H. (1977). The limits of police reform. In D. H. Bayley (Ed.), *Police and society* (pp. 219–236). Beverly Hills, CA: Sage.

BBC News Service. (2000, January 28). Rwanda: Child "serial killer" arrested in southwest. Radio Rwanda, Kigali, in English, 1145 GMT, 10 November 1999.

BBC World News Service. (1999, October 30). *World: America's Colombian child killer confesses.*

Berger, J. (1984, September 8). Mass killers baffle authorities. *New York Times*, p. 1.

Biondi, R., & Hecox, W. (1988). *All his father's sins: Inside the Gerald Gallego sex-slave murders.* Rocklin, CA: Prima Publishing and Communications.

———. (1992). *Dracula killer: True story of California's vampire killer.* New York: Pocket Books.

Bjerre, A. (1981). *The psychology of murder: A study in criminal psychology.* New York: Da Capo Press. (Originally published in 1927)

Blackburn, D. J. (1990). *Human harvest: The Sacramento murder story.* Los Angeles: Knightsbridge.

Bloch, H. (1999, December 27). The horror, the horror: As a slaughter of the innocents comes to light, a pained Pakistan searches its soul for explanations. *Time, 154*(25), Asia Week.

Bogdan, R., & Taylor, S. J. (1975). *Introduction to qualitative research methods.* New York: Wiley.

Brandl, S. G. (1987, October). *The management of serial homicide investigations: Considerations for police managers.* Paper presented at the annual meeting of the Midwest Criminal Justice Association, Chicago.

Brantingham, P. J., & Brantingham, P. L. (1978). A theoretical model of crime site selection. In M. Krohn & R. Akers (Eds.), *Theoretical perspectives* (pp. 105–118). Beverly Hills, CA: Sage.

Brearley, H. C. (1969). *Homicide in the United States.* Montclair, NJ: Patterson Smith. (Originally published in 1932)

Briggs, T. (1982, March 4). *VI-CAP memo.* Colorado Springs Police Department, pp. 1–10.

Brittain, R. P. (1970). The sadistic murderer. *Medical Science and the Law, 10*, 198–207.

Britton, P. (1999, June 27). The killers who follow in Hannibal's footsteps. *Sunday Times* (London). Features, p. 1.

Broeske, P. (1998, October 7). Blood money serial killers continue to get their stab at Hollywood stardom. *Milwaukee Journal Sentinel*, p. 1.

Brophy, J. (1966). *The meaning of murder.* New York: Thomas Y. Crowell.

Brooks, P. R. (1981). *VI-CAP.* Unpublished report.

———. (1982). *The investigative consultant team: A new approach for law enforcement cooperation.* Washington, DC: Police Executive Research Forum.

Brooks, P. R., Devine, M. J., Green, T. J., Hart, B. J., & Moore, M. D. (1987, February). Serial murder: A criminal justice response. *The Police Chief*, pp. 37, 41–42, 44–45.

———. (1988). *Multi-agency investigation team manual*. Washington, DC: U.S. Department of Justice.

Brown, N., & Edwards, R. (1992). *Genene Jones: Deliver us from evil*. Unpublished case study, University of Illinois at Springfield.

Brussel, J. A. (1968). *Casebook of a crime psychiatrist*. New York: Bernard Geis.

Burgess, A. W., Hartman, C. R., Ressler, R. K., Douglas, J. E., & McCormack, R. (1986). Sexual homicide: A motivational model. *Journal of Interpersonal Violence*, pp. 251–271.

Burn, G. (1984). *"—Somebody's husband, somebody's son": The story of Peter Sutcliffe*. London: Heinemann.

Cahill, T. (1986). *Buried dreams: Inside the mind of a serial killer*. New York: Bantam.

Campbell, C. (1976, May). Portrait of a mass killer. *Psychology Today*, pp. 110–119.

Canter, D. (1989). Offender profiles. *The Psychologist*. *2*(1), 12–16.

———. (1993). The environmental range of serial rapists. *Journal of Environmental Psychology*. *13*, 63–69.

———. (1994). *Criminal shadows: Inside the mind of a serial killer*. London: HarperCollins.

Canter, D., & Heritage, R. (1990). A multivariate model of sexual offence behavior: Developments in "offender profiling." *Journal of Forensic Psychiatry, 1*(22), 185–212.

Caputi, J. (1987). *The age of sex crime*. Bowling Green, OH: Bowling Green State University Press.

———. (1990, Fall). The new founding fathers: The lore and lure of the serial killer in contemporary culture. *Journal of American Culture*, pp. 1–12.

Centers for Disease Control. (1982). Homicide—United States. *Morbidity and Mortality Report, 31*(44), 594, 599–602.

Chambliss, W. (1972). *Box man: A professional thief's journey*. New York: Harper & Row.

Cheney, M. (1976). *The co-ed killer*. New York: Walker.

Clark, S., & Morley, M. (1993). *Murder in mind: Mindhunting the serial killers*. London: Boxtree.

Clarke, R. V., & Cornish, D. B. (1985). Modeling offenders' decisions: A framework for research and policy. In M. Tonry & N. Morris (Eds.), *Crime and justice: An annual review of research* (Vol. 6, pp. 147–185). Chicago: University of Chicago Press.

Cleckley, H. (1964). *The mask of sanity*, 4th ed. St. Louis, MO: C. V. Mosby.

CNN. (2000, March 28). Islamic council rule Pakistan serial killer's sentence violates laws of Islam.

Colton, K. W. (1978). *Police computer technology*. Lexington, MA: Lexington Books.

Connor, S. (1994, March 6). Crimes of violence: Birth of a solution. *The Independent,* p. 19.

Conradi, P. (1992). *The red ripper.* New York: Walker.

Cornwell, P. D. (1994). *The body farm.* Boston: G. K. Hall.

Coston, J. (1992). *To kill and kill again.* New York: Penguin Books.

Cox, M. (1991). *Confessions of Henry Lee Lucas.* New York: Pocket Books.

Cressey, P. G. (1932). *The taxi-dance hall.* Chicago: University of Chicago Press.

Critchley, T. A., & James, P. D. (1987). *The maul and the pear tree: The Ratcliffe Highway murders, 1811.* Boston: G. K. Hall.

Cross, R. (1981). *The Yorkshire ripper.* London: Granada.

Cullen, R. (1993). *The killer department: Detective Viktor Burakov's eight-year hunt for the most savage serial killer in Russian history.* New York: Pantheon Books.

Dahmer, L. (1994). *A father's story.* New York: William Morrow.

Daley, R. (1983). *The dangerous edge.* New York: Dell.

Damore, L. (1981). *In his garden: The anatomy of a murderer.* New York: Arbor House.

Danto, B. L., Bruhns, J., & Kutcher, A. H. (Eds.). (1982). *The human side of homicide.* New York: Columbia University Press.

Darrach, B., & Norris, J. (1984, August). An American tragedy. *Life,* pp. 58–74.

Davies, N. (1981, May 23). Inside the mind. *The Guardian,* p. 6.

de River, J. P. (1958). *Crime and the sexual psychopath.* Springfield, IL: Charles C Thomas.

Denzin, N. K. (Ed.). (1970). *Sociological methods: A sourcebook.* Chicago: Aldine.

———. (1978). *The research act: A theoretical introduction to sociological methods.* New York: McGraw-Hill.

Detlinger, C., & Prugh, J. (1983). *List.* Atlanta, GA: Philmay Enterprises.

Deutsch, J., Hakim, S., & Weinblatt, J. (1984). Injurisdictional criminal mobility: A theoretical perspective. *Urban Studies, 21,* 451–458.

Dickson, A. G. (1975). *A descriptive study of male and female murderers.* Unpublished doctoral dissertation, U.S. International University.

Dietz, P. E. (1986). Mass, serial, and sensational homicides. *Bulletin of the New York Academy of Medicine, 62*(5), 477–491.

———. (1987). Patterns in human violence. In R. E. Hales & A. J. Frances (Eds.), *American Psychological Association Annual Review, Vol. 6.* Washington, DC: American Psychological Association.

Dobson, J. (1992, Spring). Special report: Ted Bundy's last words. *Policy Council,* pp. 31–38.

Dominick, J. R. (1978). Crime and law enforcement in the mass media. In Charles Winick (Ed.), *Deviance and mass media* (pp. 105–128). Beverly Hills, CA: Sage.

Donohue, P. (1996, July 19). Zodiac told cops he envied Bundy. *New York Daily News,* p. 32.

Douglas, J. E., & Munn, C. (1992, February). Violent crime scene analysis: Modus operandi, signature, and staging. *FBI Law Enforcement Bulletin,* pp. 1–10.

Drapkin, I., & Viano, E. (1975). *Victimology: A new focus.* Lexington, MA: D. C. Heath.

DuClos, B. (1993). *Fair game.* New York: St. Martin's Press.

Eftimiades, M. (1993). *Garden of graves.* New York: St. Martin's Paperbacks.

Egger, K. (1999). [Preliminary database on serial killers from 1900 to 1999]. Unpublished data.

Egger, K., & Egger, S. (2001, forthcoming). Victims of serial killers: The less dead. In J. Sgarzi & McDevit (Eds.), *Victims of crime.* Upper Saddle River, NJ: Prentice Hall.

Egger, S. (1984). A working definition of serial murder and the reduction of linkage blindness. *Journal of Police Science and Administration, 12*(3), 348–357.

———. (1984, October). *Research in progress: Preliminary analysis of the victims of serial murderer Henry Lee Lucas.* Paper presented at the annual meeting of the American Society of Criminology, Cincinnati, Ohio.

———. (1984, March). *Serial murder—The development of a preliminary research agenda: Order out of chaos.* Paper presented at the annual meeting of the Academy of Criminal Justice Sciences, Chicago.

———. (1985, March). *Case study of serial murderer Henry Lee Lucas.* Paper presented at the annual meeting of the Academy of Criminal Justice Sciences, Las Vegas, Nevada.

———. (1985). *Serial murder and the law enforcement response.* Unpublished dissertation, College of Criminal Justice, Sam Houston State University, Huntsville, Texas.

———. (1986). *Homicide Assessment and Lead Tracking system (HALT) briefing document.* Albany: New York Division of Criminal Justice Services.

———. (1986, October). *Utility of the case study approach to serial murder research.* Paper presented at the annual meeting of the American Society of Criminology.

———. (1986). A challenge to academia: Preliminary research agenda for serial murder. *Quarterly Journal of Ideology, 10*(1), 75–77.

———. (1990). *Serial murder: An elusive phenomenon.* Westport, CT: Praeger.

———. (1990, March). *The future of criminal investigation.* Paper presented at the annual meeting of Academy of Criminal Justice Sciences, Denver, Colorado.

———. (1992, March). *Serial killing of the lambs of our dreams.* Essay presented at the annual meeting of the Academy of Criminal Justice Sciences, Pittsburgh, Pennsylvania.

———. (1994). Psychics and law enforcement. *The REALL News, 1*(7), 1, 8.

———. (1999). The history, status, and future of psychological profiling. *Journal of Contemporary Criminal Justice,* No. 4.

———. (1999, November). *Profile of the serial killer.* Paper presented at the International Workshop on Violence and Psychopathy at the Queen Sofia Center of the Study of Violence, Valencia, Spain.

———. (2000). Linked crimes, missing evidence. *The Forensic Panel letter, 4*(10). http://www.forensicpanel.com.

Egginton, J. (1989). *From cradle to grave: The short lives and strange death of Marybeth Tinning's nine children.* New York: William Morrow.

Elkind, P. (1990). *The death shift: Nurse Genene Jones and the Texas baby murders.* New York: Onyx.

Ellis, A., & Gullo, J. (1971). *Murder and assassination.* New York: Lyle Stuart.

Fair, K. (1994, July). Kenneth McDuff: Death row. *Police,* pp. 56–58.

Federal Bureau of Investigation. (1983, July). *Violent criminal apprehension program: Conceptual model.* Unpublished working document, pp. 1–4.

Fero, K. (1990). *The Zani murders: The true story of a 13-year killing spree in Texas.* New York: Dell.

Finkelhor, D., Hotaling, G., & Sedlak, A. (1990). *Missing, abducted, runaway, and throwaway children in America* (Cooperative Agreement #87-MC-CX-KO69). Washington, DC: U.S. Department of Justice, Office of Juvenile Justice and Delinquency Prevention.

Fisher, B. (1992). *Techniques of crime scene investigation,* 5th ed. New York: Elsevier.

Fisher, J. C. (1997). *Killer among us: Public reaction to serial murder.* Westport, CT: Praeger.

Fox, J. A., & Levin, J. (1983). *Killing in numbers: An exploratory study of multiple-victim murder* (draft). Unpublished manuscript.

———. (1999). Serial murder: Myths and reality. In M. D. Smith & M. A. Zahn (Eds.), *Studying and preventing homicide* (pp. 79–96). Thousand Oaks, CA: Sage.

Frank, G. (1967). *The Boston strangler.* New York: New American Library.

Franklin, C. (1965). *The world's worst murderers.* New York: Taplinger.

Freeman, L. (1955). *"Before I kill more . . ."* New York: Crown.

Ganey, T. (1989). *St. Joseph's children: A true story of terror and justice.* New York: Carol Publishing Group.

Garland, S. B. (1984, August 12). Serial killings demand new ways to analyze unsolved homicides. *Newhouse News Service.*

Gaskins, D. (as told to Wilton Earle). (1992). *The final truth: The autobiography of a mass murderer/serial killer.* Atlanta, GA: Adept.

Geberth, V. J. (1983). *Practical homicide investigation.* New York: Elsevier.

Gest, T. (1984, April 30). On the trail of America's "serial killers." *U.S. News & World Report,* p. 53.

Giannangelo, S. (1997). *The psychopathology of serial murder: A theory of violence.* Westport, CT: Praeger.

Gibbons, D. C. (1965). *Changing the lawbreaker.* Englewood Cliffs, NJ: Prentice Hall.

Gibney, B. (1984). *The beauty queen killer.* New York: Pinnacle.

Gilbert, J. (1983). A study of the increased rate of unsolved criminal homicide in San Diego, California, and its relationship to police investigative effectiveness. *American Journal of Police, 2,* 149–166.

Gilmour, W. (1991). *Butcher, baker: A true account of a serial murderer.* New York: Onyx.

Ginsburg, P. E. (1993). *The shadow of death: The hunt for a serial killer.* New York: Charles Scribner's Sons.

Godwin, J. (1978). *Murder USA: The ways we kill each other.* New York: Ballantine Books.

Goldstein, H. (1977). *Policing a free society.* Cambridge, MA: Ballinger.

Goodfellow, M. (1998, May 8). *Italian serial killer case widens.* Reuters.

Goodwin, G. (1938). *Peter Kurten: A study in sadism.* London: Acorn.

Grant, C. (1999, January 9). Spend, spend, spend killer: Like many of us Dana loved to shop. But when the cash ran out she couldn't stop so she financed her sprees by murder. *The Mirror,* pp. 26–27.

Gray, V., & Williams, G. (1980). *The organizational politics of criminal justice.* Lexington, MA: Lexington Books.

Graysmith, R. (1976). *Zodiac.* New York: Berkely Books, St. Martin's Press.

———. (1990). *The sleeping lady: The trailside murders above the Golden Gate.* New York: Dutton.

Green, T. J., & Whitmore, J. E. (1993, June). VICAP's role in multiagency serial murder investigations. *The Police Chief,* pp. 38–45.

Greombach, J. V. (1980). *The great liquidator.* New York: Doubleday.

Griffiths, R. (Producer and Director). (1993). *Murder by number* [Videotape]. Atlanta, GA: CNN.

Groth, A. H. (1979). *Men who rape: The psychology of the offender.* New York: Plenum.

Groth, A. H., Burgess, A. W., & Holmstrom, L. L. (1977). Rape, anger, and sexuality. *American Journal of Psychiatry, 134*(11), 1239–1243.

Gurwell, J. K. (1974). *Mass murder in Houston.* Houston: Cordovan Press.

Guttmacher, M. (1960). *The mind of the murderer.* New York: Grove Press.

Hare, R. D. (1993). *Without conscience.* New York: Pocket Books.

Hare, R. D., Forth, A. E., & Strachman, K. E. (1992). Psychopathy and crime across the life span. In R. D. Peters, R. J. McMahon, & V. L. Quinsey (Eds.), *Aggression and violence throughout the life span* (pp. 285–300). Newbury Park, CA: Sage.

Harrington, J., & Burger, R. (1993). *Eye of evil.* New York: St. Martin's Press.

Harris, T. (1981). *Red dragon.* New York: Putnam.

———. (1988). *The silence of the lambs.* New York: St. Martin's Press.

Harrison, F. (1986). *Brady and Hindley: Genesis of the moors murders.* New York: Ashgrove Press.

Hazelwood, R. R., Dietz, P. E., & Warren, J. (1992, February). The criminal sexual sadist. *FBI Law Enforcement Bulletin,* pp. 12–20.

Hazelwood, R. R., & Douglas, J. E. (1980, April). The lust murderer. *FBI Law Enforcement Bulletin,* pp. 1–5.

Hazelwood, R. R., Ressler, R. K., Depue, R. L., & Douglas, J. E. (1987). Criminal personality profiling: An overview. In R. R. Hazelwood & A. W. Burgess (Eds.), *Practical aspects of rape investigation: A multidisciplinary approach* (pp. 137–149). New York: Elsevier.

Heilbroner, D. (1993, August). Serial murder and sexual repression. *Playboy,* pp. 78, 147–150.

Heimer, M. (1971). *The cannibal. The case of Albert Fish.* New York: Lyle Stuart.

Heritage, R. (1994, March). *A facet model of sexual offending.* Paper presented at annual conference of Academy of Criminal Justice Sciences, Chicago.

Hetzel, R. L. (1985). The organization of a major incident room. *The Detective: The Journal of Army Criminal Investigation, 12*(1), 15–17.

Hickey, E. W. (1985). *Serial murderers: Profiles in psychopathology.* Paper presented at the annual meeting of the Academy of Criminal Justice Sciences, Las Vegas, Nevada.

———. (1997). *Serial murderers and their victims,* 2nd ed. Belmont, CA: Wadsworth.

Hilberry, C. (1987). *Luke Karamazov.* Detroit, MI: Wayne State University Press.

Holmes, R. M., & DeBurger, J. (1985, March 18). *Profiles in terror: The serial murderers.* Paper presented at the annual meeting of the Academy of Criminal Justice Sciences, Las Vegas, Nevada.

———. (1988). *Serial murder.* Newbury Park, CA: Sage.

Holmes, S. T., Hickey, E., & Holmes, R. M. (1991). Female serial murderesses: Constructing differentiating typologies. *Journal of Contemporary Criminal Justice, 7*(4), 245–256.

Howlett, J. B., Hanfland, K. A., & Ressler, R. K. (1986, December). The violent criminal apprehension program VICAP: A progress report. *FBI Law Enforcement Bulletin,* pp. 15–16.

Humes, E. (1991). *Buried secrets.* New York: Dutton.

Interpol General Secretariat. (1978). The I.C.P.O.—Interpol. *International Review of Criminal Policy, 34,* 93–96.

Isaacson, W. (1982, March 28). A web of fiber and fact. *Time,* p. 18.

Jackson, J., van Koppen, P. J., & Herbrink, J. C. M. (1993). *Does the service meet the needs? An evaluation of customer satisfaction with specific profile analysis and investigative advice as offered by the Scientific Advisory Unit of the National Criminal Intelligence Division (CRI), The Netherlands.* Netherlands Institute for the Study of Criminality and Law Enforcement.

———. (1993). *An expert/novice approach to offender profiling.* Netherlands Institute for the Study of Criminality and Law Enforcement.

Jaeger, R. W. (1991). *Massacre in Milwaukee: The macabre case of Jeffrey Dahmer.* Oregon, WI: Waubesa Press.

James, E. W. K. (1991). *Catching serial killers: Learning from past serial murder investigations.* Lansing, MI: International Forensic Services.

Jenkins, P. (1989). Serial murder in the United States 1900–1940: A historical perspective. *Journal of Criminal Justice, 17,* 377–392.

———. (1992). *Intimate enemies: Moral panics in contemporary Great Britain.* New York: Aldine De Gruyter.

———. (1995, January). The inner darkness: Serial murder and the nature of evil. *Chronicles: A Magazine of American Culture, 19,* 16–19.

Jenkins, P., & Donovan, E. (1987, July–August). Serial murder on campus. *Campus Law Enforcement Journal,* pp. 42–44.

Jesse, F. T. (1924). *Murder and its motive.* New York: Knopf.

Johnson, K. W. (1977). *Police interagency relations: Some research findings.* Beverly Hills, CA: Sage.

Jouve, N. W. (1986). *"The street cleaner": The Yorkshire ripper case on trial.* London: Marion Boyers.

Karmen, A. (1983). Deviants as victims. In D. E. MacNamara & A. Karmen (Eds.), *Deviants: Victims or victimized?* (pp. 237–254). Beverly Hills, CA: Sage.

Karpman, B. (1954). *The sexual offender and his offenses.* New York: Julian Press.

Kasindorf, J. R. (1993, August 9). The bad seed. *New York,* pp. 38–45.

Katz, J. (1982). A theory of qualitative methodology: The social system of analytic fieldwork. In R. M. Emerson (Ed.), *Contemporary field research* (pp. 127–148). Boston: Little, Brown.

Kennedy, D. (1992). *On a killing day: The bizarre story of convicted murderer Aileen "Lee" Wuornos.* Chicago: Bonus Books.

Kennedy, L. (1961). *10 Rillington Place.* London: Gollancz.

Keppel, R. D. (1989). *Serial murder: Future implications for police investigations.* Cincinnati, OH: Anderson.

Keppel, R., & Weis, J. (1993, August). *Improving the investigation of violent crime: The Homicide Investigation and Tracking System.* Washington, DC: National Institute of Justice.

Keppel, R. D., Weis, J. G., & Lamoria, R. D. (1990). *Improving the investigation of murder: The Homicide Information and Tracking System (HITS)* (Grant No. 87-IJ-CX-0026). Washington, DC: National Institute of Justice, U.S. Department of Justice.

Kershaw, A. (1999, March 27). Death on the rails. *The Guardian,* p. 38.

Kessler, R. (1984, February 20). Crime profiles. *Washington Post,* pp. 1, 16.

Keyes, D. (1986). *Unveiling Claudia: A true story of serial murder.* New York: Bantam.

Keyes, E. (1976). *The Michigan murders.* New York: Pocket Books.

Kidder, T. (1974). *The road to Yuba City.* Garden City, NY: Doubleday.

King, C. (1992). *Mama's boy.* New York: Pocket Books.

King, G. C. (1993). *Driven to kill.* New York: Pinnacle Books.

King, H., & Chambliss, W. J. (1984). *Harry King: A professional thief's journey.* New York: Wiley.

———. (1992). *A passing acquaintance.* New York: Carlton Press.

———. (n.d.). *The use of psychics in a serial murder investigation.* Unpublished paper.

Kraus, R. T. (1995). An enigmatic personality: Case report of a serial killer. *Journal of Orthomolecular Medicine, 10*(1).

Krivich, M. (1993). *Comrade Chikatilo: The psychopathology of Russia's notorious serial killer.* Fort Lee, NJ: Barricade Books.

Lane, B., & Gregg, W. (1992). *The encyclopedia of serial killers.* London: Headline House.

Laytner, R. (1998, December 6). Murderer of 350 children free to slaughter more. *Scotland on Sunday,* p. 19.

Lederman, D. (1993, July 17). Campuses search for proper response to letter bombing of 2 professors. *Chronicle of Higher Education*, pp. 18–19.

Leith, R. (1983). *The prostitute murders: The people v. Richard Cottingham.* New York: Lyle Stuart.

Leonard, V. A. (1980). *Fundamentals of law enforcement.* St. Paul, MN: West.

Levin, J., & Fox, J. A. (1985). *Mass murder.* New York: Plenum.

Leyton, E. (1986). *Hunting humans: The rise of the modern multiple murderer.* Toronto, Ont.: McClelland & Stewart.

Lichfield, J. (1999, June 18). French 'angel of mercy' is charged with murder. *The Independent (London)*, p. 17.

Liebert, J. A. (1985, December). Contributions of psychiatric consultation in the investigation of serial murder. *International Journal of Offender Therapy and Comparative Criminology, 29,* 187–199.

Lindsey, R. (1984, January 21). Officials cite a rise in killers who roam U.S. for victims. *New York Times*, pp. 1, 7.

Linedecker, C. L. (1980). *The man who killed boys.* New York: St. Martin's Press.

———. (1990). *Serial thrill killers.* New York: Knightsbridge.

———. (1991). *Night stalker.* New York: St. Martin's Press.

Linedecker, C. L., & Burt, W. A. (1990). *Nurses who kill.* New York: Pinnacle.

Long trail to find Black. (1994, May 20). *The Independent*, p. 3.

Lourie, R. (1993). *Hunting the devil: The pursuit, capture, and confession of the most savage killer in history.* New York: HarperCollins.

Lunde, D. T. (1976). *Murder and madness.* Stanford, CA: Stanford Alumni Association.

Lunde, D. T., & Morgan, J. (1980). *The die song: A journey into the mind of a mass murderer.* San Francisco: San Francisco Book Company.

Lundsgaarde, H. P. (1977). *Murder in space city.* New York: Oxford University Press.

MacDonald, J. M. (1961). *The murderer and his victim.* Springfield, IL: Charles C Thomas.

MacKay, R. (1994, May). Violent crime analysis. *The RCMP Gazette*, pp. 11–14.

MacNamara, M. (1990, November). Letters from San Quentin: Playing for time. *Vanity Fair*, pp. 80, 86, 88, 90, 92.

Maghan, J., & Sagarin, E. (1983). Homosexuals as victimizers and victims. In D. E. J. MacNamara & A. Karmen (Eds.), *Deviants: Victims or victimized* (pp. 147–162). Beverly Hills, CA: Sage.

Magid, K., & McKelvey, C. A. (1987). *High risk: Children without a conscience.* New York: Bantam.

Marchbanks, D. (1966). *The moors murders.* London: Frewin.

Mariani, T., & Stover, M. (1999, March 18). Police tight-lipped on nature of evidence sent for analysis. *San Luis Obispo Telegram Tribune*, p. 1.

Markman, R., & Dominick, B. (1989). *Alone with the devil: Famous cases of a courtroom psychiatrist.* New York: Doubleday.

Marsh, H. L. (1989, September). Newspaper crime coverage in the U.S.: 1983–1988. *Criminal Justice Abstracts*, pp. 506–514.

Masters, B. (1985). *Killing for company: The case of Dennis Nilsen.* London: J. Cape.

———. (1991, May). Dahmer's inferno. *Vanity Fair,* pp. 183–189, 264–269.

———. (1993). *The shrine of Jeffrey Dahmer.* London: Hodder & Stoughton.

McCarthy, K. (1984, June 28). Serial killers: Their deadly bent may be set in cradle. *Los Angeles Times,* p. 1.

McCauley, R. P. (1973). *A place for the implementation of a state-wide regional police system.* Unpublished doctoral dissertation, South Houston State University, Huntsville, Texas.

McDougal, D. (1991). *Angel of darkness.* New York: Warner Books.

McIntyre, T. (1988). *Wolf in sheep's clothing: The search for a child killer.* Detroit, MI: Wayne State University Press.

Megargee, E. I. (1982). Psychological determinants and correlates of criminal violence. In M. E. Wolfgang & N. A. Weiner (Eds.), *Criminal Violence* (pp. 14–23). Beverly Hills, CA: Sage.

Meloy, J. R. (1988). *The psychopathic mind: Origins, dynamics, and treatment.* Northvale, NJ: Jason Aronson.

———. (1989). Serial murder: A four-book review. *Journal of Psychiatry and Law,* pp. 85–108.

———. (1992). *Violent attachments.* Northvale, NJ: Jason Aronson.

Meredith, N. (1984, December). The murder epidemic. *Science, 84,* 4348.

Michaud, S. G. (1989, October 26). The F.B.I.'s new psyche squad. *New York Times Magazine,* pp. 40, 42, 50, 74, 76–77.

———. (1994). *Lethal shadow.* New York: Onyx.

Michaud, S. G., & Aynesworth, H. (1983). *The only living witness.* New York: Linden Press/Simon & Schuster.

———. (1989). *Ted Bundy: Conversations with a killer.* New York: New American Library.

Miller, R. (1999, June 20). The highway to hell that connects the rape and murder of 33 girls. *Mail on Sunday,* pp. 10–11.

Miller, T. (1993, September). Death row: Ray and Faye Copeland. *Police,* pp. 62–66.

Millikan, R. (1994, December 13). Backpacker murders. *The Independent,* p. 15.

Mitchell, E. W. (1993). *The Copeland killings.* New York: Pinnacle Books.

———. (1999). *The aetiology of serial murder: Towards an integrated model.* Unpublished thesis, University of Cambridge, Cambridge, United Kingdom.

Moore, K., & Reed, D. (1988). *Deadly medicine.* New York: St. Martin's Press.

Morris, T., & Bloom-Cooper, L. (1964). *A calendar of murder.* London: Michael Joseph.

Moseley, R. (2000, February 1). Setting grisly record, British doctor convicted of killing 15. *Chicago Tribune,* p. 6.

Mott, N. L. (1999). Serial murder: Patterns in unsolved cases. *Homicide Studies, 3*(3), 241–255.

Mowday, B. E. (1984, July 26–29). Computer tracking violent criminals. *Police Product News,* p. 7.

Myre, D. C. (1974). *Death investigation.* Washington, DC: International Association of Chiefs of Police.

Naisbitt, J. (1982). *Megatrends.* New York: Warner Books.

Nelson, T. (1984, March 23). Serial killings on increase, study shows. *Houston Post,* p. 11.

Nettler, G. (1982). *Killing one another, Vol. 2: Criminal careers.* Cincinnati, OH: Anderson.

Neville, R., & Clark, J. (1979). *The life and crimes of Charles Sobhraj.* London: Jonathan Cape.

Newton, M. (1988). *Mass murder: An annotated bibliography.* New York: Garland.

———. (1990). *Hunting humans: An encyclopedia of serial murder.* Port Townsend, WA: Loompanics Unlimited.

———. (1992). *Serial slaughter.* Port Townsend, WA: Loompanics.

———. (2000). *The encyclopedia of serial killers.* New York: Checkmark.

Newton, M. B., & Newton, B. C. (1985, October 18). *Geoforensic identification of localized serial crime.* Paper presented at the Southwest Division of American Geographers Meeting, Denton, Texas.

Newton, M. B., & Swoope, E. A. (1987). *Geoforensic analysis of localized serial murder: The hillside stranglers located.* Unpublished manuscript.

Nickel, S. (1989). *Torso: The story of Eliot Ness and the search for a psychopathic killer.* Winston-Salem, NC: J. F. Blair.

Norris, J. (1989). *Serial killers.* New York: Anchor Books.

Norton, C. (1994). *Disturbed ground: The true story of a diabolical female serial killer.* New York: William Morrow.

Office of Juvenile Justice and Delinquency Prevention. (1983). *National missing/abducted children and serial murder tracking and prevention program.* Washington, DC: U.S. Department of Justice.

———. (1983, November 20). *Memo.* Washington, DC: U.S. Department of Justice.

Olsen, J. (1974). *The man with the candy: the story of the Houston mass murders.* New York: Simon & Schuster.

———. (1993). *The misbegotten son: A serial killer and his victims. The true story of Arthur J. Shawcross.* New York: Delacorte Press.

Osterburg, J. W., & Ward, R. H. (1992). *Criminal investigation: A method for reconstructing the past.* Cincinnati, OH: Anderson.

Palmiotto, M. J. (1988). *Critical issues in criminal investigation,* 2nd ed. Cincinnati: Anderson.

Paretsky, A. (1991, April 28). Soft spot for serial murder. *New York Times,* Section 6, p. 9.

Penn, G. (1987). *Times 17: The amazing story of the Zodiac murder in California and Massachusetts.* San Francisco: Foxglove Press.

Pettit, M. (1990). *A need to kill.* New York: Ivy Books.

Philpin, J., & Donnelly, J. (1994). *Beyond murder: The inside account of the Gainesville student murders.* New York: Onyx.

Pinizzotto, A. J. (1984). Forensic psychology: Criminal personality profiling. *Journal of Police Science and Administration, 12*(1), 32–37.

Pinto, S., & Wilson, P. R. (1990). Serial murder. *Trends and Issues in Crime and Criminal Justice,* No. 25. Canberra: Australian Institute of Criminology.

Porter, B. (1983, April). Mind hunters. *Psychology Today,* pp. 1–8.

Pretsky, R., Cohen, M., & Seghorn, T. (1985). Development of a rational taxonomy for the classification of rapists: The Massachusetts treatment center system. *Bulletin of the American Academy of Psychiatry Law, 13*(1), 39–70.

Pron, N., & Duncanson, J. (1994, May 1). Six sex slayings may be linked. *The Toronto Star,* p. 5.

Rae, G. W. (1967). *Confessions of the Boston strangler.* New York: Pyramid.

Regional Information Sharing Systems (RISS). (1984). *The RISS projects: A federal partnership with state and local law enforcement.* Washington, DC: Bureau of Justice Assistance.

Regional Organized Crime Information Center (ROCIC). (1985, January). *ROCIC Bulletin,* p. 13.

Reinhardt, J. M. (1960). *The murderous trail of Charles Starkweather.* Springfield, IL: Charles C. Thomas.

———. (1962). *The psychology of a strange killer.* Springfield, IL: Charles C. Thomas.

Reiser, M. (1982, March). Crime-specific psychological consultation. *The Police Chief,* pp. 53–56.

Ressler, R. K. (1992). *Whoever fights monsters.* New York: St. Martin's Press.

Ressler, R. K., et al. (1982). *Criminal profiling research on homicide.* Unpublished research report.

———. (1984). *Serial murder: A new phenomenon of homicide.* Paper presented at the annual meeting of the International Association of Forensic Sciences, Oxford, England, September 17.

Ressler, R. K., Burgess, A. W., & Douglas, J. E. (1988). *Sexual homicide.* Lexington, MA: Lexington Books.

Ressler, R. K., Burgess, A. W., Hartman, C. R., Douglas, J. E., & McCormack, A. (1986). Murderers who rape and mutilate. *Journal of Interpersonal Violence, 1*(3), 273–287.

Restak, R. M. (1992, July–August). See no evil. *The Sciences,* pp. 16–21.

Reuters News Service. (1995, August 10). Station strangler is charged.

Revitch, E., & Schlesinger, L. B. (1978). Murder, evaluation, classification, and prediction. In I. L. Kutash, S. B. Kutash, L. B. Schlesinger, & Associates (Eds.), *Violence: Perspectives on murder and aggression* (pp. 138–164). San Francisco: Jossey-Bass.

———. (1981). *Psychopathology of homicide.* Springfield, IL: Charles C Thomas.

Reynolds, M. (1992). *Dead ends.* New York: Warner Books.

Ritchie, J. (1988). *Myra Hindley: Inside the mind of a murderess.* London: Angus & Robertson.

Rogers, R., Craig, D., & Anderson, D. (1991, March). *Serial murder investigations and geographic information systems.* Paper presented at the annual conference of the Academy of Criminal Justice Sciences, Nashville, Tennessee.

Rose, H. M. (1979). *Lethal aspects of urban violence.* Lexington, MA: D. C. Heath.

Rosenbaum, R. (1993, April). The FBI's agent provocateur. *Vanity Fair,* pp. 122–136.

Rossmo, D. K. (1995). *Geographical profiling: Target patterns of serial murderers.* Unpublished dissertation, Simon Frasier University, Vancouver.

Royal Canadian Mounted Police. (1993, July) *VICLAS: Violent Crime Linkage Analysis System.* Crime Analysis Report Form 3364 Eng. (93-07), 1993.

Rule, A. (1980). *The stranger beside me.* New York: New American Library.

Rumbelow, D. (1988). *Jack the ripper: The complete casebook.* New York: Berkley.

Samenow, S. E. (1984). *Inside the criminal mind.* New York: Times Books.

Sam Houston State University Criminal Justice Center. (1983). *National Missing/ Abducted Children and Serial Murder Tracking and Prevention Program.* Grant application to Office of Juvenile Justice and Delinquency Prevention, U.S. Department of Justice, Huntsville, Texas.

Sare, J. (1986, March 7). Other slaying linked to Lancaster suspect. *Dallas Morning News,* pp. 1, 43.

Schaefer, G. J. (1990). *Killer fiction: Tales of an accused serial killer.* Atlanta, GA: Media Queen.

Schechter, H. (1990). *Deranged: The shocking true story of America's most fiendish killer.* New York: Pocket Books.

Schreiber, F. R. (1983). *The shoemaker: The anatomy of a psychotic.* New York: Simon & Schuster.

Schwartz, A. E. (1992). *The man who could not kill enough: The secret murders of Milwaukee's Jeffrey Dahmer.* Secaucus, NJ: Carol Publishing Group.

Schwartz, H., & Jacobs, J. (1979). *Qualitative sociology.* New York: The Free Press.

Schwarz, T. (1981). *The hillside strangler: A murderer's mind.* New York: Doubleday.

Scott, H. (1992). *The female serial killer: A well kept secret of the 'gentler sex.'* Unpublished thesis, University of Guelph, Guelph, Ontario.

Sears, D. J. (1991). *To kill again: The motivation and development of serial murder.* Wilmington, DE: SR Books.

Sereny, G. (1972). *The case of Mary Bell.* London: Methuen.

Serial killers and murderers. (1991). Lincolnwood, IL: Publications International.

Sewell, J. D. (1985). An application of Megargee's algebra of aggression to the case of Theodore Bundy. *Journal of Police and Criminal Psychology, 1,* 14–24.

———. (1991). Trauma stress of multiple murder investigations. *Journal of Traumatic Stress, 6*(1), 103–118.

Shaw, C. (1930). *The jack-roller.* Chicago: University of Chicago Press.

Sifakis, C. (1982). *The encyclopedia of American crime.* New York: Facts on File.

Skogan, W. G., & Antunes, G. E. (1979). Information, apprehension, and deterrence: Exploring the limits of police productivity. *Journal of Criminal Justice, 7,* 217–241.

Skrapec, C. (1984). *Psychological profiling and serial murderers.* Unpublished paper.

Smith, B. (1960). *Police systems in the United States,* 2nd ed., revised. New York: Harper & Row.

Smith, C., & Guillen, T. (1991). *The search for the Green River killer.* New York: Onyx.

Smith, H. (1987). Serial killers. *Criminal Justice International, 3*(1), 1, 4.

Smith, P. (1988, May 9). The literature of the American serial killer. *Cite AB,* pp. 1933–1988.

Snider, D., & Clausen, T. (1987). *A typology of serial murder.* Unpublished paper.

Sonnenschein, A. (1985, February). Serial killers. *Penthouse.* pp. 32, 34–35, 44, 128, 132–134.

Spiering, F. (1978). *Prince Jack.* New York: Jove.

Staff. (1969, July 30). State police to take charge of co-ed murder investigation. *Detroit News,* p. 1.

Staff. (1980, December 22). FBI develops profile to change face of sex probes. *Law Enforcement News,* p. 7.

Staff. (1983). Paying a murderer for evidence. *Criminal Justice Ethics,* Summer–Fall, pp. 47–55.

Staff. (1984, April 25). Police search for killer of red-haired women. *Tennessean,* p. 1.

Staff. (1986, December 5). Police track serial killer with commercial DBMS. *Government News,* p. 78.

Staff. (1999, October 3). Trial told of butchery skills of alleged British serial killer. *The Herald (Glasgow),* p. 8.

Staff. (2000, October 18). Yates to plead guilty. *The Seattle Times,* p. 1.

Starr, M., et al. (1984, November 26). The random killers. *Newsweek,* pp. 100–106.

State police to take charge of co-ed murder investigation. (1969, July 30). *Detroit News,* p. 1.

Stewart, J. R. (1992, January). A kiss for my killer. *Redbook,* pp. 76–83.

Storr, A. (1972). *Human destructiveness.* New York: Basic Books.

Strecher, V. G. (1957). *An administrative analysis of a multiple-agency criminal investigation within the suburban district of a large metropolitan area.* Unpublished master's thesis, Michigan State University, East Lansing.

Sullivan, T., & Maiken, P. (1983). *Killer clown.* New York: Grosset & Dunlap.

Sutherland, E. (1937). *The professional thief.* Chicago: University of Chicago Press.

Swanson, C. R., Chamelin, N. C., & Terrieto, L. (1984). *Criminal investigation.* New York: Random House.

Sweat, J. A., & Durm, M. W. (1993). Psychics: Do police departments really use them? *Skeptical Inquirer,* pp. 148–165.

Tanay, E. (n.d.). *The murderers.* Unpublished report.

Thibault, E. A., Lynch, L. M., & McBride, R. B. (1985). *Proactive police management.* Englewood Cliffs, NJ: Prentice Hall.

Thomas, J. (1993, September 29). Preble County strangler: The case of the clueless cops. *Gaybeat,* pp. 2, 6, 10, 13, 16.

Thompson, T. (1979). *Serpentine.* New York: Dell.

Travis, L. F., III. (1983). The case study in criminal justice research: Applications to policy analysis. *Criminal Justice Review, 8*(2), 46–51.

Treen, J. (1993, January 25). The killing field. *People,* pp. 74–80.

Tunnell, K. D., & Cox, T. C. (1991). Sexually aggressive murder: A case study. *Journal of Contemporary Criminal Justice, 7*(4), 232–244.

U.S. Congress. House. Committee on Government Operations. Government Information, Justice, and Agriculture Subcommittee. (1986). *The federal role in investigation of serial violent crime: Hearings before a subcommittee of the Committee on Government Operations, House of Representatives, Ninety-ninth Congress, second session, April 9 and May 21, 1986.* Washington, DC: U.S. Government Printing Office.

U.S. Congress. Senate. Committee on the Judiciary. (1984). *Serial murders: Hearing before the Subcommittee on Juvenile Justice of the Committee on the Judiciary, United States Senate, Ninety-eighth Congress, first session, on patterns of murders committed by one person, in large numbers with no apparent rhyme, reason, or motivation, July 12, 1983.* Washington, DC: U.S. Government Printing Office.

U.S. Department of Justice. *Uniform Crime Report, 1982.* Washington, DC: U.S. Government Printing Office.

————. (1994). *Crime Report, 1993.* Washington, DC: U.S. Government Printing Office.

————. (1999). *Crime Report, 1998.* Washington, DC: U.S. Government Printing Office.

VICAP Alert. (1992, February). *FBI Law Enforcement Bulletin,* pp. 20–21.

Villasenor, V. (1977). *Jury: The people vs. Juan Corona.* Boston: Little, Brown.

Vollmer, A. (1936). *The police and modern society.* Berkeley: Regents of University of California.

Wade, G., Davis, R. M., & Modafferi, P. A. (1993, September). Developing a model police for the multi-agency investigation of violent crime. *The Police Chief,* pp. 27–30.

Wagner, M. S. (1932). *The monster of Dusseldorf.* London: Faber.

Walstad, B. (1994). *Police use of psychics: Results of a 1993 questionnaire.* Unpublished manuscript.

Wambaugh, J. (1989). *The blooding.* New York: Perigord Press.

Wertham, F. (1966). *A sign for Cain.* New York: Paperback Library.

West, D. J. (1987). *Sexual crimes and confrontations: A study of victims and offenders.* Brookfield, VT: Gower.

Wilkinson, A. (1994, April 18). Conversation with a killer. *The New Yorker,* pp. 58–76.

Willie, W. S. (1975). *Citizens who commit murder: A psychiatric study.* St. Louis, MO: Warren H. Green.

Wilmer, M. A. P. (1970). *Crime and information theory.* Edinburgh: University Press.

Wilson, C., & Putnam, P. (1961). *The encyclopedia of murder.* New York: Putnam.

Wilson, C., & Seaman, D. (1983). *The encyclopedia of modern murder, 1962–1982.* New York: Putnam.

————. (1990). *The serial killers.* New York: Carol Publishing Group.

Wilson, J. Q. (1978). *The investigators.* New York: Basic Books.

Wilson, P. R. (1988). *Murder of the innocents: Child-killers and their victims.* Rigby, Australia: Adelaide.

Winn, S., & Merrill, D. (1980). *Ted Bundy: The killer next door.* New York: Bantam.

Wood, W. P. (1994). *The bone garden: The Sacramento boardinghouse murders.* New York: Pocket Books.

Wroe, G. (1999, April 18). Touching evil. *The Sunday Herald,* p. 6.

Yin, R. K. (1984). *Case study research: Design and methods.* Beverly Hills, CA: Sage.

Yallop, D. (1982). *Deliver us from evil.* New York: Coward, McCann.

Zahn, M. A. (1980). Homicide in the twentieth century. In J. A. Meicude & C. Farepel (Eds.), *History and crime: Implications for criminal justice policy.* Beverly Hills, CA: Sage.

———. (1981). Homicide in America: A research review. In I. L. Barak-Glantz & R. Huff (Eds.), *The mad, the bad, and the different: Essays in honor of Simon Dinitz* (pp. 43–55). Lexington, MA: Lexington Books.

Case Study Source Material

Theodore Robert Bundy

Books

Kendall, E. (1981). *The phantom prince: My life with Ted Bundy.* Seattle, WA: Madrona Publishers.

Larsen, R. W. (1980). *Bundy: The deliberate stranger.* Englewood Cliffs, NJ: Prentice Hall.

Michaud, S. G., & Aynesworth, H. (1983). *The only living witness.* New York: Linden Press.

Rule, A. (1980). *The stranger beside me.* New York: W. W. Norton.

Winn, S., & Merrill, D. (1980). *Ted Bundy: The killer next door.* New York: Bantam.

Magazine Articles

Bundy: Guilty. (1979, August 6). *Time,* p. 22.

Camera in the courtroom. (1979, July 23). *Time,* p. 22.

The case of the Chi Omega killer. (1979, July 16). *Time,* pp. 12, 13.

Marsh, H. L. (1989, September). Newspaper crime coverage in the U.S.: 1983–1988. *Criminal Justice Abstracts,* pp. 506–514.

Newspaper Articles

Jacksonville Journal, June 19, 1984.

Lake City Reporter (Florida), May 10 and 13, 1985.

Orlando Sentinel, February 10, 1980.

Sentinel Star (Orlando, Florida), June 30, July 15, August 1, 1979; March 16, May 20, 1982; May 10, 1985.

Other Sources

Interviews with Robert D. Keppel, Investigator, Attorney General's Office, State of Washington. (various dates 1983–1985).

King County Department of Public Safety. (1974). Summary of events July 14 and September 7. Seattle, WA: King County Department of Public Safety, Case No. 74-123376.

Letter from R. D. Keppel to R. H. Robertson, September 26, 1983, regarding Bundy's travels, known victims, and list of ninety similar victims.

JEFFREY DAHMER

Books and Reports

Davis, J. (1991). *Milwaukee murders: Nightmare in Apt. 213.* New York: St. Martin's Press.

Dietz, P. (1992, February 15). *Statement of Dr. Park Dietz, M.D., in reaction to Dahmer verdict.* Press release.

Dvorchak, R. J., & Holewa, L. (1991) *Milwaukee massacre.* New York: Dell.

Fisher, H. (1992). *Jeffrey Dahmer: An unauthorized biography of a serial killer.* Champaign, IL: Boneyard Press.

Jaeger, R. W., & Balousek, M. W. (1991). *Massacre in Milwaukee.* Madison, WI: Waubesa Press.

The Mayor's Citizen Commission on Police–Community Relations. (1991, October 15). *A Report to Mayor John O. Norquist and the Board of Fire and Police Commissioners.*

Norris, J. (1992). *Jeffrey Dahmer.* New York: Shadow Long Press.

Schwartz, A. E. (1992). *The man who could not kill enough: The secret murders of Milwaukee's Jeffrey Dahmer.* Secaucus, NJ: Carol Publishing.

Simon, R. I. (1996). *Bad men do what good men dream.* Washington, DC: American Psychiatric Press.

Journal and Magazine Articles

Black men tragic victims of white Milwaukee man's gruesome murder spree. (1991, August 12). *Jet,* pp. 16–17.

Caplan, L. (1992, March 2). Not so nutty. *New Republic,* pp. 18–20.

Chin, P. (1991, August 12). The door of evil. *People Weekly,* pp. 32–37.

Chin, P., & Tamarkin, C. (1991, August 12). The door of evil. *People,* p. 34.

Dahmer. (1984, November 26). *Newsweek,* p. 106.

Davids, D. (1992, February). The serial murderer as superstar. *McCalls,* p. 150.

DeBenedictis, D. J. (1992, April). Sane serial killer. *ABA Journal,* pp. 22, 78.

Dietz, Dr. Park. (1992, February 12). Court testimony. *Court TV.*

Gelman, D. (1991, August 5). The secrets of Apt. 213. *Newsweek,* pp. 40–42.

I carried it too far, that's for sure. (1992, May–June). *Psychology Today,* pp. 28–31.

Jeffrey Dahmer. (1991, January 6). *People Weekly,* p. 70.

Jeffrey Dahmer. (1992, December 30). *People Weekly,* p. 25.

The jury finds Dahmer sane. (1992, March 2). *Jet,* p. 15.

Kaufman, I. (1982, August). The insanity plea on trial. *New York Times Magazine,* p. 18.

Kaplan, D. A. (1992, February 3). Secrets of a serial killer. *Newsweek,* pp. 45–51.

Mackenzie, H. (1991, September 23). Infamous in Milwaukee. *MacLean's,* p. 28.

Masters, B. (1991, November). Dahmer's inferno. *Vanity Fair,* pp. 183–189, 264–269.

Mathews, T. (1992, February 3). Secrets of a serial killer. *Newsweek,* pp. 46–49.

Mathews, T. (1992, February 10). He wanted to listen to my heart. *Newsweek,* p. 31.

Miller, A. (1991, August 12). Serial murder aftershocks. *Newsweek,* pp. 28–29.

Post-mortem on the Dahmer trial coverage. (1992, February 29). *Editor & Publisher,* pp. 9, 125.

Prudhome, A. (1991, August 5). The little flat of horrors. *Time,* p. 26.

Prudhome, A. (1991, August 12). Did they all have to die? *Time,* p. 28.

Restak, R. M. (1992). See no evil: Blaming the brain for criminal violence. *The Sciences,* July–August, pp. 16–21.

Salholz, E. (1992, February 3). Insanity: A defense of last resort. *Newsweek,* p. 49.

Schneider, K. S. (1992, March 2). Day of reckoning. *People Weekly,* pp. 38–39.

Secrets of a killer. (1992, February 3). *Newsweek,* pp. 44–47.

Secrets of a serial killer. (1992, February 3). *Newsweek,* p. 49.

The Socrates option. (1992, May 24). *Reason,* p. 47.

So guilty they're innocent. (1992, March 2). *National Review,* pp. 17–18.

Tayman, J. C. (1991, August 12). The door of evil. *People,* pp. 32–35.

Toufexis, A. (1992, February 3). Do mad acts a madman make? *Time,* p. 17.

Treen, J., Toufexis, A., & Tamarkin, C. (1992, August 20). Probing the mind of the I-70 killer. *People Weekly,* pp. 37, 75–78.

Wroe, G. (1995, November 19). The real life Hannibal Lecter. *Mail on Sunday,* p. 49.

Newspaper Articles

Dahmer is given life in prison. (1992, February 18). *Boston Globe,* p. 3.

Dahmer shocks even expert on deviant psyches. (1992, February 18). *Los Angeles Times,* p. B4.

Defense gears for battle over Dahmer's sanity. (1992, January 26). *Springfield* (Illinois) *State Journal Register,* p. 3.

Expert: Dahmer sought control. (1992, February 9). *Boston Herald-American,* p. 4.

Expert says killer lived for morbid sex fantasies. (1992, February 6). *Boston Herald-American,* p. 3.

Expert tells of Dahmer's twisted acts. (1992, February 5). *Boston Herald-American,* p. 1.

He wanted "excitement, gratification." (1992, February 3). *USA Today,* p. 3A.

A horror warning for Dahmer trial. (1992, January 28). *Chicago Sun-Times,* p. 14.

Juror: Dahmer is a con artist. (1992, February 16). *Springfield* (Illinois) *State Journal Register,* p. 1.

Jury debates Dahmer's sanity after hearing final arguments. (1992, February 15). *Springfield* (Illinois) *State Journal Register,* p. 3.

Killer-cannibal Dahmer declared sane by jury. (1992, February 16). *Boston Herald-American,* p. 2.

Lawyer: Dahmer drawn to sex with the dead. (1992, January 31). *Springfield* (Illinois) *State Journal Register.*

Necrophilia drove Dahmer. (1992, February 9). *Decatur* (Illinois) *Herald & Review,* p. A4.

Officers dismissed in Dahmer case lose bid to get their job back. (1992, November 29). *New York Times,* p. 35.

Officers in Dahmer's case try to regain jobs. (1992, October 12). *New York Times,* p. 7.

Police in Dahmer case admit making error. (1992, October 17). *New York Times,* p. 14.

Psychiatrist: Dahmer gave up idea of freeze-drying victim. (1992, February 13). *Springfield* (Illinois) *State Journal Register.*

Psychiatrist says Dahmer fought his necrophilia. (1992, February 4). *Chicago Sun-Times,* p. 5.

Two serial killers' day in court. (1992, January 28). *USA Today,* p. 3A.

Victims' kin bring anger for Dahmer. (1992, January 29). *Chicago Tribune.*

Witness: Dahmer said he'd "eat my heart." (1992, February 1). *Springfield* (Illinois) *State Journal Register,* p. 3.

JOHN WAYNE GACY

Books

Gacy, J. W. (1991). *A question of doubt: The John Wayne Gacy story.* (C. I. McClelland, Ed.).

Kozenczak, J., & Henrickson, K. (1992). *A passing acquaintance.* New York: Carlton Press.

Linedecker, C. L. (1980). *The man who killed boys.* New York: St. Martin's Press.

Sullivan, T., & Maiken, P. T. (1983). *Killer clown: The John Wayne Gacy murders.* New York: St. Martin's Press.

Magazine Articles

Darrach, B., & Norris, J. (1984, August). An American tragedy. *Life,* pp. 58–74.

Double life of a clown. (1979, January). *Newsweek,* pp. 24, 93.

Wilkinson, A. (1994, April 18). Conversation with a killer. *The New Yorker,* pp. 58–76.

Newspaper Articles

New York Times, December, 23, 24, 25, 28, 29, 30, 31, 1978; January 1, 2, 3, 8, 9, 10, 11, 12; March 1, 3, 11, 17; April 8, 10, 24, 1979; January 28, 29; February 2, 7, 16, 17, 22, 23, 24; March 8, 9, 11, 12, 13, 14, 16, 27; April 1; May 4, 1980; September 8, 1984.

Washington Post, March 3, 1980.

Other Sources

Osanka, F. (1980, March 6). Sociological evaluation of John Wayne Gacy for W. J. Kunkle, Jr.

"HILLSIDE STRANGLER"

Books

Schwarz, T. (1981). The hillside strangler: A murderer's mind. New York: Doubleday.

Newspaper Articles

Bellingham (Washington) *Herald,* January 1, 1980.

Glendale (California) *News Press,* February 22, 1979.

Houston Chronicle, February 5, 1984.

Los Angeles Daily News, August 18; November 16, 19; December 2, 1982; January 7; March 20, 28; April 27, 29; May 4; June 22; August 3, 8; September 3, 29; November 1, 4, 7, 9, 11, 14, 15, 17, 18, 19, 20, 23, 25, 1983; January 5, 11, 14; March 19, 1984; January 14, 1985.

Los Angeles Herald Examiner, March 8, 1978; January 7; March 30; April 29; November 14, 15, 16; October 2, 16; November 2, 20, 21, 23, 25, 1983; January 8, 11; March 19, 31, 1984.

Los Angeles Times, November 22, 1977; August 22, 1978; January 1; March 5, 20, 27; May 6, 8, 12, 13; June 13, 17; September 11; October 3, 4, 6, 22, 25; November 14; December 4, 6, 1980; January 6; February 6; March 15; July 7, 8, 11, 13, 22, 23, 27, 29, 30, 31; August 6, 7, 9, 10, 11, 13, 14, 21, 28, 29; October 5, 23, 1981; February 8, 11, 27; March 2, 3, 4, 8, 9, 10, 11, 12, 15, 17, 19, 24, 25; April 6, 9, 14, 27, 29; May 31; June 5, 24; July 1, 8; October 4, 13, 26; November 1, 8, 10, 1982; January 7; February 24; September 2; October 21; November 1, 2, 4, 6, 8, 9, 10, 11, 12, 15, 16, 17, 19, 30, 1983; January 5; March 9, 19; August 19, 1984.

New York Times, February 24, 1979.

San Francisco Chronicle, May 7, 1994.

Other Sources

Barnes, M. (Producer and Director). (1984). *The mind of a murderer* [Videotape]. Washington, DC: Public Broadcasting Service.

Interviews with Frank Salerno, Sergeant, Los Angeles Sheriff's Office. (various dates, 1983–1985).

HENRY LEE LUCAS

Books

Call, M. (1985). *Hand of death: The Henry Lee Lucas story.* Lafayette, LA: Prescott Press.

Larson, B. (1984). *The story of mass-murderer Henry Lee Lucas.* Boulder, CO: Bob Larson.

Magazine Article
Cuba, N. (1985, July). The life and deaths of Henry Lee Lucas. *Third Coast,* 4(12), 44–59.

Newspaper Articles
Atlanta Constitution, April 10, 1985.

Atlanta Journal, December 21, 1984; April 22, 1985.

Austin American Statesman, June 29; July 3; November 23, December 8, 1983; March 9, 12; April 4, 18, 24; May 11; July 26, 1984; April 21, 1985.

Avalanche Journal (Lubbock, Texas), June 3, 4, 5, 6, 28; September 2; October 31, 1984.

Baltimore Sun, February 20, 1984.

Beaumonth Enterprise, July 1, 29, 1984.

Dallas Morning News, June 30, July 7, August 3, 11, 25; December 8, 1983; June 8; August 1, 2, 9; October 28, 1984.

Dallas Times Herald, August 11, 1982; June 24, 26; August 13, 25, 26; November 26; April 5, 7, 11, 14, 23, 27; May 11, 17; October 6, 27; September 7, 1984; April 14, 15, 16, 17, 18, 19, 20, 23, 24, 1985.

El Paso Herald Post, October 26, 27, 1984.

Fort Worth Star Telegraph, January 16, 29, 1984.

Herald Dispatch (Huntington, West Virginia), December 11, 17, 28; April 7, 13, 23; May 12; June 2, 17, 23; August 1; September 7; October 6, 1984; January 14; April 15, 16, 18, 22, 23, 24, 25, 30; May 4; June 24, 1985.

Houston Post, June 30; August 11, 28; September 8, 9, 22, 23, 30; October 1, 4, 5, 8, 22, 23, 25; April 5; July 1; August 18, 1984; April 15, 16, 18, 19, 20, 1985.

Law Enforcement News, September 24, 1984.

New York Times, April 18, 24, 29, 1985.

Rocky Mountain News (Denver, Colorado), September 13, 1984.

Tampa Tribune, June 9, 1985.

Toledo Blade, January 17, 19, 20, 1960.

Other Sources
Egger, S. A. (1985, March). *Case study of serial murder: Henry Lee Lucas.* Presented at the 1985 annual meeting of the Academy of Criminal Justice Sciences, Las Vegas, Nevada.

Henry Lee Lucas Homicide Task Force Investigative Reports:
- Index of confirmed homicides
- Court action involving Henry Lee Lucas
- Index to supplements of synopsis
- Synopsis of confirmed homicides
- Daily log activities of Lucas and Toole

Interviews with Henry Lee Lucas:
- June 5, 1984

- June 22, 1984
- July 18, 1984
- August 2, 1984
- August 14, 1984
- September 25, 1984
- February 8, 1985
- March 22, 1985

Mattox, J. (1986). *Lucas report.* Austin: Office of Texas Attorney General.

Regional Organized Crime Information Center. (1985). Travel movements of Henry Lee Lucas and Ottis Elwood Toole, 1952–1985. Nashville, TN: ROCIC.

Psychiatric Reports

Transfer to Ionia State Hospital, Michigan, July 14, 1961.

Ionia State Hospital diagnosis, August 10, 1961.

Ionia State Hospital record, January 28, 1965.

Psychological evaluation, Center for Forensic Psychiatry, Ypsilanti, Michigan, November 17, 1971.

JERRY MARCUS

Books

Douglas, J. E., & Olshaker, M. (1995). *Mindhunter: Inside the FBI's elite serial crime unit.* New York: Scribner.

Egger, S. (1998). *The killers among us: An examination of serial murder and its investigation.* Upper Saddle River, NJ: Prentice Hall.

Hickey, E. (1997). *Serial murderers and their victims,* 2nd ed. Belmont, CA: Wadsworth.

Matza, D. (1964). *Delinquence and drift.* New York: Wiley.

Ressler, R. K., Burgess, A., & Douglas, J. E. (1985). *Sexual homicide.* Lexington, MA: Lexington Books.

Interviews

Grant, Agent Jerome, Alabama State Police, telephone interview, 1998.

Jones, Ken, Public Information Officer, Mississippi Department of Corrections, personal interview, Jacksonville, Mississippi, 1998.

Lindley, Captain David, Starkville Police Department, personal interview, Starkville, Mississippi, 1998.

Lindley, Captain David, Starkville Police Department, personal interview, Starkville, Mississippi, November 1999.

Marcus, Jerry, Personal Interview, Parchman Penitentiary, Parchman, Mississippi, November 13, 1999.

Marcus, Ruth, personal interview, November 12, 1999.

Owens, Arthurlene, personal interview, November 12, 1999.

Patrick, Captain Lester, Tuskegee Police Department, personal interview, Tuskegee, Alabama, 1998.

Journals

Doener, W. G. (1975, May). A regional analysis of homicide rates in the United States. *Criminology*, 13, 90–101.

Hickey, E. (1986, October). The female serial murderer. *Journal of Police and Criminal Psychology*, 2(2), 2–81.

Newspaper Articles

Marcus may be linked to Knoxville death. (1987, April 22). *Starkville Daily News*, p. 1.

Town dumbfounded by murder charges against Marcus. (1987, April 23). *Birmingham Post-Herald*, p. 3C.

Police Records

Starkville Police Department; Marcus, Jerry case file, April 16, 1987.

JOSEPH MILLER

Books

Canter, D. (1994). *Criminal shadows*. London: HarperCollins.

Egger, S. A. (1990). *Serial murder: An elusive phenomenon*. Westport, CT: Praeger.

Newspaper Articles

Car of missing woman found on East Bluff. (1993, September 24). *Peoria Journal Star*, p. A6.

Meidroth, T. (1993, October 27). Indictment returned in woman's vanishing. *Peoria Journal Star*, pp. A1–A2.

Moll, D. (1993, October 17). Search yields no clues. *Peoria Journal Star*, pp. A1–A12.

Moll, D. (1993, October 29). Sexual assaults preceded deaths. *Peoria Journal Star*, pp. A1–A2.

Okeson, S. (1993, September 28). Parents feared for daughter. *Peoria Journal Star*, p. A1.

Okeson, S. (1993, October 12). Volunteers will search for woman. *Peoria Journal Star*, pp. A1–A2.

Smothers, M. (1993, October 6). Miller's prosecutor hoped for execution. *Peoria Journal Star*, pp. A1–A2.

Williams, C. R. (1993, September 18). West Bluff woman, 88, missing nearly 3 weeks. *Peoria Journal Star*, p. A6.

Williams, C. R. (1993, September 19). Two bodies found nude in ditch. *Peoria Journal Star*, p. A1.

Williams, C. R. (1993, September 22). One murder victim stabbed, another asphyxiated: Coroner. *Peoria Journal Star*, p. C1.

Williams, C. R. (1993, September 27). Body found in county. *Peoria Journal Star,* pp. A1–A2.

Other Sources

Federal Bureau of Investigation. *Criminal history record: Joseph Miller.*

Illinois Department of Corrections. (1978, September 27). *Intake assessment report: Joseph Miller.*

Illinois State Police. *Criminal history record: Joseph Miller.*

Interviews with Lieutenant David Briggs and Detective Steven Schmidt, Peoria County, Illinois Sheriff's Police, February 9 and February 23, 1996.

Official autopsy photographs and records. (1993).

Perry, J. K. (1993, October 18). Leads report list.

Perry, J. K. (1993, November 10). Timeline for case M930004, Peoria County Sheriff Department.

Pyatt, T. (1993, October 5). Incident report.

Special Task Force investigative reports and materials, Joseph Miller case: Peoria County Illinois, Sheriff's Police; Peoria, Illinois Police Department; Illinois State Police; et al. (Obtained via Freedom of Information request, February 23, 1996.) Including: Taylor, C.D. (1994, February 1). Field report.